S0-BCV-486

LIVING THE DREAM
IT'S TIME!

A Chronicle of the Gathering of Equals

Mark Conrad and Keith Varnum

Pura Vida Publishing Company

Pura Vida Publishing Company
Post Office Box 379
Mountlake Terrace, WA 98043-0379

Edited by Ariele Huff and Judee Pouncey
Cover art by Ray Pelley
Cover design by Shawn McKell
Illustrations by Ken Susynski

Manufactured in the United States of America
1 3 5 7 9 10 8 6 4 2
This book is printed on acid-free, recycled paper.

Publisher's Cataloging-in Publication
(Provided by Quality Books, Inc.)

Conrad, Mark J.
Living the dream: it's time: a chronicle of the Gathering of Equals/Mark Conrad and Keith Varnum - 1st ed.

p. cm.
Includes index.
Preassigned LCCN: 97-75697
ISBN: 1-891569-19-8

1. Self-actualization (Psychology) 2. New Age movement.
3. Self-help groups. I. Varnum, Keith. II. Title.

BF637.S4C66 1998 158.1
QB197-41482

For Mom and David

TABLE OF CONTENTS

If one advances in the directions of his dreams,

and endeavors to live the life which he has imagined,

he will meet with a success unexpected in common hours.

Henry David Thoreau

Acknowledgments

We would like to acknowledge the huge contribution of the following people whose works have been an inspiration to us while writing this book: Kevin Benedict, Brad Blanton, Julia Cameron, Deepak Chopra, Elizabeth Kubler-Ross, Dan Millman, Marlo Morgan, Georgina Murata, Carolyn Myss, Arnold Patent, James Redfield, Marianne Williamson, Neale Donald Walsh, and Gary Zukav. By speaking from their heart, they have let their light shine so that we all may see more clearly.

These are the wonderful people who shared from their inner knowing and gave us permission to use their names: Allen, Amy, Anne, Audrey, both Carols, Carolyn, Chris, Chuck, Claudia, Darline, David, Debra, Dell, Duncan, Fran, Helaine, Inge, Jane, Janet, Jill, Joanna, John, Kate, Laurice, Laurie, all five Lindas, Lynette, Marianne, Marie, Mia, both Michaels, Nelson, Ray, Renee, Sam, Steven, Suzanne, and Venita. There were many other participants for whom we used pseudonyms for one reason or another. Their wonderful anonymous words will live on!

A heartfelt thanks to Judee Pouncey, Linda Costello, and Michele Rogalin (the most wonderful woman in the universe), for all of their editing help and moral support.

The Seattle, Austin, and San Francisco *Gatherings* were not highlighted, but there was a lot of beautiful wisdom shared by the people in those cities. That truth greatly influenced the book and is sprinkled throughout. There were also numerous individuals who kindled the spirit of *Gatherings* but were not included in print. You all contributed greatly with your love and intent. Thank you.

Introduction

Welcome to *Living The Dream.* The human consciousness is evolving at an accelerated rate, and we're *all* along for the ride. This book is about waking up to our inner knowing and starting to play in the universe as we deserve and are meant to, as true equals with each other and with all of the great spiritual beings of the past, present, and future. We will share the way that many people have gained *conscious* control over every aspect of their daily existence. It happens by learning how to live each day and each hour fully and consciously in the moment.

Magic happens! Have you ever felt as though you want more, that you can *have* more? Have you wondered what your *spirit* is up to and why you're here on the planet? It's time to know! That's what *Living the Dream* is about.

When Keith Varnum received this message from within, he knew it was time.

"We are the fail-safe seeds to ensure that this creation does not go on forever. Within us are the seeds of knowing how to undo this particular creation, this creation of being unconscious, of not knowing who we are, of suffering because we don't know who we are. We haven't known what's happening, and we've not allowed ourselves to have our natural power. The seeds of knowing are within us, and when given the right environment, these seeds will grow."

We, as humans, are waking up the sleeping spirit within each of us. It is now *safe;* it's okay to know great things and share what we know with others. It's time to *awaken* to the dream.

Jesus and other great masters have all said the same thing: *"All of these things we have done and more, will you do."* Abundance and sovereignty await each of us as we awaken to love and lift the self-imposed, truth-obscuring veils. There is no limit to what we can do for ourselves and others if we tap into our own inner power, that part of God which lives within us, and begin to live the dream.

In the book, we follow others on their intuitive journeys directly to the "vibration" of their individual truth and bliss. tap into our own inner power, that part of God which lives within us, and begin to live the dream. We are witnesses as they go "inside" to discover who they are and discover the qualities and vibrations they prefer. Instead of the popular approach of "peeling the onion" of doubt and misunderstanding, the process is simplified, *starting* at the truth, our "inner knowing," and casting aside veils from that "space." Many of the basic approaches used in The *Gatherings* have been advocated by great spiritual leaders for centuries. They are remarkably simple, which makes it seem at once sad and absurd that we've chosen not to fully understand and use them consciously and continuously until now.

Many of the people who now attend the *Gatherings* say they have been "going inside" alone for some time and are pleased to find spiritual playmates. As the critical mass of people who are "waking up" grows, each *Gathering* builds on the last one and a natural, organic evolution takes place. *Living the Dream* is about this phenomenon and the incredible shift in consciousness that is changing the world. The *Gatherings* and this book are a bridge between the present reality and the future when we'll get together intuitively, at the right time, without the need of a leader. We'll no longer have the restrictions of a belief system, philosophy, or any spiritual or religious order.

The successes of Deepak Chopra, Carolyn Myss, Marianne Williamson, James Redfield, Neale Donald Walsh, and many others is a clear sign the way has already been paved. The materialistic 80's have given way to a search toward simplifying life, relationships, and discovering the true essence of our being. Over the entire planet, people are looking for spiritual solutions to worldly problems. They're looking for a way to experience the true meaning of love and life.

The book chronicles the *Gathering* event, a fun, playful four-day event of conscious equals coming together to celebrate and explore each other's unique "vibration," essence, and gifts. We call the events playful because they are a joyful emergence of knowledge and innocence. It's remembering who we are, then going forth and living in harmony with others and the universe. People who have gathered at these events and on their own are taking their heightened states of awareness to the workplace and beyond. As we do, and as our numbers increase, we're creating the largest paradigm shift in the history of mankind. As more people begin to resonate with their true energy of knowing, the whole world is changing.

This book is the story of the *Gatherings,* how they started, where they are now, and where they're going. The first chapter describes how Keith Varnum consciously awakened after decades of searching for an answer. It shares how I, logically minded, corporate, and convention-bound, was magically drawn to the *Gathering* without any idea what it was about. Most of the book is a chronicle of the *Gatherings,* a word-by-word account of people sharing the voice of their intuition. In a twelvemonth adventure that began with my first Seattle *Gathering* in June 1996, the book takes the reader on a spiritual journey from city to city and heart to heart. From Seattle to Costa Rica, San Francisco to Tallahassee, Phoenix to Philadelphia, and lots of cities in between, these workshops have gathered human spirits who are coming together to learn from others as they rediscover the God within themselves.

In *Living the Dream,* we capture the essence or major themes of one or more *Gatherings* in a chapter. We follow, through stories of direct personal experiences, the evolution of awareness and consciousness that is unfolding.

In the second chapter, we explained the general format and basic tools used in the *Gathering* events. These will be beneficial to those wishing to experience the magic at home or in small local groups. We encourage you to attend the events held by Keith Varnum in your area or start them on your own. Our goal is to reintroduce you to some of what you've always known but forgotten and to provide some basic and powerful tools to help you to operate consciously and more often from your intuition or "inner knowing."

Keith and I, as well as others participating in *Living the Dream,* are living out our purpose. We're delighted to be sharing this experience with you. You are literally making our dream come true, and we're glad you've taken this step toward fully experiencing your own personal dream. You're ready. It's time! That's why you're reading this now. We hope you enjoy *Living the Dream.* You may be surprised at how familiar some of this feels to you.

LIVING THE DREAM

IT'S TIME!

A Chronicle of the Gathering of Equals

Humankind falls into three classes,

Those who are immovable,

Those who are movable,

And those who move.

Arab proverb

Chapter One

JUMP AND THE NET WILL COME

Keith's Story with an Introduction by Mark

GEORGINA MURATA WAS NINE YEARS OLD WHEN she came to the *Gathering*. Shortly before, in a flurry of inspiration, she had composed several poems about coming into her own personal power. She felt *The Dream - A Gathering of Equals®* was the appropriate place to share the music from her soul. At the Friday night introductory session, Georgina sat there timidly and listened while her dance teacher read her poetry to the group.

The roomful of adults was stunned, inspired, and humbled at the profundity and innocence of her poetry. It speaks of the wisdom, power and light within us all. *Living the Dream* is about awakening to recapture those gifts. The quickening is upon us. It's time!

Georgina had no conscious way of knowing that her poetry would be highlighted in a spiritual book for adults. How did she come to write such profound wisdom from the heart at only nine years of age? Was it a coincidence that she presented it at the *Gathering* and, consequently, to thousands of readers? There is a reality which many of us have only had glimpses of throughout our lives. It's an existence in which nothing happens by chance, "coincidences" abound, magic is commonplace, and abundance prevails. It comes into being simply by becoming fully conscious, fully alive. Georgina was there. Lots of our children are there. Now it's time for *us* to return to that part of our being that makes magic happen.

Many of us are awakening to discover we need to re-establish a relationship with our inner knowing, that all-knowing God voice within. It's pure love and pure light, the state we have all touched but then forgotten. Why do we forget? It's part of the game, this fast-paced game of effort we call living. In the space of true essence, *your* true essence, there is no time, there is no space, and there is no struggle. *Living the Dream* is about a different kind of existence, one I only began to fully discover a short time ago.

My name is Mark. I am the scribe, the one who was called upon to write what you're about to read and who will serve as your guide to tie the shared thoughts together as we go. Writing this book has been a profound and transformational experience for me. I've had the good fortune to first attend the *Gatherings* then listen and transcribe the notes and audio recordings of the *Gatherings*. These activities have integrated into my life and changed me in wondrous ways.

Two years ago, I would have thought you were crazy if you told me where I would be and what I would be doing today. I was on the treadmill called a "normal" life with more "success" than many because of my tenacity and ambitious drive. Way deep down inside, I knew there was more, but it was *way* down there.

As a child, I connected with some of the true spirit of God

and Jesus in church services. I loved singing the old hymns and looked forward to Sunday when I could sing them with others. Very early on, I could tell that people were going through the motions and not really *living* what they talked about in the churches. I noticed when many of them sang, though, they brightened up, were touched by spirit, and began living pure joy in the moment. Suddenly they were real, and I wanted to be with them. By the time I was seventeen, I had become greatly disappointed by the hypocrisy. I knew that if the people in the churches would only take the spirit of the music into their hearts and keep it there, things would be better.

I became disillusioned with the experience and convinced myself I was an atheist or maybe an agnostic who enjoyed singing hymns. I had always loved science and turned to it as the ultimate answer to everything. Science became my religion.

My analytical self convinced me that coincidences were simply chance happenings, mere bleeps in the steady flow of reality as we know it. Science and logic prevailed. I could see the God of science in nature, but Jesus, Buddha, and all of the rest of them were fairy tales. To me, they were pacifiers for the masses like Santa Claus and the Easter Bunny. Anytime I personally experienced psychic phenomena or knew events before they actually occurred, I dismissed that as a quirk or something that must have a scientific explanation.

I went to college and worked steadily up the corporate ladder. For eight years preceding my recent jump into the new reality, I worked my way into a very good management position with a major food company. I commuted an hour and a half or more a day from the suburbs of Seattle to work about fifty hours a week. I saw my two wonderful children for about an hour and a half a day during the week and a little longer on weekends. My wife and I juggled our time with them along with the mowing, painting, entertaining, going to business functions, and doing all of the other things done by "successful" people at our age and in our position. I was married to a person who had similar interests and goals, a very good business person and supermom who kept an immaculate home. We shared a lot of good times, especially with the children, but basically had become two hardened corporate beings who did not have enough time to kiss, hug, or have intimate conversation. We were just too busy with other important things. We told ourselves and each other we were doing it for the kids. We believed it.

I was going through all of the appropriate motions and doing it quite well. I was saving money for retirement to build up enough "security" so that, in twenty years, I could follow my heart's passion and write. I had sold my soul to the routine and in return held onto hopes that I could do anything I wanted to "as soon as:" I retire, the large lawn is mowed, the pile of wood is chopped, I get the next promotion. As soon as... I was dying in tiny pieces, a day at a time.

There was no time for spirituality in my life, no way to schedule it. My calendar was booked solid with lots of things that other people expected of me and that I expected of myself. I began to realize there is more to living than working, saving and working some more, and sleeping. My awareness of another way came with the birth of my two children. There was something about the purity and innocence of my children that jarred me back into my present reality, *living,* not in the old way, but with a renewed sense of love and vigor. I credit my children with saving my life, rescuing me from the treadmill of drudgery to which my surrender to mainstream thought had sentenced me. It was truly their influence that ultimately resulted in the living of my dream.

Only a few years ago, some of my suppressed inner yearnings started to become stronger and stronger. I was becoming more conscious of the food I ate and the company I kept. Somehow, even in the business tapes I would listen to while commuting to and from my stressful job, I began to notice spiritual messages. My demeanor slowly began to shift, and I became more sensitive about the environment and about life. I began to capture and release spiders we found in the house rather than smash them. My children had a great influence on me during these early stages of my transformation.

At work, I began to consider the needs of my employees first and those of the company second. I became more concerned about their personal well-being than the profitability of the company. All of these changes were slow and gentle until several key events occurred in my life in very quick succession. It's difficult to say if any of them had more impact than the others, but they all set me up to take several large leaps of faith. Somehow, during that time, I began to listen to a soft voice deep within my being. This was a huge step because I did not believe in intuition. Finally, I read the words in a book somewhere and they resonated within me as none had ever done before. "Jump and the net will come." It gives me the chills, or what I call a huge "rush" to write it even now. I have since learned to run *toward* rather than *from* the rush. *Jump and the net will come.*

About that time, I went on a body cleanse diet, deciding before I started it that I would eliminate red meat and greatly reduce the amount of poultry in my diet. After the cleanse, an increasingly stronger voice from inside told me to give up meat entirely. This caused some domestic turmoil and was a catalyst for dealing with several other more major issues. I was becoming desperate to do what was really right for myself and what I knew would also be best for those around me. A "normal" life was not right for me anymore. Deepak Chopra calls a lot of the "normal" things society expects of us "the psychopathology of the average."

I was having stronger and stronger intuitive messages that I needed to do something spiritual. I needed to deliver a message of peace to the world. It would not happen living and working where I was. This was scary and I thought I might be going off the deep end. I was very tentative when approaching my spouse about this because it was so clear she wanted us to remain exactly who and where we were. She had worked her entire lifetime to build the lyfestyle in which we existed. So had I, but I was realizing that the whole thing, our whole reality, was not really what we thought it was. I was beginning to suspect that security is an illusion. The more you struggle to build it around yourself, the less you really have. The pesky voice of intuition was one I could no longer ignore.

Through a string of bizarre "coincidences," I found out about a workshop called *The Dream - A Gathering of Equals* that was, "coincidentally" coming to Seattle within a week. Just hearing the name, I *knew* I would go, and I could feel it would be a major step for me. I managed to get the time off work to go. Through the *Gatherings* experience that voice from within was handed a megaphone, and I have never been the same since. I am now living consciously. I have jumped off the treadmill and am consequently able to manifest marvelous things in my life.

For most of my life, I had fantasized about writing a book, one that spoke the message of my heart. Then, just over a year ago, while in my new green station wagon, commuting on the way home during rush hour, it hit me. It was an epiphany, a huge enlightenment, right in the middle of stop-and-go traffic on an interstate highway north of Seattle! My voice from within was shouting again. I had recently discovered that small miracles began occurring in my life as I learned to become truly *"present"* more of the time. My epiphany in the car was like seeing a spectacular sunset and being so caught up in the beauty that I felt as if I were floating. The feeling of joy was so encompassing I cried. I was filled with such an overwhelming rush of peace that I *knew*, beyond any doubt, that *everything* was okay. *That* is being fully present. I did it in rush hour traffic, at that time, one of the most stressful parts of my life. I realize now that all stress is completely self-imposed. The universe spoke, as it always does, but that time I listened. I knew, *absolutely knew*, everything is okay. I knew I was to write this book.

As I write this and continue to explore my inner God voice, and see God in *everything*, miracles are becoming a part of my daily life. In marvelous ways, I have manifested a new life. It includes my soul-mate and our new beautiful baby, a publishing business, travels, and a house nestled in the woods. The drawing at the front of this chapter is of our back yard, a lush oasis of fir trees, ivy, and ferns. Through a series of miracles, my wife Michele and I manifested our ideal house and yard. We now receive virtually everything we want and need. This past year and a half has been a wonderful adventure in living, and I know it's just beginning!

The majority of this chapter is about Keith Varnum's life. As the founder of the workshops highlighted in this book, his story is relevant to an understanding of how *The Dream - A Gathering of Equals* came into being. His story is a journey into another reality. He came from a considerably different background than I did, as you will soon see. I presented my recent past as an illustration that *anyone* can break free and truly live the dream. Truth is in the same place it has always been. *It* hasn't moved; *we* have. We can get there from anywhere. Since Keith and I come from such opposite ends of the spectrum, it makes a convincing case for the possibility that anyone could be here. Where is "here?" "Here" is living *consciously, in the moment, with heart and intuition* in control, in the driver's seat. The brain is in the back seat where it belongs, performing its vital functions, and assisting when called upon.

Two years ago, I would have thought the following stories were the fantasies of a spiritual nut, a raving counter culture guru who could not hold down a real job. Now I believe them as the truth as Keith knows it, and am discovering that I am open to experiencing all kinds of new wisdom, joy, and surprises of my own. For the first time in over twenty years, Jesus is real to me again, but in a fresh, new, alive way. I have heard messages from Jesus and other ascended beings as well. As crazy as it might sound to people who are as close-minded as I was, I even listen to *trees*.

As I go "inside" and find out who I really am, the line between magic and "the real world" becomes more and more vague. I am beginning to remember events like Keith's that have occurred in my own life and am looking forward to more. It's amazing what we forget! Now sit back and enjoy some new reality. Set your judgments aside and read with your heart.

The remainder of this chapter is an abbreviated version of key events in Keith Varnum's life, in his own words, that led up to the *Gatherings*. We hope you will have as much fun reading this as we have had in bringing it to you.

KEITH VARNUM'S STORY

One day recently, I sat me down on my living room couch while spirit came and presented my entire life to me in a short but profound vision. This comprehensive review was clear, precise, and inspiring. I saw that every experience I'd had in my life so far has been brilliantly and deliberately designed to train me to successfully facilitate *The Dream - A Gathering of Equals.* This four-day play/workshop is the current expression of my life purpose and my soul's joy.

Even at five years old, I was being exposed to a full spectrum of spiritual options. My mother wanted to raise me Unitarian, so when I was five years old, my parents drove forty miles every Sunday to a Unitarian Sunday School. That school taught as much about Buddha and Lao Tzu as it did Jesus. After a couple of years, I couldn't go anymore because it got to be too difficult for my parents to travel through winter snowstorms in the Pennsylvania mountains. After that,

I was exposed to a more conservative mainstream religion in the hands of a Protestant Church. I went to Sunday School during the year and Bible School every summer. I loved Bible School mainly because of the stories they told about Jesus. I noticed, though, that every Sunday School and Bible School teacher and church minister interpreted those stories very differently. Basically, I could tell they didn't know what Jesus was *really* saying.

I heard many stories from the Old Testament about disastrous things happening to people who could not understand why God acted that way toward them. In one case, God told Abraham to kill his son. I remember hearing about the trials of Job. There's the tale of the prodigal son, about two sons; one is good and works really hard, and the other goes off and spends all the money his father gave him on riotous living. He returns, though, and the father takes him back. I loved those stories, but even as a kid I could tell that the religious leaders barely had a clue what the *real* import of these stories is. When I asked questions, they would mumble, fuss, and give all kinds of varied and vague answers. I decided then I needed to discover the true meaning of these biblical stories on my own.

I really didn't have a personal relationship with God or Jesus at that time because of the way the teachers talked about him in Sunday and Bible Schools. The picture they painted for me about God and his son was that they were wrathful, that you would be condemned, go to hell, or be famine-stricken if you screwed up. It did not feel accurate or real to me. I felt deep conflicts between what the people in the church were saying and what I understood from the Bible and felt in my heart.

I was an acolyte, an altar boy, in the Methodist Church for many years. I lit the candles before the service and extinguished them at the end. I liked the job because I got to leave the sanctuary during the sermon and relax backstage until I was needed again to put the candles out. I didn't want to listen to the insincerity and the inconsistencies of the sermons. It was so much more uplifting to hang out in the spacious loft behind the sanctuary altar. I would see angels in the rafters when the organ music was really loud.

Spiritual hymns and music were powerful to me at that time. *In the Garden* is still my favorite song. It talks of going to the garden alone and meeting Jesus while the dew is still on the roses. "And the voice I hear calling on my ear, the son of God discloses. And he walks with me, and he talks with me, and he tells me I am his own, and the joy we share as we tarry there, none other has ever known." That music would fill me completely. I could feel it in my soul. In gardens I feel the peace of Jesus and God. I have planted beds of flowers and vegetables everywhere I've lived since childhood. I also loved singing Christmas carols. I would go out with the church on Christmas season nights, singing carols at people's homes. I have always made contact with spirit through music and song.

The first time I consciously realized there was something more grand going on in life than what I was being taught was when I was fourteen taking drawing lessons at a summer resort. My art class convened at in old community called Lilydale in New York State. It's a summer headquarters for spiritualist mediums. About a hundred resident clairvoyants there presented talks and seances for thousands of visitors. People would come to have the mediums contact their dead relatives and friends. We aspiring young artists came to draw and paint the old Victorian houses, hotels, gazebos, and the majestic trees in the deep, dark virgin forest surrounding it all. The original buildings and grounds with lakes and ponds were preserved with great care and love. Nothing had changed for over a century. Lilydale had an enchanting, timeless quality to it. When we were done sketching for the day, we would go to a trance session or a seance just for fun, to check it out in the spirit of fourteen-year-olds.

In my art class, I met a kid my age from Wisconsin. One day, he got up the nerve to raise his hand and talk to one of the mediums. As she was speaking, suddenly my friend's deceased uncle started speaking through this woman and said, in the uncle's voice, "You really have to quit breaking parking meters. You're going to get caught next time." As the deep voice talked on about these parking meters, my friend turned ashen white and started shaking. After the seance, he said he and a buddy *had* gone out and smashed parking meters in his hometown. His father was the chief of police in the little town he was from in Wisconsin. The meters cost thousands of dollars and no one had ever discovered who wrecked them. Neither of us could imagine any possible way the medium could have known. The rest of that summer I kept contemplating that mystery. I realized there was something going on in Lilydale I wanted and needed to know more about. This is my first memory of beginning to suspect there are more realities happening here on the planet than I was being told about at school and at home.

I remember starting to read spiritual books at around fifteen years of age. I would visit bookstores in Erie, Pennsylvania, the only real "city" near the tiny town where I grew up. I'd find these out-of-the-way bookstores run by crotchety old men. Dust and cobwebs layered everything in the store. I used to come home with Zen stories and strange, little spiritual books. These volumes were a treasure to me. I couldn't explain them because I really didn't understand them myself, but I loved them. I'd read from the books to friends who would give me blank stares in return. They could never feel the magic I felt in those words.

About the same time, I experienced a lot of near disasters with cars. I noticed that when I should have rationally gotten in a car wreck, or even been killed, an "inevitable" accident didn't occur. One time, for example, I was driving with friends and decided to pass a car. Once in the other lane, we encountered a truck coming straight at us and going in the opposite direction. Speeding toward the truck, we were so close we could see the truck driver's face through his windshield as our headlights lit up the inside of his cab. By all known laws of physics, we should have smashed right into that truck. We were going at least fifty miles an hour and so was he. All of a sudden, without realizing what had happened, we were safe and unscathed on a grassy knoll on the side of the road. There is no way, physically, we could have gotten there. Similar enigmas happened to me throughout my teenage years.

It was also about then that St. Germain started appearing in my bedroom. St. Germain is an energy being, an expression of my higher self, who is very wise. He is commonly spoken of as one of the Ascended Masters. They're called "ascended beings" because they have mastered and ascended the influence of their emotional programming. St. Germain ascended and agreed to stay in contact to help us do the same thing he has done, to master human limitations and remember who we are. Ascended beings play consciously in form in order for us to be able to see them. Actually, for them to be able to appear and to be experienced as separate from us, they have to be in form. Jesus is one. Buddha, Lao Tzu, Mother Mary, and Sai Baba are others. There are some who choose to remain nameless.

St. Germain and I spent a lot of time together, sometimes four hours at a time. He would talk and show me life lessons on the wall. I would joke and say to him that this method of instruction felt like when my football coach would project training films of last week's game on the white wall of the locker room. St. Germain's visual presentation was of the *future*, however, not of the past! He'd show me how my life was going to unfold and how I could prepare for it. Much of what he had me focus on was my interaction with individuals and groups. He said

I would need all the love, understanding, and skills I could muster to facilitate large *Gatherings* someday. At the time, my memory of these nighttime sessions was very vague. Usually in the morning, I'd just shake it off as a dream. Deep down within myself, though, I knew it wasn't a dream at all. I was fully awake, walking around in my bedroom, and talking with St. Germain as I would a close buddy. I would get up and go to the bathroom in the middle of our discussions. These meetings went on through high school and college and into my twenties. As the visits became more frequent, I would run into businesses such as the St. Germain Hair Salon, St. Germain Dress Shop, and receive mailers from the St. Germain Book Co. I knew then, that these reminders were appearing in my life to help me keep my sanity and to know that the rendezvous were real.

Also during these same years, I would have numerous out-of-body experiences. Typically, I would be standing with a group of friends, and at the same time I'd be about twenty feet above them! I would actually look down on the group. I would see other people coming long before they could see us, because I could see so much further from that elevated vantage point. I was completely conscious of leaving my body, just floating, and I knew it was okay for me to do that. I'd tell my friends, but they thought I was crazy, so I learned to keep it to myself.

One time, I was climbing a six-hundred-foot cliff with a girlfriend and at one point, we both slipped. As we began sliding down the cliff, my whole life flashed in front of me, all my happiest birthday parties and other special times. As we were falling, with five hundred feet to go, we suddenly stopped sliding. The next second we found ourselves at the bottom of the cliff sitting in a small pool in the creek bleeding and staring at each other. We had certainly been scratched, but we were not dead or injured. On many occasions during my early years, I experienced numerous jumps or gaps in time and space like that day at the cliff. Whenever these time lapses occurred, I got more and more curious about what was *really* going on.

I was in college at the University of Michigan in Ann Arbor during the height of the sixties' awakening and I did all of the stereotypical hippie things. I found the spirit was very real in the "Make Love, Not War" movement and I experienced genuine brotherhood and sisterhood with many different people. My friends were very caring and authentic. We lived together in groups and freely shared our money, food, bodies, emotions, and ideals. Many strong, positive seeds were planted for my future unfoldment.

At the same time my spiritual perspective was being pried open by these adventures, I was shutting down on other levels. I was very angry at society, and at my institutional schooling in particular. I was initially excited about college, but soon discovered it was no different than high school and not the expansive place I had hoped it would be. Everything seemed like such a lie. I was discovering that very little of what I was told about the world was turning out to be accurate.

All of my kindred spirit friends were having the same experiences. There was a huge contrast between what we saw in the world and what we were told was going on. We knew the truth, but weren't able, yet, to live it. The paradox was just too much for most people. Some of my friends went crazy. Some of them died due to hepatitis and other diseases, but most "checked out" with drug overdoses or motorcycle crashes. They found a way to die because they couldn't find a way to live in the conventional world. A lot of the others eventually "sold out," just decided to forget what they felt in their hearts and work at mundane corporate desk jobs. Some friends went "back-to-nature" to homestead in northern New England, Alaska, or Canada. A few died or disappeared up there. Most came back, got burned out, and slowly died at jobs. The track record wasn't very good; not many of us were able to keep our spirit alive.

Before my senior year at college, I went to Europe, to the roots of Western civilization, where I felt I might find some answers. There maybe I could make sense of it all and find a way to fit into the world. While in France, I went to a 2,000-year-old Roman coliseum that was still being used for bullfights. It was originally the site for gladiator exhibitions and other forms of public entertainment, pageantry, and expression of imperial Rome. I was engrossed in this monumental piece of architecture and the throngs of French and Spanish people who were the descendants of ancient civilizations. I then watched as all of this collective energy was focused on killing the aliveness of these vibrant, majestic bulls. Very slowly, spear by spear, the life force was drained from these beautiful creatures.

As I watched the slaughter in horror, I fully realized I wasn't going to fit into this culture. It is not a natural part of me. My heart wouldn't allow me to remain any longer in this society. It wasn't a judgment, it was simply a recognition that my spirit didn't fit. At that moment, I experienced a sense of my true nature and my true destiny. I wasn't yet at the point of being able to fully express or describe it, but I did know that I needed to go in an entirely different direction. My being was here to express and evolve totally outside of the human culture I had grown up in. To protect my spirit, I needed to find a place this culture doesn't even know about. I knew that this civilization is, fundamentally, a killer of souls. I realized, sitting there in the Roman coliseum, that everything I had been taught about Western civilization was false; nothing was really as it appeared. If Western culture really had heart and wisdom, it could not continuously use a structure for 2,000 years toward the destruction of the spirit, toward the killing of the life force in beings. *(This discovery is explored in more detail in Chapter 10 - The Message of the Volcano.)*

Soon after leaving the coliseum with these realizations, I went to Amsterdam where I met a new friend at a youth hostel. One night, he took me out into this big forest on the outskirts of the city. We peeked through the bushes and saw naked babies there. Naked men and women danced and chanted. There were blood sacrifices of lambs and goats and bizarre sexual things going on. It was some sort of satanic rite or ritual. As soon as I got a glimpse of it, I accidentally stepped on a stick. My friend said, "Run! Who knows what they will do to us if they catch us here." So we ran and got away safely. The very next morning, though, I woke up and my eyes were inflamed and wouldn't open.

I flew to my parents' home in Pennsylvania to try to heal my eyes. However, the condition got progressively worse and I effectively lost my eyesight for over two months. I realize now that I had to hide deep in the darkness, out of the sight of my society. I needed to find a way to put my spirit, trust, power, and gifts into something other than the culture I'd been brought up in. The divine purpose in this was for me to withdraw until I found my sovereignty, until I found God within myself. That's what happened. I started talking to God to see if s/he really existed. S/he talked to me and we made a deal. I swore that instead of complaining, I would go deeper. I would look behind the appearances until I found the truth, until I found a reality more fundamental than what was showing up on the surface of human experience. I would go deeper and deeper until I found the fire inside, my true essence. Within hours of making this agreement with myself, events started to unfold which led to the restoration of my eyesight.

With my sight recovered, I began to make films my senior year in college. Over Christmas vacation, my filmmaking friends and I decided to drive up to Montreal to shoot a documentary about an international spiritual group that taught Yoga and other spiritual techniques. I'd heard of the group from my friend, Rhone, who was the nephew of the group's leader, Gaston Bourdage.

With no forewarning from Rhone, I called my friend's uncle to see if we could film their group's activities, and he said, "Oh, we have been expecting your call. Yes, you can come and stay at our house." About halfway to Montreal, I got really sick. I was physically ill the whole time there and for a year afterwards. I had nausea, intestinal flu, and diarrhea. My body was trying to tell me something, but at the time, I wasn't able to listen. When we got to Montreal, we arrived at a large home that looked like a very typical suburban residence. It was the meeting place of their secret society consisting of about two hundred members. They all held regular jobs but met at nights and on weekends in this big house. As we went inside the center, it started to snow heavily outside. Before long, we were snowed in under six feet of snow. The drifts were so deep there was snow up to the top of the door, so we couldn't go outside at all for five days.

Consequently, we were stuck inside with this man, Gaston, and his partner, Edith. They told us they were not human, and they just took human form for our comfort and so they could communicate with us. With me, were three guys and two women. We were all filmmakers and not very spiritually minded. (I was at that time still in complete denial regarding St. Germain and my agreement with God.) As far as we consciously knew, we simply came there to do a documentary as journalists. Yet, to our shock and surprise, here we were sitting down hearing stories from people who said they were not human. Gaston and Edith proceeded to take us through five days of spiritual initiation. First they told us the true history of the planet and about who we really are. I have since heard the same story, in different words, from every other spiritual teacher I have had. Earlier, in my young life, St. Germain had prepared me for these revelations.

They told us who we were as human beings. They said we are souls who have come here to experience that the whole creation is made up of polarities, dualities—right and wrong, good and bad, up and down. We all buy into these beliefs, and that's what makes matter and earth possible, as well as the whole pretend game we're playing. All of this information went right over our heads; but, I know now, it went right into my soul. Then they took us for five days of soul travel, also called past life regression, astral projection, or awareness technique. We lay on a bed and allowed our intuition or soul to open us to other lifetimes, either our own or others. In present time, several of us went, in spirit, to the Himalayan mountains between Tibet and India. We delivered verbal messages from the people in Montreal to friends of theirs in Tibet. When we did this, it was as real as a conversation in everyday life, not foggy or vague in any way. Then they took us on a fantastic ride through various lifetimes of our choice.

In each other lifetime we visited, we would vividly experience being physically born in that lifetime. Then we'd observe and feel significant moments of the life in a very tangible way. We'd fully experience dying in that lifetime. While doing this, we were 99% present in the other lifetime with only about 1% of our consciousness aware of our body on a bed in Montreal. That's how real it was. Every time we opened to another lifetime, we were very aware that the purpose was to learn about the effects of greed, selfishness, revenge, jealousy, and other human emotions and feelings. We were experientially realizing how being stuck in a certain narrow point of view can dominate and debilitate a person's whole life. It was quite an extreme exploration of all the various human conditions and frailties. In addition to going through death over and over again, we also experienced what it is like *between* lifetimes. In the in-between-lives state, we'd meet with our spiritual advisors, talk about how we had fared the last lifetime, and choose what qualities and experiences we wanted to explore in the next lifetime. It was very powerful and transforming. I learned so much that I was able to use it professionally to benefit other people years later in Boston.

Then Gaston gave each of us a personal reading. For three hours, he told each of us who we were personally, as a soul, why we were here and what we came to do. He said that originally there was only Oneness. When the Oneness decided to reveal itself in form, we each chose to express different aspects of the totality, each embodying and radiating more of one aspect than the others. Some of us carry more of the vibration of space, of love; for others it's innocence; for some it's courage. We have different jobs to do. Gaston shared that my essence is predominantly the frequency of peace and harmony. He told me that my soul was from a place, or actually a space, of peace. I was here on a mission of peace to observe humans and society and see how people interact. When I had learned enough, I was going to assist people to heal, re-connect, and wake up. At first, I would learn ways to counsel and help people make peace with themselves and each other. Eventually, I would embody the vibration of serenity so much that if people were arguing and I walked down the other side of the street, they would just quit arguing from the effect of the calming quality of my radiance. It's interesting because my first teacher after that was Michio Kushi, a Japanese teacher of macrobiotics and natural healing methods. The whole reason he lives is to bring peace to the world. As it has turned out, I've spent my life assisting people to become whole, tranquil, and happy—through meditation, yoga, Zen, counseling, therapy, rebirthing, natural foods, acupuncture, and other methods of self-empowerment and integration. Gaston also showed us a way to open the chakras, the energy centers of the body. Before we left, we met some of the other members of the society. They were professors, lawyers, doctors, and police officers, a cross section of society—very open, friendly people.

When we got back home to the University of Michigan, three of our group became so overwhelmed and scared that they went to a "white witch" in Detroit. She taught them different spells and rituals to protect themselves. The three of them had decided that the people in Montreal were evil and must be in some sort of satanic cult. They went home and put salt over all of their doorways. Then they went to a Catholic church and got holy water to sprinkle on everything. All three were eventually committed to mental institutions. They went to psychiatrists and couldn't be helped. They went completely off the deep end. I wanted to go see the people in Montreal again, but I didn't because I was still so physically sick. It was too soon for me. I had expanded too fast and needed to integrate what I had uncovered within myself. Gaston wanted us to share with other people what we had learned, but I wasn't able to do that for about ten years. I know now that the sickness was a way for my soul to slow me down so I would heal and rearrange my universe before I transformed any further. I needed to develop more strength, compassion, and wisdom before I opened to more spiritual exploration. The fifth member of our group did not freak out or get sick, but he did seek assistance from Findhorn, the spiritual community in Scotland, to understand and assimilate what happened to him in Montreal.

The purpose of the secret spiritual society in Montreal was to bring people together to awaken. It was a gathering of equals. They considered everyone in the group of equal ability and worth. The technique they used, which was similar to the *dream outs* we do in the *Gatherings,* was to have people become aware of their spiritual nature. That way, they would realize they are eternal and all-knowing beings. The experience of the soul travels we did with them pierced a permanent bubble in our belief that we are just a personality in a body living only this lifetime.

The year after Montreal, I was so sick I couldn't work. I slept a lot, was freezing all of the time, and very weak. I had graduated from college and was about twenty-two. I had no money left, so I moved in with my brother who was going to law school in Boston. One night for dinner, my brother was cooking live lobsters in a big pot on the kitchen stove. I watched the lobsters trying to crawl out and sat there with the same feeling I had had in the Roman coliseum with the bulls. I realized I needed to leave. I could not stay. I didn't feel judgmental toward my brother, but my spirit knew that at that time it was not helpful for me to have to sit by and witness the killing of innocent animals again. I had nowhere to go, no money or friends, and I was sick. I didn't tell my brother I was leaving. I just grabbed my suitcase and left. Something was propelling me out of there toward my next step.

An hour later, I found a natural food store where I could buy some ready-made food to eat. At the cash register, there was a young man who had a bright glow around his whole body, who was buying a fifty-pound bag of whole wheat flour. I thought no one would buy fifty pounds of whole wheat flour unless they lived in a commune or with a group of people. My inner voice told me to go talk to him, but I was very shy about talking to strangers. He left the store and I suddenly experienced a jolt of inner panic. I heard an insistent command from deep inside, "You have to talk to this person!" I left the store and saw him way down the street. Chasing after him, I ran past people in the mud and slush. I finally caught up to him and said, "I couldn't help noticing that you have all this flour and I figured you cooked for a bunch of people. Maybe I could come and eat with you." He said, "Sure, come on over."

He didn't live with a group of people. He and his girlfriend lived in a two-bedroom apartment. They loved making homemade whole wheat bread, chapatis, tortillas, cinnamon rolls, and muffins from scratch; they just used lots of flour between the two of them. There was an empty bedroom because a roommate had just left. I moved in that night and stayed for a year. We became really good friends and they introduced me to Michio Kushi.

Michio and I recognized our soul connection right away. I was soon helping to run his natural food stores. He helped me to understand and integrate the Montreal experience. By being with him, eating simple foods like brown rice, and getting a whole new world view, I regained my health very quickly. We would meet after his macrobiotic lectures and he'd talk to me for hours about being a free being. He taught that everyone is equal in all ways, and that we are all inherently able to do anything we choose in life. He spoke to me about sovereignty and the importance of working for one's joy, not just for money. He used to levitate and taught me how. Michio's whole purpose was to bring people together to become whole again and wake up. He told me someday I would be leading large groups of people to freedom. He said, "You will, and you must, go far beyond me. You must leave me behind. You're going to teach something much bigger and yet much simpler."

I moved to Los Angeles to run Michio's East-West Center, a villa and gardens in the Hollywood hills. It was a thirty-room mansion with magnificent porches and balconies looking out over the city. We had a staff of eight people to keep it clean, cook for the residents, and maintain the grounds. There were avocado, lemon, lime, grapefruit, and orange groves on the property, as well as an evergreen forest, a rose garden, and a grape arbor. It had a gate house that was bigger than most people's homes. There were four huge fields in which I grew organic vegetables for our own food consumption. There were two meals a week for the public as well. Movie stars used to come to eat natural foods. The Center offered classes in Tai Chi, acupuncture, massage, macrobiotics, paper folding, flower arranging, and many other spiritual and Japanese disciplines.

It was in the East-West Center gardens where I first tuned into the vibration of plants. I learned to hear plants speak and I've been able to do it ever since. By my listening to the plant spirits and doing what they suggested, the gardens thrived and gave us an abundance of food. The plant devas told me I did not need to water them; I could save money on the water bill. They said, "Plants don't need water, soil, or nutrients to grow; they grow from consciousness and love, just as humans do." They proved it to me. Following their instructions, I never watered the vegetables, flowers, or shrubs, yet they all grew healthy and strong. I would go up to the fields every day and lie in a hammock, and then tell everyone in the Center that I had been watering the gardens for hours.

The plant devas implored me to tell people I was watering the fields. They told me that if people found out that the gardens were not being watered, the plants would have to conform to the human belief in the necessity of watering. They would have to wilt and die in order to be in harmony with the collective consciousness. Also, following the advice of the devas, I planted a smaller garden, about twenty by twenty feet, exclusively for the deer, rabbits, snails, fungus, and bugs. This garden had all of the vegetable varieties of the larger fields. It was devastated all the time, eaten to pieces by insects and animals. They left the main fields alone. I was enraptured by the experience and did everything the plants told me to do. There was a part of me that would completely relax and trust them. At that time, if you told me to do anything that was 180 degrees opposite of what society says, I did it! "Don't water? Great! No problem!"

My life shifted abruptly once again after running the East-West Center for about a year. One night I went and saw a movie called "Sunday Bloody Sunday." It's about people following the urgings of their heart. I came home from the movie and immediately got on a bus to the L.A. airport. I flew to San Francisco leaving my car and all my belongings behind because I knew intuitively I needed to move on. I made myself get on a plane that night because I knew if I "slept on it," I would have second thoughts and not leave at all.

The next day in San Francisco, I began to feel regret that I had possibly left Michio's Center in the lurch. After all, I was the director and it was a busy place with hundreds of people coming in and out. It was not a small thing from which to walk away. I called the Center to tell my staff I was in San Francisco and never coming back. Before I could say anything, the head cook told me that Carolyn had called. She was the person who ran the center before I did, and we had not heard from her for a year. I called her and she said, "Look, I am kind of up in the air, could I come back and be your assistant or help in some way?" I said, "Well, you can have the whole place back if you want it." She said, "Wonderful!" So I was able to tell Michio, "Hey, I've left and Carolyn's back running things." I was able to leave in a totally responsible way, even though, on the surface, it looked as if I was being irresponsible. I've found that when I make a move intuitively, following my heart, spirit takes care of the responsibility part and all of the other synchronicities necessary to maintain harmony.

In San Francisco, I developed my interpersonal skills further by helping to run a communal natural foods restaurant called the "Good Karma Cafe." My experience at the cafe lived up to its name. It was a very healing and nurturing place for me. My daily routine was to arise at dawn and buy fresh produce directly from farmers at an outdoor market at the edge of town. I would spend the rest of the day cutting vegetables and fruits in a very meditative way and prepare them in soups, sauces, and specials for two hundred people to eat each evening. Surprisingly, making all decisions concerning the restaurant as a group was a very smooth, enjoyable, and easy process! The cafe was well known in hippie circles and was a crossroads for people traveling from Hawaii to Machu Picchu and from Alaska to some ashram in India. After a blissfully contemplative, very California year, I was ready for more challenging exploits; I traveled to Boston to assist Michio with his booming natural food business there.

In Boston, I helped take Michio's macrobiotic food company from one little retail store to the largest natural food manufacturing company in the world at the time. I learned to blend the financial with the spiritual. My social and managerial expertise blossomed. I discovered I was good at assisting people to open to new possibilities and tapping into previously unknown capabilities. I loved transforming *with* people.

During this period, I entered into the wild, adventurous world of rebirthing. Rebirthing is a way of releasing emotional and physical blocks in order to open to spirit. Wearing a snorkel to breathe, people would float face down in a hot tub. This environment simulated the womb experience and would invariably trigger people to re-experience their birth and the trauma of the soul coming into a body and into this physical world. It was very powerful and often very dramatic. Often people would stop breathing and their body would turn white and then blue from lack of oxygen. It was in these crises that I learned to call on and trust grace. Asking for divine intervention, we'd intuitively massage and hug the body of the person, lie next to them, and talk to the person's heart. Eventually, they would start to breathe again, come back to life, and feel ecstatic. We never lost anyone. We were watched over by their guardian spirits and our own. I know it was our innocence and pure intention to serve that guided us through each rebirthing safely.

When I was rebirthed for the first time, I opened so much that I entered into the realm of angels for a period of two weeks. Every morning I'd wake up and whisper quietly to myself, "They're still here." I felt very honored and blessed. I just sat in my living room for two weeks straight and soaked up the energy of this heavenly host. I was receiving daily vibrational healing, cleansing, and briefings on my next mission. I'd call in to work every day and tell them I couldn't move. Every day my partners and co-workers understood and would leave food off at my home. Finally, I was able to go outside. I went to a large park across the street, and the sky was filled with hundreds of angels going all the way up into the heavens as far as I could see. It was a glorious event. I still carry with me the feeling of awe and the infinite I embraced that afternoon.

Eventually, everyone in our company got rebirthed. We had naked truck drivers rebirthing each other. That sounds crazy, but they did it. Their hearts told them to. The next day, they would not even talk about it. It was funny. Somebody would refer to the rebirthing the night before, and they'd say, "Don't you ever mention that again." Yet, the next evening, they'd be back to get rebirthed again, holding each other like babies for hours, naked in a hot tub. It was completely spiritual and not sexual in any way; there was too much grace to feel anything else. It was very healing and magical.

As everyone at the company rebirthed and freed their bodies and spirits, our sales took off, and we tripled our market in just a year. Customers loved dealing with our salespeople, order takers, and especially our open, personable truck drivers, who delivered the wholesale food orders to retail stores across the Northeast. One day, though, the three of us who ran the company, the president, the general manager, and me, the vice-president, had a meeting. We had a little extra money, and my two partners wanted to buy a new fleet of trucks. We had a lot of manufacturing equipment to grind nut butters and fill bags. Some of the machinery was getting old and breaking down and severely injuring the operators. The three of us always voted on major issues. The two of them voted on spending the money to buy new trucks; I voted to spend it on fixing the machinery and safeguarding our workers. They saw no profit in fixing the machinery but a large one in buying new, more efficient trucks. When they out-voted me, I got up and just left. These were my friends who were being maimed by the faulty equipment. I couldn't remain at a company that had lost its heart.

Soon after leaving the health food company, I bought and ran two gourmet natural food Mexican restaurants in Boston. Owning my own restaurant had been a dream of mine for my entire life. I always wanted to prepare chef specials and then mingle with the clientele, inquiring how they enjoyed the specials that night. For a while, it was a lot of fun; but once satisfied with the thrill of ownership for a year, I wanted out of the business. Within a week of deciding to get out, a businessman who owned big steak and seafood houses up and down the East Coast offered to buy the restaurants for a hundred thousand dollars. That would wipe out my debt and give me enough money to go to acupuncture school. But the restaurants weren't worth that much. We were fifty thousand in the hole. I felt I needed, in good conscience, to tell the potential buyer the truth of how I felt. I said to him, "Look, you don't want these restaurants. They can't make money; there aren't enough tables." He thanked me, but went ahead with the deal. I told the truth and *still* got the money. It was a very clear and powerful demonstration to me that speaking one's truth allows whatever is mutual and harmonious to unfold.

My next adventure was as an acupuncturist. I combined acupuncture with Reiki hands-on healing very effectively with my clients. As I allowed more transformative energy to flow through me, I met my next teacher, Medicine Cloud, a Hopi medicine man. From him I learned to work with the spirit animals of my clients. The spirit animals of a person would tell me what was really going on with their energy field and guide me to harmonize their system with acupuncture and Reiki. This collaboration allowed me to become a lot more conscious, comfortable, and accurate dealing with the beings in "so-called" other dimensions. When the time came to begin the *Gatherings,* I was energetically more versatile and relaxed, because I had worked all those years with Medicine Cloud, spirit animals, and vibrational healing.

After many years of playing doctor of Chinese medicine, I shifted the course of my life direction once more in a matter of a few hours. My brother had developed what his doctor called "terminal" cancer. I assisted him to feel his feelings and change his beliefs to heal himself. After I witnessed my brother free himself of cancer with intention alone, I couldn't continue to present myself as "the healer." The morning my brother called to say he was cancer-free, I told my office secretary to cancel all of my appointments. I just left my practice that morning after years of being an acupuncturist. I knew it wasn't acupuncture that was healing people; it was the power of their intention. I drove home without any conscious idea of what I would do next in my life. As I walked in the door to my house, the phone was ringing. A spiritual teacher I had visited in Arizona was on the line. He asked impishly, "Do you want to come out to Arizona and assist me in helping people change their consciousness?" He already knew! He had never called me before, but at that moment, he knew I was ready to leave my old universe. I said, "Sure! I'll be out in four days." For three exciting years, I assisted Lester in Arizona to help people to release stress and emotions and to free their consciousness of limiting beliefs.

After being with Lester, I facilitated a group course called "Avatar" for five years. It was also a way to assist people to improve their lives by transforming the beliefs that shaped their world. I delivered that training in major cities across the country quite successfully. I learned how to set up a network and co-create with people on a national scale. This valuable experience was a perfect final step in preparation for the exciting new phenomenon we call the *Gathering.*

The Dream - A Gathering of Equals is the adventure of people showing up as conscious equals to play for four days as the creative, knowing beings they are—clear, powerful, and free. It's a coming together of people who know they are equal in wisdom, compassion, and in their ability to transform their reality—without the need for a leader, a belief system, or spiritual structure. People share their individual unique gifts and vibration as equals to each other and as equals to those spiritual beings, teachers, and authorities they have previously considered higher or wiser than themselves. At the *Gathering,* people open permanently to their knowing, to that part of them that knows their destiny, their purpose, and the right thing for them to do each moment in life. The *Gathering* unfolds in the realm of vibration, energy, essence. Drawing from personal, direct life experiences, people go directly to the quality they want and allow that core vibration to manifest itself as a reality in their present life. Reclaiming innate wisdom, inner strength and natural aliveness, people make profound and lasting life changes with ease.

I've heard about the *Gatherings* from every spiritual teacher I've had. Each one talked to me about a time when people would come together intuitively to share what they know in their heart, in their beingness, in their essence, from their deep inner wisdom. The first time I encountered this was with St. Germain. Most of my life, I've experienced miracles, spontaneous healings, and a very fluid, magical personal universe. Even with all of that, I still had a lot of doubt, reluctance, and fear. I know now it just wasn't time for me to wake up and to start utilizing these awarenesses. Then, finally, something happened that really was undeniable, that made it impossible for me to go back to sleep.

One evening I was in a hotel restaurant in Florida with a new friend I had recently met. On this occasion, we were talking about very safe subjects like sports and business. After dinner, we walked outside and my friend asked me if I wanted to go to a 7-11 convenience store a mile down the street and get some bottled water. Noting the time and feeling it wasn't too late, we decided to walk to the store. Just as we were beginning our walk, my friend asked me, "What do you know about St. Germain?" Considering the tone of our dinner conversation, this question seemed totally "out of the blue." I had rarely mentioned my lifelong encounters with St. Germain to anyone and had never breathed a word of that, or anything "spiritual," to him before. To our shock and surprise, when our first foot hit the ground, we were in front of the convenience store! We had gone that mile in one step. We quickly looked at our watches in front of the store and discovered that no time had gone by. We checked the wall clock in the store; no time had elapsed. In a daze, we bought the water and walked back to our hotel in silence—the hard way. It took about 20 minutes.

After a long uncomfortable silence, we began to talk about other times we had experienced the stretching or contracting of time. As people now do as a main element of each *Gathering*, my friend and I were intuitively making space in our belief system for something new. We would share personal, direct experiences of similar *extra*ordinary events. As we acknowledged to ourselves the reality of what we had just done, two lights began to fill the room—a purple radiance and a golden glow. Soon we were sitting there with St. Germain and Jesus in the hotel room. They began to speak to us in a very informal, familiar way. We conversed back and forth as old soul mates. They told us about our lives, what we were each doing here this lifetime and what our relationship was to each other, to them, to God, and to the overall plan. They met with us every evening for a week. Because I had a witness in my friend and because the connection was so vivid, powerful, and conscious over so many days, the whole experience was impossible for me to deny, discount, or invalidate. For the first time, my knowing of who I really am would not sink quietly back into my unconscious.

After this encounter, I continued to open to my true nature at a greatly accelerated rate. One particular night, I was lying in bed feeling very frustrated and lonely. I started to feel something in my heart, in my chest, that I had never felt before. It felt very different, very strange. It was a slight burning sensation. At first I thought maybe it was indigestion or heartburn. But it felt good. Then I got a momentous realization from deep inside began to dawn on me. This feeling was *me*; it was a part of me that was coming alive again. As I lay there, opening gingerly to this warmth, this fire coming to life in my belly, a strangely familiar voice—the voice of my heart, my knowing, my higher self, began to speak. "This is not heartburn. This is *you*. This is the *real you*. It's not what you *think* is you, but the you that really exists behind your identity, your body, and the appearances of life. This is the *essence* of you. Right now, it's only a small flame, a pilot light. Your only job is to nurture this radiance. Protect it. Keep it safe. Allow it to grow." This mandate to nurture the primal fire within soon lead me to the volcanic islands of Hawaii.

For the next several years, I spent as much time on the Hawaiian Islands as I could. The inviting ocean, the balmy breezes, and the protective palm trees, allowed me to relax in a much deeper way than

I generally would anywhere else. I felt safer and more connected with the earth than I did in most other places. The Big Island with its active volcano attracted me in particular. On that island by the shore one evening, I was unwinding and allowed myself to open. I surrendered to the rhythmic waves lapping on the rocks. I merged into a connection with spirit, oneness, self, to a greater degree and for a longer time than I ever had before. I'd had glimpses of this experience before, brief moments when I knew the whole score, the blueprint of what I was here on the planet to do. Until this moment, though, I'd only stayed in that state for seconds at a time, not the forty-eight hours to come.

I discovered the more I allowed myself to enjoy and surrender to these waves of love and acceptance, the deeper and more powerful the joy got. I allowed wave after wave of total non-judgmental, unconditional energy to pour over me. Gently, tenderly, I was gathered into the arms of the earth. I was held childlike by life itself. Each breath of wind spoke to me of the love that was my essence. The only word I know that comes close to describing this state is *grace.* I had used the word before, but at that moment, I finally knew what it meant. As this ecstatic embrace continued throughout the night, I realized it wasn't going away this time. I wasn't going to deny it or run from it. It felt like home. I started to really trust it. I began to let surface the unresolved problems and painful traumas of my life—the issues that still hadn't cleared up with my parents, friends, body, and finances. As I felt my way through my life, old confusions lifted, ancient terror melted, and the horror of separation dissolved. Clarity came. I knew true peace for the first time in my life.

After two full days of this divine energy, I was sharing my excitement with friends at a seaside cafe. Suddenly, piercing the afterglow of this inner calm, a very familiar memory, vision, nightmare swept over me. I had been hounded by this remembrance my whole life. It recurred every time I was in a safe and expanded state. I knew the story well:

I was a member of a group of twelve beings whose job, and greatest joy, was to bring light and consciousness to the places in the creation where there was still darkness and unconsciousness—where awareness had not yet arrived. We loved this adventure, but there was one place we were not ever supposed to go. This was very frustrating because our very essence was to be light-bearers. One day, I convinced the others to go to this forbidden space. As we approached, I, being in front as the ringleader, saw the nature of this prohibited place and was able to stop myself from going any farther. Despite my warning, my cohorts, however, could not stop soon enough and went into the outer zone of this space and were repelled into a kind of spiritual limbo for eons.

Even though I had worked on this trauma with every technique and teacher in my life, I had not been able to resolve the heavy guilt, regret and sorrow about having gone against the will of God, broken a divine trust, and sent my closest soul friends to a state of perpetual purgatory. I also had never been able to remember or discover what this place was that was so off-limits to everyone. That evening, however, as I remembered the hopeless tale one more time, I saw with total clarity the reason we were not supposed to enter into this place. *It hadn't been the right time!* I was chilled by an ominous breath of wind, as I sat there in an open cafe watching the golden sun retire into the depths of the ocean. I realized with equal clarity that now it *is* time to know this final piece of the puzzle: *This previously prohibited place is the space of knowing—knowing how to undo the whole current creation—and knowing that it is now time to do it.* As the primal force of this awareness moved up through my body and being, the phrase was triggered and expressed: *We are the fail-safe seeds to ensure that this creation does not go on forever.*

With the dawning of this awareness, I knew it was time for *Gatherings* to commence. I had been told of the *Gatherings* my whole life by my human and celestial teachers, by Pan, and by my own heart. They told of a time when people would intuitively begin to gather around the earth to share, from the core of their beings, the wisdom of their own unique knowing—once again each person freely expressing her/his own individual particular gift, vibration, aspect of the Oneness, and in doing so, return us all to wholeness. The *Gatherings* would be a fertile space for the seeds of knowing, planted by us so long ago, to germinate and to blossom. Just as the 6,000-year-old wheat kernels found in Egyptian pyramids sprouted when given the right environment for growth, so our absolute knowingness will come forth organically when provided with the warmth of the heart and the safety of innocence. In the timelessness of grace and in a space free from duality and judgment, our ancient wisdom will naturally begin to flow forth again. This will be the magic, the alchemy of the *Gatherings.*

I knew, right at that moment, exactly what we gatherers would do when we came together. We would ask for and enter the state of *grace;* we would go to our knowing; and we would allow ourselves to know what our purpose is here and how to go about it. Our knowing would direct the rest of the *Gathering,* and the rest of our lives!

When I got back from Hawaii to my home in Arizona, I discovered that my friend, who had shared with me the encounters with St. Germain and Jesus, also knew it was time to do *Gatherings*. We used our intuition to decide which friends to phone. We called friends around the world to tell them what we intended to do. Twenty-five souls came from New Zealand, Hawaii, and from across the country to the first *Gathering* in Sedona, Arizona, in the summer of 1994. As with current participants, these first people showed up because their intuition guided them to come.

Right before the first *Gathering,* my friend and I felt we needed to open to more inner direction for this initial reunion of soul mates in Sedona. We hiked deep into a remote canyon in northern Arizona. Our intention was to wake up to who we were individually, what our relationship was to each other, and to St. Germain, Jesus, and God. On the fourth day, spirit spoke to us. "What you are seeking, you can find by going to what you know—go to what you know from personal, direct experience." We started playing with this by the river in the canyon. I'd say something and then my friend would say, "Well, do you know that for *sure*?" I'd say, "Well, no, that's what the Bible says, or Jesus, Sai Baba, or Buddha." He'd respond, "Okay. That's fine. Their words and their experience are helpful. But what do you know about it *for sure* from your *own personal, direct experience*?"

Up until this time, I had tried meditating a lot. I'd tried going to my intuition in the past. Sometimes I got an answer, and sometimes I didn't. Sometimes I got an answer, and I didn't trust it; I couldn't tell if it was my intuition or not. As we sat there in the silence of the canyon, with our intention very strong to just allow this to work and allow ourselves to wake up naturally and gently, answers *did* come. Our inner voice came through loud and clear with answers from our own direct, personal experience. The more questions we asked about life, death, money, sex, and spirit, the more quickly and easily answers came from our knowing. The channel to our intuition became clearer, stronger, and more fun!

We began to feel ourselves coming alive again—ignited, burning with joy and passion for life we hadn't felt since childhood. Our sense of who we really are, our essential being, got deeper, richer, and more tangible. As we filled with the power, wisdom, and compassion of our soul's direct life experiences, we noticed our fears, doubts, confusion, and spiritual forgetfulness, were lifting naturally. We knew then, that this is what we'd do at the *Gatherings*. We also knew then, that just as we discovered scores of buried, personal direct experiences, so too would people at the *Gatherings* uncover their own direct experiential answers to their deepest questions.

The next chapter, *The Dream: A Gathering of Equals,* goes into some of the basic, experiential techniques Keith uses to help the people in his workshops access their own inner knowing. It gives a good background before the theme chap-ters. In those, we follow along as Keith assists the workshop participants to access their "knowing," then openly share their experiences.

The breezes at dawn have secrets to tell you.

Don't go back to sleep.

You must ask for what you really want.

Don't go back to sleep.

People are going back and forth across

the door sill where the two worlds touch.

The door is round and open.

Don't go back to sleep.

Rumi

Chapter Two

THE DREAM - A *GATHERING* OF EQUALS

Freeing Attention, Unveilings, and Dream Outs

A COMPLETELY NEW LIFE OPENED UP FOR ME AS I began to actively seek spiritual answers to my ques tions about life. For some time, the universe had been sending me messages that I was not on the right path, but I hadn't been acknowledging them. I had actually felt murmurings from my intuition for a few years, but I dismissed them. It wasn't time for me to open to them yet.

Then a magazine came to me at work. It was a published by a group that teaches spiritual workshops around the world. At first, I was irritated that it was mailed to me at work, but I was intrigued enough to look in the back and call up a local contact in Seattle.

I called a toll-free number and connected with a wonderful woman named Vicky on the island of Hawaii. By my standards at the time, she should have seemed a little eccentric to me, but she *didn't*. She spoke to me from her inner knowing, and I was so unaccustomed to it, I was fearful when talking with her. She knew so much it literally gave me the chills. Frightened yet fascinated, I talked to her on the telephone several times over the next few days. Finally, she told me I didn't really need her workshop now. I could come to it another time. She told me there was going to be a *Gathering* in Seattle within the next few weeks, her very close friend was conducting it, and I would be *ready* to go.

"A what?" I was actually stalling because I heard what she had said quite clearly, so clearly it almost knocked me off my feet. The instant she elaborated with the name *The Dream: A Gathering of Equals,* I knew my life had changed. I was terrified, but absolutely *knew* I'd be going and that it was the beginning of a new life for me. I had no spiritual affiliations, thought traditional religions were hopelessly lost, and non-traditional new age stuff was garbage.

Vicky, my telephone friend and spiritual mentor gave me the Internet web site access number for *The Dream* and I downloaded some of the following. I decided for sure when I read the statement at the bottom of one of the pages that read, *"If you know the quickening has begun and you're ready to play, please join us."*

Keith and I thought it would be fun to introduce you to the *Gathering* and the remainder of this book by sharing some of the same materials I read before going to my first *Gathering*. These will lead into a more in depth explanation of some of the basic approaches used in the *Gatherings* and some examples of how they are actually experienced by the workshop participants. These, as with the rest of the book, are from actual dialog recorded during the workshops. Of course, it is impossible to duplicate the spirit, vibration, and feeling that exists

when there are voices, bodies, and spirits present. The electricity in the air can't be captured in print. We hope to have captured enough of that essence to intrigue you and help you to reconnect with your own dream.

Presented here is some of the material from the brochures:

The Dream: A Gathering of Equals is four days of aliveness, alchemy, and awakening flowing from the well of your own personal power, sovereignty, innocence, and grace. In an atmosphere of total respect for your own intuitive style and timing, you will learn how to:

- Live from your heart, not from your fear.
- Reclaim your lost vitality, magic, fun, and spontaneity.
- Manifest your soul's design with no effort or doingness.
- Weave the life of *your* dreams, not of your parents or the culture.
- Lift the ancient veils of scarcity, struggle, sickness, and secrecy.
- Enjoy the love you deserve...with a partner and with yourself.
- Reconnect permanently and intimately to Universal life force.
- Make profound and lasting life changes with clarity, joy, and playful ease.
- Share your unique vibration and wisdom honestly, openly and safely in the world.
- Open fully to universal supply and attract abundant resources, money, opportunities, and friends.
- Keep your attention, creating energy, focused solely on your desires, not the distractions of life.
- Wake yourself up in a way and at a pace that is compassionate, graceful, and perfect for you.
- Create freely with the most fundamental and effective force in existence...pure vibration.
- Know directly who you are and exactly what you are here to do this lifetime.
- Bring the amazing, the magnificent, and the miraculous into your daily life.
- See through the eyes of your soul, not your personality.

WHAT HAPPENS AT THE GATHERINGS?

Master Your Attention

You retrieve your attention from the places outside yourself where you have given your power away. You regain your orphaned energy and soul fragments.

Go to Your Knowing

You focus your newly freed attention on what you know for sure, from personal direct experience, from your absolute knowing.

Unveil

If anything gets in the way of your having or knowing what you want, it is a veil, a veil that covers up your essence, blocks your power, and hides your divinity. Veils are intuitive devices deliberately designed by your real self to control your awakening/forgetfulness and keep you safe until you can take over the same protective, regulating function consciously, using your knowing awareness. Veils operate as unconscious masks, identities, conditioning, limiting beliefs, fears, illnesses, and lies. When you recapture enough free attention and absolute knowingness to be able to intuitively protect yourself and consciously manage your life, the veils dissolve naturally. The power that the programmed, automatic, unconscious controlling device had over you fades organically…from lack of sustaining attention, because it is intuitively no longer needed. You recover more of your awakeness, your sovereignty, your soul.

Rediscover who you are and why you are here

Focusing full attention and knowing on your own unique vibration, you re-experience directly and absolutely the real reason you are here, the *dream* that excites you, the personal blueprint that resonates in every cell of your body, the unique energy/gift that is you and that you came to express. Now, as you direct your full attention to your real dream, it unfolds organically, without effort or programmed doingness. Also, when you are following your true design in being here, that destiny is in perfect harmony and alignment with God's purpose (divine will, the universal blueprint). Thus, every human being, animal, plant, and rock is naturally assisting you to manifest your real intention.

Become whole and fully conscious again

From knowingness, you explore personal and collective archetypal spaces (gateways, portals), such as Innocence, Universal Supply, Grace, Ascension, and Trust. You recover lost aspects of your true self. At your own individual pace, you return gently and intuitively to your whole natural self, to your true power, to your full consciousness. You dance with the universe as an integrated, complete being.

Reconnect with your greater self

The journey home is primarily an individual one, but we come together now to assist each other on the adventure by each offering his or her piece of the ancient puzzle, each unique, individual vibration, essence, gift. The *Gathering* is an opportunity for you to re-connect with your original excitement and zest for life and with the people with whom you are destined to play in this adventure. A collective knowing and explicit memory draws on each group: We planned this get-together for exactly this purpose...a long time ago from the highest level of consciousness. It is time to gather as fully conscious, whole, divine equals to live our shared dream...heaven and earth as one...again.

What's different about
THE DREAM: A GATHERING OF EQUALS?

- Attention is focused on what you want, not on what's in the way of what you want.

- Each *Gathering* is unique, reflecting the current awareness of the group at the moment and evolving with the timing of the awakening of each person. There is no set agenda or plan. Each get-together explores consciousness in a fresh, spontaneous, organic way and develops into something very new and timely for the particular people present.

- Each *Gathering* is deliberately designed to be a bridge between the present and the future, a gentle, conscious transition from the current collective paradigm to the next step in the creative expansion for humankind. During the four days, the usual "leader/follower" format intuitively and gracefully transforms into a dance of emerging equal beings. As people unveil their forgetfulness, the flow of the *Gathering* flows from the typical facilitator/participant (teacher/student) framework into an exciting expression of the new playground...conscious equals openly sharing and living the real dream, whatever that is for each person.

- You are encouraged to share whatever you want from the *Gathering* with whomever you want in whatever way you want. There is no confidentiality or secrecy.

- The *Gathering* goes beyond words, ideas, and technology. You play with the transformative power of live, real vibration, not concepts, beliefs, or formulas. What at first appears to be "technique" soon reveals itself as your own re-found natural ability. Transformation occurs from the inside out instead of from the outside in, as in trying to strip off limiting beliefs and stuck emotions, layer by layer, to uncover the real you. You go directly home by reconnecting with times when you were in the vibration you prefer. As you allow yourself to vibrate at your own unique, natural frequency, the ever-increasing vibrant energy flows right through and past the old limits and patterns.

- In the *Gatherings*, our attention is focused solely on what you know for sure, from personal, direct experience. Relying on other people's life experiences and conclusions leads to confusion, conflict, and complication. Listening to your own personal, direct knowing brings simplicity, harmony and clarity.

In the rest of the chapter, we'll give you guidelines for some of the basic tools used in the *Gatherings* then follow them with actual examples. There are others used in the workshops, but we'll limit the scope of this chapter and the rest of the book to three of the most fundamental. They are, *Freeing Your Attention, Unveilings,* and *Dream outs.* Since each of the remaining chapters has two or more actual *dream outs,* we did not include any examples in this chapter.

WAYS TO FREE YOUR ATTENTION

(so that your creative energy is available to fund your dream)

1. Where is my attention right now? Is it where I want it?

If not, allow a suggestion to arise spontaneously from your inner knowing by asking:

***Intuitively*, where else *could* my attention be right now?**
Immediately experience where your attention has shifted by asking:

Where is my attention right now?
Repeat until you feel an authentic shift in your whole being, not just in your mental state.

2. For more clarity in any situation, ask the following until you experience a state of absolute knowing and peace:
What do I know for sure?

3. To free your attention from any fear or any emotional blockage, overwhelm or confusion, ask the following until you experience a breakthrough or release into a state of absolute knowing and peace:

Emotionally, what would happen if? Then what? What next?

ALLOWING THE FEELING (Freeing Your Attention)

(A process inspired and used by Arnold Patent.)

1. Feel the *feeling* as energy, vibration, power, movement, aliveness, life force, essence, sensation.
Feel the feeling free of any thoughts about it. Allow yourself to sense the feeling in a fresh, new way. Feel the energy, the vibration of the feeling. Experience the feeling as power, your *own* power. Resonate, vibrate, flow with the energy of the feeling. Allow the energy to move beyond the boundaries of the body.

2. Feel *love* for the *feeling*.

Acknowledge the existence of the feeling. Allow the feeling to just be. Be with the energy just as it is. Say "yes" to the feeling. Feel acceptance for the energy in the feeling. Feel the energy loving you. Feel energy recognizing energy. Feel life force connecting with life force.

3. Feel *love* for *yourself* feeling the feeling.

Acknowledge yourself for feeling the feeling. Appreciate yourself feeling the power of the feeling. Feel love for yourself feeling your own power. Feel love for yourself feeling the feeling. Feel compassion for yourself freeing your attention. Feel compassion for yourself freeing your spirit. Allow the feeling, the love, and yourself to be free.

Here is an example of the "Freeing Your Attention" process from a *Gathering* in Phoenix. This exercise took place on the morning of the first day of a four-day workshop:

SULANA - **(In tears)** This is a replay, this is a pattern. Last night I got home and I felt the millions of falsenesses in my life. And I felt like "I can't lift all of these veils." I felt clarity and then I sank down again.

KEITH - Do you want to try something right now? Where is your attention right now, your energy? Is it on what you were speaking about?

SULANA - My attention is on sadness and fear. That's all I feel.

KEITH - So, allowing yourself to be open—and anyone else can do this too if you want. Right now, in *this* present moment, intuitively, would you allow your heart to speak to you? Would you allow an opening for something to speak or communicate with you, *other* than the sadness and the fear? Just allow a space and ask, intuitively, where else *could* your attention, your focus be right now? Just leave that opening, for your inner self, spirit, heart, to offer a suggestion. Where else *could* you be focusing your life force right now? **(Quietly to Sulana)** Could you share when you get an answer, a suggestion, a vibration, a feeling?

SULANA - At first I felt love, then I just felt energy. I feel a lot of energy. But in life...

KEITH - Forget about "life." See how that's taking you out of the moment? It's draining your power. Right now, what came from spirit was some energy, love. So *right now*, right now is all there is. Right now, where would you *prefer* to play, to live, to experience? Where your attention *was*, or to *this* energy? Which is more attractive? Where does your energy, your attention, your focus *want* to flow?

SULANA - It wants to be here now.

KEITH - With what? That energy, the love? Or just here? Which is more attractive? Where do you want your attention? On the sadness and fear? So what else is available right now that's pulling you, stronger than that? Is it a vibration, an energy? You don't even have to name it.

SULANA - There's a space and an energy.

KEITH - Okay, could you, right now, just plainly and simply allow yourself to go there, be there with that energy, that space? Could you do that? Right *now*, where do you want your attention? Where does it feel good?

SULANA - The energy I'm feeling burns. I don't like it.

KEITH - Okay, so right at this moment, could you ask your heart, your spirit, where else could your attention be right now? Ask for a suggestion, for something that doesn't burn, for something that's attractive; right for you. Tell me when you get a suggestion that's attractive, desirable, that *pulls* your heart, your attention, your soul. Could you allow it to move toward something desirable, pleasant, enjoyable, and nurturing. Could you allow it to flow that way?

SULANA - I feel a light space and I also feel heavy.

KEITH - Okay, between those two, where would you like to hang out, in the light space or the heavy space?

SULANA - The *light* space.

KEITH - So could you allow yourself to move toward the light space?

SULANA - I'm afraid I'm going to die if I say, "Yes." **(crying)**

KEITH - So what would happen if you die?

SULANA - I don't know.

KEITH - In your knowing, what would happen if you died...right now?

SULANA - Well...in my knowing I realize nothing would happen. I can't die.

KEITH - Is it okay to move on?

SULANA - Yeah, everything's okay **(laughing)**.

KEITH - We actually did three of the exercises there all at once, thanks to Sulana. Just so you can get a sense for what we just played with, it seems like a technique, but it really isn't. What we use is an overall playful approach and attitude to guide your attention toward something that will shift you and get your energy moving again. Where is my attention other than where I want it? This is when you're in something you're not enjoying, a space that's not pleasant for you. You have some attention somewhere that you don't want it. It's stuck; it's fixed; it won't go away. So you can ask yourself, intuitively, where else could my attention be, *right now*? It seems like a structured way of asking it, but everything we are doing here in the *Gathering* is really that same question. Everything we are doing is *that* question in another form, in another way.

The spirit of that question is saying, "Hey, you have a choice. There are alternatives. There are other spaces, other places, other emotions, other feelings, where you could be *playing* right now. There are other places where you could be focusing, feeling, allowing your attention to flow, allowing your life force to flow, putting your awareness, your concentration." It's just to remind you that you have a choice. There are other spaces in the universe other than the one you're in. In fact, there are *billions* of places to be other than the one you're in.

When we're in our stuff, when we're in a feeling, when our energy's stuck in our back or a headache, or terror, or sadness, it feels like the *only* place available. It feels like this is what we've *got* to experience.

It's so powerful, so dominating. But there are an infinite number of other possibilities. We don't ask, "Where else would you *like* your attention to be?" Can someone intuit why? If you go into *thinking* mode, go into your mind, it's usually a mental answer you get. Guess what? Guess who already has you right where it wants you? Your *mind* does. You don't want to go to your mind. It's not going to lead you out. It will lead you to a cult or to a fourteen-hour-a-day, six-day-a-week job you hate. It'll lead you somewhere, but it won't lead you out. My friend Lester used to say "Your mind will never assist you to free yourself from the mind." My experience of that is that it's true. The mind will make it *look* like it's leading you somewhere nurturing, better, but it won't.

Intuitively, where else could my attention be? In other words, we're opening to spirit, to God, to intuition, to heart, to infinite wisdom, to the great spirit. That's what we're opening to. We're saying great spirit, universe, intuition; give me a suggestion which will be *so* attractive, so right for me, so enticing, that it will actually pull me out of this funk, out of this migraine headache, this depression, this terror. Give me a suggestion that will be so powerful and attractive, in a positive, fun way, that it'll draw me *out* of here. It's the same as praying. They are just different words. Everything we do here is *this* simple, instead of going to your head for a suggestion, we're going to our heart. We're going to our essence. Instead of the past, we're going to the present.

The reason we're presenting a lot of different ways of saying the same thing is because sometimes the *mind* will find a way to block some of these approaches. One of these will work if you keep trying to use them all, using your intuition, using playfulness, a little humor. Being gentle with yourself, you can get yourself to *move*. Once you've moved, where are you going to move to? Where's your heart going to be drawn? Where's your spirit going to go once you get it unstuck? In your experience, in your knowing, where does your spirit go once it's moving?

GROUP - Love, realness, safety. The real trick is to just get yourself moving, unfixed, untraumatized, unparalyzed, unhypnotized.

KEITH - Every approach that we use in the *Gathering* is to make a crack in your world, is to **(Keith claps his once loudly.)** break the spell. That's what it's all for, so a little light can come in. "Oh my God, there's something more than the world being polluted, and I'm overworked and tired and a victim. There's something else out there.

There's an alternative."

Each of these approaches are a way to snap us out of the spell we're under. We're actually hypnotized. We're under a spell of our mind that we wove a long time ago. We wake up, but then we go back under the spell because we wove it so well. It was supposed to last for a while, but we made it *too* well. How many people have spoken to ascended masters or other wise beings? They talk about this whole experiment on earth, that we constructed the veil of forgetfulness *too* well. We wanted to explore physical dimension, victimhood, suffering, polarity, aloneness. We wanted to explore all that, right? So we all went and explored it. Hardly anyone came back. Almost everyone got lost in it. And they sent these beings down to wake us up. Jesus, Buddha, Lao Tzu. They haven't been successful yet. Look at the earth. Everyone's still under the spell. They nailed Jesus to a cross. They made religions and structure out of their teachings. They killed the spirit of the others. What I know is that I *still* get trapped. I *still* fall asleep. I *still* am under the spell at times. What I want to share with you are ways that are working for me to break the spell.

All of us are gathering as equals, tapping into our own knowing to share with each other ways we have found to break the spell in a way that *lasts*, that really works. These approaches are ways that have been working for us, for the last three years, to keep the spell from taking us over again. They wake us up to the fact that there's an alternative. The one thing that's unique in the *Gathering* is that we're going to our knowing for answers as opposed to anywhere else. Then, if you can, receive it, let yourself hear it, sense it somehow. Then you start moving toward it.

The whole breakthrough for me was just before the first *Gathering* when I experienced two days of complete grace. For the first time, I was going *toward* something rather than *away* from something. I'd been going *away* from pain my whole life, away from suffering, away from slavery. Moving away from the undesirable worked for a while, but then the old patterns would catch up to me. For the first time, I felt myself going *toward* love, light, home. No matter how I felt, there was this part of me being drawn toward harmony. It's been that way ever since, no matter how deep my depression, how strongly an old program, danger, or terror comes up. I've had a lot of issues arising lately, but I still feel that I'm going home. In fact, I *am* home. I just forget sometimes. Actually, I don't even forget. This is part of what I call "playing out." We're all playing it out.

These approaches allow us to go to our *knowing*, rather than our head. They allow a suggestion from a place other than your programming or ingrained belief systems.

Another approach in the *Gathering* is a means of getting past all of the issues keeping you from your own inner truth. This *unveiling* is a means of clearing all of the obstacles which are between you and your dream:

UNVEILING

A veil is a feeling (thought, belief, pattern, condition, or fixed attention) you feel is in the way of allowing you to experience the present moment exactly as you prefer to experience it.

Allow a suggestion to arise spontaneously from your inner knowing by asking:

What beneficial purpose has the veil served for me?
How has it protected me or kept me safe?
What has it tried to bring my attention to?
What has it maintained or controlled for me?
What has it helped me to handle or deal with in my life?
How has it helped me to experience the things I wanted to experience in my life?
How has it regulated the pace or timing of my life plan?
What deliberate role has it played for me in the overall design of my life?

Wait for an answer on the level of a realization, insight, revelation, or recognition. A feeling of appreciation will spontaneously accompany an authentic realization.

As I begin to know for sure that my intuition can serve the same purpose as the veil, do I allow the unconscious influence of the veil to lift?

The genuine recognition that *your intuition can now do the same thing for you the veil has been doing* has the power to de-activate the influence of the veil.

What is the gift on the other side of the veil?
What aspects of my wholeness, my *true being* has this veil been covering up? At a loving, intuitive pace, do I now allow myself to integrate and live as the natural part of my *real self*?

Here is an example of the *unveiling* process from a *Gathering* in Phoenix. Here Keith explained what an unveiling is, then assisted the group members as they *unveiled* experientially:

UNVEILING

KEITH - The key question is, "What beneficial purpose has this veil served for you right now or in the past? Once you get an authentic, real, genuine answer to that, the rest flows naturally. When you get a genuine realization as to how it's actually served you, when you go to that level where you see that you put it in place *deliberately,* it begins to lift. At that point there should naturally be a sense of appreciation, awe, and recognition. Usually, once you see the purpose it serves, you are already at a level of consciousness where you can take over the same purpose. You don't have to have an automatic program anymore.

As you do take over and the veil begins to lift, go off automatic, you begin to sense what it was covering up all along. It could be your power, clarity, sense of well-being, divinity, grace, trust, whatever. Let yourself shift permanently into a place where you're in the power, in the space, to do that same thing for yourself that the veil has been doing up until now. When you consciously take over the function of the veil, the veil won't even try to reactivate. Unveiling is going to your knowing and allowing an answer to come from there. What's the *real* reason? How has it served you? When you see that, the rest naturally unfolds.

Very often there are other veils that protect us from undoing the veil we go after. They may come as regret, self-recrimination, going to sleep, spaciness, distraction, or others. The veils were originally put in place to keep you from freeing yourself and keep you from taking off the main veil. You can deal with the distracting veils individually as they come up. What else do we call veils?

GROUP RESPONSES - Onion skins, blocks, heavy metal iron armor, denial, pretense.

KEITH - Identities, programming, conditioning.

GROUP - Masks, your shadow, reaction, thought forms.

KEITH - Limiting beliefs. I have a question for you. Is there any belief that is not ultimately limiting?

SHAWN - No, there isn't.

KEITH - We just call them all *veils*. At the very beginning of the *Gatherings*, we called them "cloaks" because they felt like those heavy draperies in a castle or heavy wool cloaks. Then they started feeling lighter, easier to part, and we started calling them veils. I have another question for you. If there is another living being that is bigger and more powerful than you and this being is out to get you or eliminate you, what will you do?

GROUP - Resist. Grow. Try to take charge.

KEITH - Try to take charge?

GROUP - Get bigger.

KEITH - What does all of this sound like?

GROUP - Anger, fear, ego.

KEITH - The veils are actually the ego, the mind, our beliefs. We spontaneously discovered something in playing with veils. We took the point of view and approached the ego much in the way that you were sharing this morning, of looking to see the beneficial value. Examine the positive intention or the beneficial purpose of these veils, of the ego, emotions, patterns and see what true part they played in our purpose, our whole design, our blueprint. In other words, we didn't approach the veils with the attitude and intention of eliminating them.

Instead we approached them from the point of view of intuition, from the deepest level of knowing. Why is this here? Why did my higher self create this? What true purpose does it serve?

Using this approach, we found it increasingly easier to *find* the veils. They would show up; they'd stick out. They didn't need to hide from us anymore. Our intention was to *include* them, *embrace* them, rather than extinguish them, judge them, or make them wrong. It has made an amazing difference. That's the main way we *unveil*. When we say *unveil*, it's really not so much lifting the veils, it's lifting the *unconscious* power the veils have over you. It's lifting the *automatic* control that the veils have over you: the ego, beliefs, fears, and emotion. It's lifting the programmed influence the veils have over you.

Veils are automatic and ingrained. They are a lot like cruise control. You're zooming down the road just great at 85; the car's on automatic, then all of a sudden, you're heading straight for the rear of a semitruck right in front of you. The truck is only going 55 miles an hour. What are you going to do? Take your car off automatic and go to manual. We have a whole bunch of patterns, beliefs, and behaviors that we've put on automatic to protect us, to keep us safe, to give us love. They also allow us to gain *other* experiences. Believe it or not, we've actually set up these experiences of suffering, victimhood, and betrayal by our own choice. We wanted to see what it's like to be poor, or to experience scarcity, loneliness, and desolation. What else do veils do?

GROUP - Help you to survive. Keep us operating the way we're accustomed to. Protect us from the unknown.

KEITH - The veils help us keep our forgetfulness in place until it's time to wake up, to make sure we don't wake up too soon. If we start to awaken too soon, a veil kicks in and we go back to sleep.

A veil is anything in your way of being happy, anything you are experiencing that's preventing you from experiencing life the way you want to. It's really a feeling. Whether it's a belief, idea, concept, or pattern; it's the *vibration* of it we're playing with here. You don't need to be able to describe or explain it. It's that feeling of something preventing you from being joyous, playful, open, trusting. It doesn't matter what it is. When you experience blockage, that's the veil.

In fact, some of the most *vague* feelings are the *most* powerful veils to lift. A lot of people have had lifelong undercurrent feelings that have *always* been there, like feeling melancholy, lost, depressed, anxious, insecure or unsafe. Those are prevalent undercurrent veils you can't even describe; they're a kind of background noise, background feelings in life. A lot of people think that's the way life is. They have never experienced life without these veils. Those are *wonderful* veils to lift. Once you lift them, the energy flows and new, exciting, and nurturing things start to happen to you.

A veil can be anything you consider to be a veil. If it doesn't feel good, if you don't like it or enjoy it, it's a veil for you. You decide. The group doesn't decide. The belief system doesn't decide; *you* decide if something is a veil. You don't need to know anything more about it. In fact, knowing more about it can really stall the whole process, bog it down. That can be a veil itself: needing to know what the veil is. Veils block the free flow of energy and life. The effective way to lift these patterns is to ask, in our knowing, "What is the actual *beneficial* effect of this veil?

We know about the negative effect it has; we know how it's blocking us. But from the higher self, from the overall blueprint design, why was it put in place? What did it help us to accomplish? How did it protect us? What we're looking for is the answer in the form of a realization, an "aha," an insight. If it doesn't feel fresh, new, and invigorating, it's probably a *mental* answer, rather than an awareness from your knowing. If it is from your knowing, there is usually a sense of awe, appreciation, and gratitude for the insight. Wait for an epiphany. Sometimes it might take awhile, a few minutes, but wait for something *authentic*. When it is, you'll feel a rush of energy; you'll feel lighter. Your life will get brighter. Things will seem clearer. You'll get a sense of the big picture, a broadening. Then the question is: do you want this particular pattern on *automatic* anymore? Do you want it running your life? Do you want it to come up and control you every time you're in that situation to make sure you stay safe, remain protected?

Could you now substitute your intuitive awareness in the moment? Could you use your own knowing to keep you safe, to protect you, to regulate things instead of being on automatic power? Could you consciously and deliberately do the same thing that the veil has done for you up until this moment? Do you want it on automatic, or do you want to be in charge?

JANET - It's interesting. The unveiling process has taken me off of automatic so that I can fully experience a situation. My awareness has shifted for me in many ways.

KEITH - That's really what we're doing when we review automatic behavior and decide what we're going to do about it right now. Do we want to keep it on automatic or deal with it consciously in the moment? Do you want to try one? Can everyone feel something you would consider a veil right now? Let's have examples of some veils that are up for you right now in your life.

GROUP - Scarcity of money, not understanding, tightness, anxiety, being distracted, frustrated, irritated, any botheration disturbing your peace, your joy? Wanting too much? Anything could be a veil. A sense of dissatisfaction could be a veil, uneasiness.

JUDY - Just the fact that we're talking about this is making my chest tight.

KEITH - That's why we're doing it. We're trying to bring up a veil. **(Laughter from the group)** Does everybody have one now?

JANET - Keith, what if you're not feeling an intense discomfort....do you make one up? I have plenty I have experienced, so I can choose one.

KEITH - How about right now, when you ask that question, what are you feeling?

JANET - I feel like there's something wrong with me. Maybe that's a veil.

KEITH - A good veil to choose is often one that is really up right now, operating right at this moment, really bothering you *right now*.

Here Keith led the group in an actual *unveiling* exercise:

KEITH - As you allow yourself to focus on this pattern or feeling, ask yourself, "Has it come up in your life before?" Right now, relax into your beingness. Allow, in its own time, its own way, an answer to come from your knowing, from the deepest part of your own wisdom, from that part of you that knows the overall picture. What beneficial purpose has this veil served, either right now, or in the past? How has this veil, this pattern, helped you, assisted you? Has it helped you to stay safe, to protect you, helped you regulate or control something? Has it helped you to deal with or handle something in life? Has it wanted to draw your attention to something? Has it assisted you in having certain experiences in life you've wanted to have? Allow yourself to go to that level of knowing, and discover what role this pattern is playing in that overall design. Just allow the answer to become clear.

Allow yourself to enter into that level of knowing where both the designer and the design reside. How has this veil actually served you? Has it kept you safe or helped you to handle stress in some way? Allow the answer, the clarity, to come. Open to what is right for you to know. What is the beneficial purpose of this veil?... Did it serve you well?... Do you have a sense of appreciation, gratitude, awe for what it has done?... Do you choose to take over the same function deliberately?... What is the gift on the other side of the veil?... At a pace that feels compassionate and loving towards yourself, could you allow the veil to lift?

After a silent period of about twenty minutes, Keith lightly rang chimes to indicate an opening for people to begin sharing what they experienced. After a few minutes of shuffling back into their seats, people began to share their experiences. Shawn started with a humorous veil:

SHAWN - I got that my job is a veil. In fact, every day my job *tells* me it's a veil. I monitor mainframe on-line systems for (a major) bank in Brooklyn. So every day, I jump out of bed at 3:30 in the morning, that is 5:30 east coast time, and I check the status of all the on-line systems. The computer screen reads "available, available, available, available...". So, a few months ago, I figured, to save time, and to save space, I'd shorten the word "available" to the letters a-v-a-i-l. And now I jump out of bed at 3:30 in the morning, log onto the system, and the screen says "avail, avail, avail, avail...". **(Lots of laughter and clapping from the group)** So, I got that the job is telling me it's a veil. And it's going to happen at 3:30 tomorrow morning when I do it again. Until something changes. Then I got stuck in the fear of "How do I replace my job?"

That's where I got stuck. Then I figured, let me handle the veil of fear. Instead, what came up was the fact I was living flat line. I was living a steady life. My job pays my bills, allows us to live comfortably without going into debt, but without saving money. I was living flat line. We just moved here from Florida, one of the flattest states in the union. The biggest height is, I think, the garbage dump outside of Miami. We moved from Florida to Arizona which is all mountains and valleys. So this idea of living flat line became real evident to me. I discovered I was, at this point in time, really afraid to take a risk, to take a loss. So maybe this move means something. I got stuck again in the fear of "but what am I going to do about replacing this job?" I don't have any alternatives right now. So that's where I got stuck again.

DAVID - I had a neat unveiling this time. I was frustrated that I'm not getting the feedback I want in the work I'm doing. I got the message, "David, what you *really* want to do is the thing you actually *flow with.*" And I wasn't doing that. What I was doing wasn't flowing. It's *that* simple. And I looked at all kinds of things where I want recognition. I discovered I don't want or *deserve* recognition in areas where I'm out of the flow. It was *so* great.

LINDA - The answers came really fast. Frustration has been a development to keep me in my flow. At the end, the gift was the *journey*. You know, *being* ***in*** *that flow*. It is a development, to keep me in my flow.

AUDREY - I was working on a veil of being *comfortable*. Then all of a sudden I noticed that a Beatles song was playing in my head. It was the song "All You Need is Love." You don't need to *do* anything. It was going for quite awhile.

JANET - For me it became simple to get an answer. I was exploring frustration and *immediately* finding the gift in it and thinking "This is too easy, I'm doing it wrong. There's something wrong here." Then I realized that's been my veil recently. I thought it needed to be complicated to be powerful. I realized, going through that *unveiling* that I'm letting go of that belief.

SULANA - I got really angry. That *veil* lifted easily too and under that I felt power. I realized I was angry because I am feeling my own power now. I know when I don't combine it with love or compassion, it can be very harmful. So I have some work to do with power. (**She laughs.**) I'm afraid of power. I feel it right now.

MARK - I had a veil. I asked, "Why isn't my eyesight better?"

KEITH - It's because you don't have your glasses on.

MARK - Oh, that's it. Thank you. It's a miracle! All you need to do is ask. **(The group laughs.)** The answer I got was that my glasses were literally a veil; they were hiding my eyes, the window to my soul. I've been hiding behind my glasses. Then I got a clear visual image of the cosmos. It was like a giant eye looking at me and extending out until it disappeared into the stars. I am part of the whole universe. So what's to be hiding? Why should I be hiding *anything*? It's all power, all knowing, all everything. What set that off for me was that earlier in the day my vision was better than it's been in a long time. It reminded me there's something I need to get rid of. I recognized the beneficial purpose of this veil was that it wasn't yet time for me to see certain things. Now it's time, so I have decided to consciously take over the job.

MARIE - One of the veils I recognize in myself is that I used to need to understand everything and put it into a form before I would speak. Now I'm just speaking. Internal answers have come to me here, where I was always reaching outside of myself before. For example, in a *dream out* yesterday, I went to another universe and I faced a bird that stared me in the eyes and said, "You *know* that you know." We merged and became one. When that being left me...talk about *changes* **(crying)**, it left very abruptly. I'm on my own now. This morning, when I got up, we heard a noise. It was a bird that had somehow gotten into our bedroom. To me, it looked exactly like the bird **(sobbing)** I was connected with yesterday, in one of the exercises we did when I remembered where I put my heart. I opened up the shades so it could come out because it was flying behind the shades and didn't know *how* to get out. I opened up the back door, and I said, "Okay, you're free now." And the bird said to me "Okay, *you're* free." Then I said, "Okay, fine" and off the bird went....

The *dream out* is what Keith sometimes refers to as the "main event" of the *Gatherings*. Here are the basic guidelines for a *dream out*. The rest of the book consists of major theme *dream outs*. This approach is deceptively simple and remarkably effective in escorting people to their own inner knowing. It is the stuff that true life is made of.

DREAMING OUT (an intuitive journey)

Is there anything in your life that is not exactly the way you want it?

Go to a time in this lifetime when that aspect of your life was exactly the way you wanted it.

Allow a vibration, time, place, awareness, energy, or experience to arise spontaneously from your inner knowing to open a gateway for you to the vibration you want.

Let your intuition guide you. Ask, "Am I in the right place?"
If you are not certain it's the right place, let it go and open to another vibration.

Be there emotionally, resonate with it, become it, merge with the vibration.

Move past viewing or witnessing it.
Be fully conscious in the present as a vibration.

Dream out exactly the way you want that vibration in your life.

Allow the vibration to unfold in the moment and open you spontaneously to whatever experience is right for you at this time on your path.

The *dream out* is the basic tool in the Gathering to access the inner knowing part within each of us. Now the book moves along to the theme chapters, the heart and soul of the book. Chapter three we explores rediscovering our magic and connecting to universal supply.

I am holding a key
and so are you.

I can open the padlock
into your circle

And you can open mine

Let us keep opening padlocks
That have been
long forgotten.

Georgina Murata

Chapter Three

THE SANDBOX AND THE LILAC BUSH

Where Did You Hide Your Magic?** and **Universal Supply

MARIE HANTHORN EXPERIENCED A VISION ON THE second day of a *Gathering* in Phoenix. Her dream was a vivid recollection of a scene from her childhood, another place, another time, where magic lived and creation abounded. It was a place of innocence where joy reigned supreme and the sun was always shining. It is a place to which we all need to reconnect in order to find our dream.

MARIE - I went back to a place where I was happy. What I remember is the sensation of being two years old and coming out of the back of our house. I remember opening the back door and seeing the sunlight shining on my sandbox, and I remember running across the back yard without any shoes on. I was barefoot and running to the sandbox and jumping right in and running my hands through the sand, playing with rocks and pretending they were little vehicles. I had a feeling, a very strong sense, I could create *anything* in that sandbox. And right next to the sandbox was the lilac bush. Whenever I wanted to, I could crawl into it. The lilac bush was a place where I could always hide, and I could talk to the different beings who lived in the lilac bush. They were there, so happy to see me and to be with me. I really did have the sensation, at that age, that *I* could *create anything*. The sunlight would caress and support me with its soothing warmth. I knew that I was loved and protected. I was *so* connected with that sandbox and the lilac bush, just like I am here, now, with all of you.

The *Gatherings* in the Phoenix area have a special feeling to them. Since Keith lives there, they are held frequently, about every three months. As the home base for the *Gathering* movement, there is a sense of ownership in Phoenix, fostering a familiarity that assists the group in getting to a deep state of shared oneness sooner. Keith's introductory workshops in the area provide the opportunity for more local exposure and a continual source of new gatherers who bring renewed innocence and awe to the group.

Because I scheduled a late airline flight, I arrived after the Friday evening session had already begun. It was a completely dark November night when I arrived at *The House of Eos* in the rural desert north of Scottsdale, Arizona. I was struck by the thousands of stars dimly lighting the desert cactus and brush with the flickering light of the heavens. I walked slowly toward the door of the beautiful stucco ranch style home. I could hear the voice of the night desert and feel a mystical, surrealistic pulse coming from the silhouettes of the sage bushes and majestic saguaro cacti surrounding the house. The warm air contrasted with the damp cool atmosphere in Seattle. This world was so different from the one I had just left, and the spirit of the desert was strong and alive. I stood for a few minutes, staring up at the brilliant star-filled sky and felt amazingly connected to the earth and the universe.

In that space, I hesitated, thinking maybe I didn't need the *Gathering.* I felt I was already "there." A primary focus of the *Gathering* is to get connected with your inner knowing and the universe. At that moment, I was as connected as I had ever been. I gathered myself, under the desert sky, and lost all sense of space and time. Yet the porch light, intensely bright in contrast with the vast darkness all around, called me. In my trance like state, I walked toward that large, beautiful home. As I approached the door, the old world brick tile and fountain in the piazza fueled the dreamlike state I was in. I opened the door slowly, to find the inside of the house as beckoning as the outside entry way. It was as though I had entered an ancient *Gathering* place. I felt an amazing sense of *deja vu,* a feeling I'm now learning to associate with the fulfillment of my destiny, or doing exactly what I'm supposed to be doing.

Inside, Keith was talking to those who had gathered for the evening. I could hear the hum and cadence of his words and feel the energy of their intent, but my mind was not yet focused on the content. As I walked through the Spanish hacienda foyer, I was captured by the magical spirit of the house. The entry way opens directly into a huge sunken living room. The far wall consists entirely of huge stones. The wall adjacent to that is almost exclusively windows, opening, at that time, to the dark desert night. A panel of French doors overlooks the fountain and the front piazza. The cathedral ceiling, constructed of huge wooden beams, opens the entire space and yet pulls it all together into a unified architecture of peace.

I removed my shoes, then walked across the saltillo brick tile floor. I tried to be as inconspicuous as possible in order to not disrupt the powerful concentration and energy I could already feel from the group. As I walked closer, Keith's words became audible. I could feel a strong connectedness from the twenty people who were listening intently to Keith's soothing words. He was describing a *dream out*, one of the basic tools of experience people use in the *Gatherings.* Keith introduced me as "Mark from Seattle" and I received a lot of polite smiles and nods before everyone quickly returned their attention to Keith.

Because of the euphoric state I was in after bonding with the night desert, I connected, on a very deep level, with a number of the people in the *Gathering* when I walked in the door on Friday night. The depth of feeling, so early in the process, was partly because of the strong bond the group had (many of them had been together in earlier *Gatherings* in Phoenix), and I felt an amazing sense of peace come over me. After the first and second *dream outs* on Friday night, there were already phenomenal coincidences going on. As people shared their *dream out* experiences, I discovered many of theirs were quite similar to what I experienced. I was already beginning to feel energetic surges or "rushes" as people were truly speaking from their hearts, from their inner God-voices. Opening to our hearts is the intention of the *Gatherings*, and it usually took me three days to experience it fully. Keith has pointed out that since the first *Gathering* nearly three years ago, this phenomenon has evolved. Each *Gathering* seems to build on the previous ones, even if there is a completely different group of people.

On Saturday morning, Keith started the *Gathering* when the group was ready. Keith suggested a group meditation on "Why am I here at this *Gathering*?" We all got quiet and went to our "inner knowing" to ask what was there for us to embrace, to receive, to know. Once I was able to rid my mind of racing, unrelated thoughts, I felt a strong message that I was there to become more aligned with my purpose and to learn about love.

Each of us shared our names and a little bit about ourselves with the group. It was obvious the group dynamic was going to be good. I was still a little tentative about announcing that I was writing a book. I planned to ask the group's permission to audio record the sessions without divulging why. Before the *Gathering*, Keith and I discussed not revealing there was a book being written until it was time. Someone had heard about the book from Keith, but didn't realize that we were keeping it quiet at that point. She announced to the group that I was writing this book about the *Gatherings*. We asked the group's permission, and it was unanimously agreed upon. It was time for the recorded history of the *Gatherings* to officially begin.

Janet began sharing by telling us why she came and what she was looking for. It opened the space for others to speak from their hearts.

JANET - I'd like to express that I came here very scared, and feeling very vulnerable, and feeling like every part of me (crying) is being *stripped away* so I can fully accept who I really am, the power I can bring through *in the moment*. Why the hell does this scare me so much? I know in my heart it's because I have *wanted* it for so long. I want to make sure it's there, that it's not just something I've been longing for all my life. I want to experience, in this workshop, my freedom, and touch upon my joy and my abundance. It's really important to come from the place of love I know I am, in *all* moments. Because I know, I've done it, I've experienced it where I was part of a *gridline of light* and I felt, actually experienced, what and who God is. I remember it. I wasn't even a body; I was just stretched out on these gridlines about four years ago, and I said, "My God, this is what God is. This is what being part of everything is." And yet I still knew I was Janet, in a body. I knew it was a *gift* given to me. That experience was so damn powerful. That's what I'm longing for. That experience.

ALLEN - I've conditioned myself to be hard, but when someone comes from the space you just did, there's a love inside me that wants to become one with you, in every aspect of your pain, from your highest to your lowest. I know that state you've been in, and I know a lot of people in this room have been there. We have the memories of that and it keeps us going. I love the yearning of spirit. When someone comes from that same energy you just exhibited, only cloaked with some sort of hardness about it, I don't know what it is; it makes me want to run. When you come out with that energy unveiled, it's what I want to join with. Last June, in this room, I got into a terrible funk the very last hour of the last day. And somehow I got out of it with the help of Keith and people in the room. I finally came from that space that you were just in. I received *so much* at that time, whereas, before, I wasn't going to receive diddley squat because I was coming through a cloak. My intention is to drop those cloaks in this physical world, not in my dream world where I had all of these connections with God and spirit. I want to do it *here and now, in the physical*, to give and receive.

JOHN - I've got to say that I want what both of you want, too. I so very much want to become connected with people. What stops me is my own defenses and fears, judgments and separations. All my life I've been seeking on some level more of those few rare moments where you lift the barriers, lift the veils, and suddenly your heart is open. I want not just my heart, but for everyone else's heart, to be open so we can be open to each other and experience the joy that's *always* there, to be conscious and present at all times as an ongoing way of life. Janet, I want to thank you for expressing the tears I feel.

JANET - You're welcome. Believe me though, there wasn't a choice. Well, there was, but I chose to allow myself to let go.

KEITH - I just had a clarity as you were speaking, Janet. My experience of what we have done and what we are doing right now in the *Gathering* is that it's not positive thinking; it's not affirmations. There's something different that's happening. We are opening a space to allow an authenticity and a deep yearning blended with intention, to allow whatever is real to unfold. As you said, "I think," then shifted it to "I know," you invoked all of your presence, your power, which allowed all of the real you to show up. To me, the intention I feel with the people who gather is to love, allow, and embrace all aspects of ourselves. With our heart's desire and intention, we move toward who we really are. We allow it all, but don't linger in the confusion and the fear of the veils, the illusions.

What I've been doing lately is saying "Thank you very much" to my veils. "Thank you, but, no thanks. Thank you, but no more. Thank you, but I'm moving on." I feel like you did, Allen. Anything that comes up here is fine with me, but I'm not going to stay with the shadow self. I'm going to move toward the light, toward God, grace, freedom. I'm going to move. Period. I'm going to keep moving and let my spirit be free. That's what I find is working. This helps me to purge the worst depression and hopelessness. It also allows me to let people be just the way they are and the world to be just the way it is. When you feel something completely, you move.

I've been realizing that, what I, and what most people say is "feeling," is not feeling. It's expressing. It's lingering. If you feel or experience something fully, you show up right away in the present and are real and authentic. You don't linger! You move; the feelings transform. Alchemy happens immediately. So that's what I'm learning to do, to surrender to the moment, to feel things fully. I just experienced it in you, Janet. When you're totally real, you don't have to do a technique, you don't have to remember your intention. Things change automatically.

Where do we move, when things move? Where do we go naturally? Self, God, joy, spirit...naturally. We don't have to do anything or remember anything. To me, that's the magic happening at the *Gatherings.* It's not about positive thinking, or affirming, or making and keeping intentions. It's simply doing what you just did and what Allen has done in the past when he's come. It's being 100% real.

And yeah, it's uncomfortable sometimes, but look at where we go with it!

As people begin to go toward 100% realness, to the essence of their beings, they begin to remember there have been numerous instances of magic in their lives. Many of these incidents have been effectively veiled; these occurrences have been experienced and then completely forgotten about. In the *Gatherings,* one of the favorite *dream outs* is discovering where we lost our magic in order to reconnect with it. Keith explains:

WHERE DID WE HIDE OUR MAGIC?

KEITH - There's a *dream out,* or intuitive adventure, people have found to be very helpful, especially at the beginning, to help them to play during the rest of the *Gathering* and beyond. We go and retrieve the aliveness and magic we lost, hid, or camouflaged at some point in our life. At some point, we decided we couldn't be as open, as spiritually strong, playful, or honest as we are. We decided we couldn't be who we are in the world, just as we are. At some point we made a decision that we couldn't be that spontaneous and real. A lot of children have spiritual abilities they lose or hide because they think it will get them into trouble. They know things like sensing when their parents are coming home, knowing events are going to occur before they happen, or knowing what people are thinking or feeling. Where did we hide our power and passion? Where did we lose touch with our power and passion, and quit using it?

DAVID - In adopting the belief that other people thought we ought to be doing something else or behaving in another way.

KEITH - The inspiration for this *dream out* came from a book I read years ago. It was about a man who started a school where the children were allowed to follow their heart, their inspiration, and do whatever they wanted to do. At any time they wanted to, they could do mathematics, painting, whatever, and just develop through their own intuitive evolution. It lasted for many years. The fellow who started the school noticed that there were several of the children who were watching him, kind of secretly, for years. One day, these children started showing up, independent of each other, at his home and his office to talk to him. They wanted to speak with an adult, but an adult they could trust. That's why they were watching him for so many years. What they all wanted was to talk to him individually, in private, and they all had the same things to say. They said there was a point in their lives when they were able to see nature spirits like Pan, elves, fairies, and gnomes. They were able to move objects with their will. They could see through walls, know the future, know what people were thinking and feeling, see angels, talk to God, and enjoy many other natural spiritual abilities. Then a parent, relative, teacher, or some other authority figure who noticed would say something about it. Sometimes the adult just outright told the kids what they were doing wasn't okay. At that point, the children made a decision that it wasn't safe or they weren't permitted to do these things anymore. They picked up that it was best to hide these abilities in secret for awhile. But they still played with their natural magic, but only when they were alone or with other children. The reason the children wanted to talk to an adult was because they discovered they were losing the ability to do these wonderful things at all, even in private. That's what had them really worried.

In the very first *Gathering* in Sedona, we allowed our intuition, our awareness, to take us to a time when we made a major decision about our aliveness, our passion, our spontaneity; about being seen for who we are, as knowing, powerful, playful, open, and trusting. What else does magic mean to you? What's magic for you so this can be a real personal journey?

GROUP - Making the make-believe real. Seeing the beauty of our existence, the magic in everything. Spirit is magical.

KEITH - When was your spirit broken? That's what the spirit of a wild stallion talked to me about when we encountered each other in an Arizona canyon. He said, "Keith, your spirit has been broken, just like a horse that has been saddle trained." It was really painful, but once I recovered, I went searching for my spirit and found it. That's what this *dream out* is about. Even if you don't know what part of your spirit you've lost, you can go find it. Your heart knows; your intuition knows. There's something missing, something lacking. That hole, that bottomless pit people try to fill all the time with cars, fame, money, adventure, music, art. Did someone say chocolate? No, let's not pick on chocolate. That's getting a little close to home. **(laughter)** That pit that people try to fill and can't fill. What used to fill that pit? What would fill that pit, that searching, that longing? That's what this *dream out* is about. It's allowing yourself to go to where you lost whatever it is you're searching for, what you're yearning for, what your heart is longing for.

One of the wonderful things people have discovered doing this *dream out* in the *Gathering*s is that, once they rediscover their magic, it begins to bloom again in their lives. Just remembering the decision they made to hide their real self, undoes the decision. It opens that door again. Then organically and naturally, people start owning their magic as it comes back.

When I did this *dream out* the first time, I went back to when I was a little boy. I discovered I had hidden my heart behind a waterfall. Then, several of years ago, the person who laid the flagstone at my house told me that he builds waterfalls. I decided to have a waterfall built in my back yard. One night I was sitting near it and felt a presence next to me. I looked over and I could see Pan, and feel Pan, as I had when I was a child. I had forgotten. I then looked at the waterfall and could see water sprites and devas. I glanced at the garden and I saw fairies, elves, and gnomes. That whole world came back for me. It's still coming back. It's wonderful. I realize now my higher self had me build the waterfall in order to bring my magic back. Other people have had similar experiences. It has explained a lot about people's lives, why certain objects like flowers or treasured objects are really important to them. Their magic, their aliveness, was stored for safe-keeping in those objects. It's really fun to discover where we hid our childhood essence and to open that door again.

I also lost some innocence and openness at another time when I was a little boy. We had "show and tell" day in first grade. We were assigned to bring a nature project to school. I brought a small planter full of moss and flowers. On the way to school, several girls were laughing, probably not even at me, but I decided they were. I hid behind a tree, and then it took me about an hour to get to school because I had to run from tree to tree to not be seen. I didn't want anyone to know I loved those flowers and that moss. They would laugh at me. I decided there must be something wrong or not normal about it. That decision put the lid on it. Seeing how we shut down is sad at first, but then you realize, "Wow, that's what I did." Now you know that, you can feel the feelings around it and undo it. The aliveness comes back.

JANET - I attended a workshop in Sedona and we went on a vision quest. There was an opportunity for several of us to go up to a mountain the night before to meditate on bringing through the spirits and asking if we could go into a shaman's cave. I was thinking, "You mean we are going to go out there all night without any lights or anything? Oh, my God!" But I still wanted to do it. I thought it would be a good opportunity for me. One girl with us was from Colorado, and she likes to travel with all of the comforts of home, no matter where she goes. She brought this *huge* sports bag. We were all climbing on the top of the mountain, and she has this *huge* sports bag with her. The rest of us only brought some cushions for the ground because we were going to stay up all night and do some prayer work. It was *so wonderful* because in the middle of the night, when we were doing prayer work, she pulled out fairy dust and started spreading it around. We had candles and we could see beautiful colors everywhere. I said, "What *else* have you got in that bag?" She then pulled out these magical flashlights with beautiful purple colors. She was one of these fairy godmothers who had a bag that held treasures and surprises way beyond its capacity. It was just so *magical*. It *reminded* me to get back in touch with the fact that it's not just about this *serious* prayer work. It was very much about really getting to the *heart* and *playing*. It was incredible.

Here Keith guided the group through a *dream out* on *Where did we hide our magic?*

DREAM OUT: WHERE DID WE HIDE OUR MAGIC?

KEITH -Where did we hide our magic? Where did we hide our play? Want to find out? Open to a time, place, experience, or an energy where you hid your magic, where you camouflaged or changed your aliveness, your power. Go to a time where you made a major decision about life, about revealing yourself, about it being safe to be who you are, to be seen as powerful, playful, magical. Go back to a time when you lost your spirit, when you lost your passion, you lost your sense of fun, play, spontaneity, your sense of openness, trust, support. Allow yourself to open to the perfect time or place, experience or energy, that will open a gateway again to your magic, your power, your play, your passion. Allow your heart to take you on a journey, a discovery, an adventure, an opening. Allow it to unfold. What happened to your magic?... Did somebody say something?... What is it that you heard?... Who was there? Was your mother there, your father?... What happened?......

The room got quiet for about fifteen minutes while group members opened to their soul communicating to them about where their magic went. Typically, after a *dream out* has finished, it takes a few minutes of shuffling and settling in as the group members, most of whom have been lying on the floor during the *dream out,* settle back into their seats. The group gets back together to share their *dream out* experiences with the others.

LINDA - Well, that totally surprised me. When we were talking earlier about where we hid our magic, our power, I was very aware of that *empty* feeling in me that I've been feeling for as long as I can remember. I've had a feeling of not being nurtured. I've done this *dream out* many times, and the one place I tend to go back to a lot is this little stuffed monkey I had when I was about three. What I remember most about this monkey is that it had a hard plastic face with a soft body. I used to lick its face all the time, cleaning it like a mother cat cleans her kittens. I was *nurturing* the monkey. I used to nurture that monkey because I was not being nurtured myself at three. I then explored the question "When did I stop having fun?" I was about two and my mother was pregnant with my younger brother. I don't remember the exact words. I just remember I was basically told it was time for me to be responsible. So I was, always, all my life. In my marriage what wore me out was that my ex-husband was very ill, and I always took care of him. That was the major dynamic in our marriage, me taking care of him. Again, I never got the nurturing, never. And when I left my marriage, that was a step toward nurturing myself.

JOHN - In this *dream out,* suddenly I remembered the movie *Fantasia*, my first real contact with music. The last time I remember seeing that movie was with my grandfather. He took me on a trip to the big city, to Denver. That movie was at the center of the whole experience. During this *dream out,* I realized that was the last time I was completely carried away into music. I remember going down the road. I loved to rest my head against the window of the car and hear the wind whistling and feel the motion of the car. I could hear full choruses, *grand* choruses singing, and somehow, they were *me*. I didn't know or understand how that worked. I just enjoyed it. During the break we just had, I went over to the piano and played for a little bit, and it felt so good, just like back then. It was incredible to be back at the piano, *back in the magic of the music from my youth.*

JUDY - In this dream out, after passing through and banging down a lot of doors and opening them with keys, I entered into a cavern. It was all lit up in golden light. There were devas, tinkerbells, and fairies. They had a little angel dust so there was something going on there with fairy dust. And it was just *so beautiful.* So I asked where my magic was. That's where I went and the last thing I heard was *"You already have your magic."* It was a most incredible experience.

In opening myself more fully in the past year, the amount of synchronicity, "magic" and extraordinary events in my life, has been staggering and wonderful. As I tune in to who I am and live from the heart, I also recognize how magical "ordinary" things are. The message Judy received is true for all of us. The magic is everywhere! All we need to do is open to it.

AUDREY - I came to realize that I lose my magic when I'm trying too hard.

After others had praised Laurie for her courage in being able to express herself in physical movement during the *dream out*, Laurie spoke.

LAURIE - I have to say, this is just amazing for me to be here and *just be who I am* and hear the impact I'm having on other people. For me, the experience was very brief. What I got was that my *spirit* is here. I then remembered the horse telling you (**Keith**) your spirit had been broken and just feeling it *here.* It's *here!*

KEITH - One thing people have found in the *Gathering* is that this is an ongoing story. More pieces fall in place, more things get revealed during the rest of the *Gathering*, in the evening, at night, in dreams and the next day. So we're really just opening the exploration. More unfolds, more gets clear, as we go.

DAVID - What happened to me was that I had an understanding of when it was I lost my magic. It was something that happened when I was about six months old. I don't really remember very much about it, so I was just allowing myself to go back into that space of "where was I?" I moved into a space where I was experiencing enjoying the freedom of *just doing what I want to do, being in the flow, instead of trying.* And then I'm not sure whether I fell asleep or whether I just zoned out somewhere. Is that a common experience? Is it likely to be a veil? I had a distinct feeling there was a healing that took place in that, because as I came up after the bell rang, I felt much more *free*.

KEITH - What you just said is the way I, and a lot of other people, look at that phenomenon. What matters is how you feel when you come out of that state. If you feel dead, groggy, like you took a nap, you probably took a nap. If you feel lighter, freer, somehow purged, different, then the sense is, "something happened there." You went to another level of consciousness to experience and explore. That often happens for people during the *dream out*s and *unveilings*. People will go into what they call, "unconsciousness," what I call "another level of consciousness." When they come out, they feel different, like something's shifted. They're lighter, more open, something moved. Sometimes when people come out of this state, they experience a resolution to a troubling issue or an answer to a current question. I used to go to that level of consciousness a lot, and what I started to ask spirit for was the ability to remember or to stay conscious during the experience. Now I'll go to that altered state but stay completely aware and awake when I'm in it, which is really fun. So you can lift those as veils, the veil of not being aware, the veil of not staying conscious for the adventure.

Often, an unveiling exercise will move in a direction the group wants or needs to explore together. In this instance, David explored the veil of not having prosperity. It opened up the space for a discussion and *dream out* on universal supply:

UNIVERSAL SUPPLY

DAVID - I really had a neat time this last unveiling because what I worked with was the anti-prosperity syndrome. What I came to understand was that *I have been keeping myself away from* the level of *prosperity* that can be mine. I wasn't doing the right thing. I kept doing stuff that was what *other* people thought I ought to be doing or what *I* thought other people thought I ought to be doing. I kept denying this ability that developed when I was four years old and my mother taught me how to project my voice to the back of the room. I'd see people doing presentations and say, "I can do that." Occasionally, I would do it. It would work really well, and then I'd go back to whatever else I was doing. What I came to appreciate in this particular unveiling on a level I haven't ever appreciated before was not only that I *can* do that, but I *am* doing that. I appreciate and honor the fact that I have had myself in a series of intermittent, and sometimes, quite uncomfortable financial pickles. A voice was always coming back to say, "David, *you're not doing what your passion is.*" To me, it was almost as exciting as when I first listened to The *Dream* tape and heard Keith talking about some of the things he had done. It was really dynamite.

KEITH - How many people have had resources, funds, money, financial assistance, gifts or material things, come from an unexpected source, out of the blue, from somewhere you would never have imagined, at some point in your life? How many people have found themselves in a physical state where they, at least for a certain period of time beyond normal for you, didn't need to eat? How many of you have found yourselves having an inner regulation, either a coolness or a warmth, that enabled you to easily be in conditions that would ordinarily be too hot, too cold, or too uncomfortable? How many of you have been in a fix or a situation where ordinarily you would have done something in a usual or methodical way, but you didn't have the time, the right equipment available, or you weren't in the right place and, yet, that predicament or situation you were in got handled anyway?

These, to me, are examples of universal supply, a direct personal connection with independent universal energy, a direct connection to your own energy, love, joy, fulfillment, or peace. There are many people who think they need to get energy and love from others. They develop control dramas as ways of getting energy, in all its forms from others. I've come to realize that if I can always, at will, tap into my own energy, my own internal love, supply, approval, grace, I won't need to be controlling or change others. I've learned I can exchange energy and love with people instead of negotiating and manipulating for it. That is very exciting to me.

The first time I went to Hawaii, on the plane ride there, I read a tourist brochure that turned out not to be entirely accurate, but I believed it. It said there were no poisonous insects, plants, snakes or anything of that nature in Hawaii and no wild animals that would attack you. On the second day there, I climbed up to this mountain top, and I stayed there two or three nights sleeping without a blanket. It was fine. It rained and I dried off without getting cold. For someone coming from the Northeast U.S., this was quite exceptional. When I got hungry, I ate the fruit growing in the trees and on the ground all around me. It was national park land so I was free to stay as long as I wished. All of a sudden, it occurred to me I could just sit there forever. I'd never be moved; I'd never have to go anywhere; I'd always have food. There was nothing that would harm me. I didn't need shelter, because I could stay warm without it. I could just sleep, eat, and live. Once this sunk in, I had a lot of tied up energy leave me for the next four hours. It felt like shields of holding myself a certain way, alertness, and watchfulness, were lifting off.

I'd grown up in Pennsylvania mountains in the cold and snow. It was all those aspects of myself falling away, my survival training and social conditioning to pay attention to weather, temperature, wind, food and shelter so you could stay safe and comfortable. Also important was to stay watchful and alert for dangerous and poisonous animals, snakes, insects, and plants. All of a sudden none of this programmed protection was necessary for my survival, or even for my comfort. For hours, I experienced wave after wave of energy release, sheets of armor and anxious alertness fell away.

It was a wonderful experience and now it's happening again, but on a deeper level. It doesn't have to do with being in Hawaii. It's being here on earth and knowing I have an *internal connection* to warmth, protection, safety, energy, and love. As I'm realizing this natural supply is available to me always, the same kind of dropping away is happening. The function of the old maintenance project, of controlling your personal energy, the planet and everyone on it, is all for survival and comfort. Now I've tapped into the personal universal well of warmth, strength, love, peace, and connection. All need to maintain anything externally has been falling away. And that, to me, is direct connection to universal energy. The key is to be able to be truly sovereign but also to be truly loving, allowing, accepting, harmonious, and sharing.

What is universal supply to you? To me, it's way beyond just financial and material abundance and prosperity. It's having exactly what you need when you need it, as you need it, and not needing to pay any attention to the past or future or any conditions anywhere. You just know you will have exactly what you choose to have *as* you choose to have it. And because we've noticed this infinite supply comes in so many new, fresh, inventive, and unexpected ways, we now call it "universal surprise!"

DEBRA - One of the things that came to me recently was this *tremendous* sense of detachment, far greater than anything I've ever experienced. What concerned me was, as I looked at my children, I felt love for them, but it was different. It was so detached, almost as if they weren't mine. It was like that with *everything*. Everything in my house, everything I wore, everything. A part of me that made a decision that I no longer wanted the overly attached, anxious, crucial, clinging, and controlling relationship to people and things I used to experience, and considered "normal."

DAVID - People are frightened by real freedom. The reality is we reach a point when we're virtually alone and recognize we're alone. It's uncomfortable at first, until we've accepted our sovereignty.

KEITH - I just want to share that my experience has not been the way you normally view a feeling of detachment. I've actually felt closer to everything and less alone than I've ever felt in my life. I felt more intimate, more connected with everyone and everything as I become more sovereign, available, open, and receiving.

JOHN - A lot's been happening for me this weekend. One thing is that other people have been thinking and speaking my thoughts. I'd want to share it, then not want to share it then someone else would share it, so I'd say [to myself], "Good, now I don't have to." I've been noticing that minor little wishes I've been wanting have been being fulfilled. After the last exercise this morning, when everyone had left, I felt incomplete. Then Audrey came over to me and said, "John, do you feel complete?" I said "No." Then I shared my experience with her, and I felt complete with her. After the break, when Linda put the music on, I was in an empty space. I had my eyes closed, and out of nowhere, Janet, you came over to me and held my hand. There was just such grace happening. Then Dave, you came over. I'm just noticing that my thoughts and desires are really manifesting. There was also something that happened in the unveiling. I realized I have held myself back. I have not reached out to people, so I would not be boisterous, would not make a commotion. So I made a decision several hours ago to put myself out to more people. I don't think I've done that physically, it seems like people have been putting themselves out more to me, just as I'd made that decision. I'm seeing things manifest very quickly here. And yes, I feel very safe, protected, cared for, and very in touch with universal supply and abundance.

KEITH - Shall we explore that in a *dream out?*

ALLEN - I'd very much love to, but before we do, I'd like to admit I don't feel supported by the physical world *at all,* and it scares the crap out of me. I feel supported by my idea of spirit, but I feel like the physical world is just part of this agreement we made, some sort of set of rules to play in, and all the rest of universal supply can't come into the physical world. The *only* thing I can do is take whatever situation comes up and do the best with it. I don't believe that money is going to come my way at all, just when I need it. There's nothing in my physical reality that I have noticed that says I am supported. My fear is, even though I earn decent money right now, in four weeks, I could be homeless. I know many people who are close to homelessness.

KEITH - Would you be open to your heart, your spirit, God, grace taking you to a time or place or to a vibration to open a gateway to change this, to transform it, open some supply for you? Would you be open to that right now?

ALLEN - I've got a voice that says, "Yes," and a voice that says, "No."

KEITH - Are you open to your own heart, your own self, your higher self, assisting you to find an opening, a gateway, that might transform, or at least loosen up your situation? Would you be open to that, to movement in that area, totally directed by your own being? To me, that's what the *dream out* is. It's just allowing, from wherever you can allow it, some movement, some loosening at an appropriate, safe, gentle pace. Does that feel good? Could you say okay to that?

ALLEN - Okay, I'm scared, but I'll trust I'll be taken care of.

SULANA - I'd like to add something. I was experiencing what Allen was talking about, and I'm finding such great gifts and value in opening to something new. There's a part of me which does not want to let go of the poverty, the lack, and yet I do want to. I want to because there are a lot of gifts waiting for me. It's time to move, Allen.

KEITH - May I ask you a question, Allen? Will that aspect of you that's scared and doesn't want to let go of the old, familiar limitations, take into account that your own intuition, spirit, higher self is going to be directing your experience in this *dream out*. The key to the approach we're using is that intuitive safety, control, and pacing is an integral aspect of giving permission for something to move and evolve. It's using the part of you that knows best exactly where you are and how you might be opened in a safe, gentle, organic and natural way. Does that help? May I ask you another question, Allen? I understand your use of the word "trust," but could you also say it's a knowing? Knowing is even deeper, stronger, more powerful than trusting. Do you know that you will be taken care of? Deep inside is there a knowing?

When I realized that universal supply was about a lot more than the first of the month and finances and money, I've been able to open and have a lot more movement and transformation with this wider perspective. I started to realize abundance is about the temperature of your body, not needing food, having love come in, synchronicity, people giving you touch, letting things happen when you need them and want them. It's a kind of magic, sensitivity, responsiveness with the universe; it's play. When I realized all of that is universal supply, I could let all those things in. Along the way, while I'm learning how to let all that in, some of the more basic things, like money, are happening. So that's the reason I suggested it in a much broader context than abundance, prosperity, money. It is much broader.

DREAM OUT: UNIVERSAL SUPPLY

KEITH - Somewhere, in everything that's been discussed in the last hour about this, could you let something new, something fresh, happen? Allow your own self-love, your own internal wisdom open a door never opened before. Could you allow there could be a door that you haven't opened yet in terms of self-love, supply, independence, freedom, sovereignty, receiving, allowing? Could you say "yes" to the possibility that such a door might exist and that your own heart, your own soul, might actually find a way to seduce, cajole you into finding that door and maybe actually opening it and stumbling over the threshold? Could you allow your own soul to be playful with you, to understand you've been hurt, disappointed, betrayed, that you're tired and frustrated and that you don't want to run down the same dead end road again?

Could you allow your own soul to show you, to open you to a way that's gentle and considerate of your whole past, your whole history, your emotions, and your feelings right now? Right now, could you allow your heart to take you to a time or a place, an energy or a vibration that will compassionately open a gateway, a new door, a fresh door, a way for you to let in your own sovereign joy? Open an avenue for resources, opportunity, friends, love, money to reach you. Allow it to come in a safe, nurturing, organic, natural way. Allow yourself to find that door.

A twenty minute group *dream out* followed after which people shared their individual experiences:

SULANA - I had a lovely experience. I let in my appreciation for people I hadn't previously felt any appreciation for. All my life, I had an abundance of everything I needed, and I was miserly with it. I had so much, and I had very little appreciation for what I had. I experienced the value of being where I am now, which is not much at all in the way of material things. I felt a real appreciation and love for it, and I hadn't been able to see that in my life when I had so much more. Now my life has become so simple and basic that when I make a dollar, I appreciate it. So I went to appreciation and that just opened it all up.

JILL - I got excited and immediately knew what it was that I wanted to explore. The *dream out* state is a lot like sex for me. If I hang in there long enough, I know I'll get a good one. But this *dream out* was the *fastest* I've ever had, and I got *so* much *so* quickly. It's because I asked! I immediately knew what door I wanted. I had been in front of that door many, many times in *dream outs*. It's been a fascination for me. It's totally purple. There have been many times I have had a curiosity as to what's on the other side, but it's always been with the knowing that I'm not ready to open that door yet.

When Keith said that about the new door, I said, "It's time." It *felt* right for me. I immediately went to find out where God was hanging out, and, as usual, it was this visual of patience like "Where have you been?" And I said, "I want to know what's on the other side of *that* door." He just looked at me and said, "Everything you ever wanted." I said, "I'm asking. I want you open it." And he said, "*You* open it." At that point, what came up was a little interaction, and he said, "Do you remember all of the babies you had? Do you remember when they always whined and cried, and you had the feeling that if they could just talk to you and just tell you what they wanted, you could fix it for them? You *get it*?" And then we just took this amazing walk through this beautiful garden together. It's so simple. Just *ask*. Quit whining and *just ask*.

JOHN - I had a profound experience with that one. People were talking about money and abundance, and I got in touch with other things coming to me. I felt I really have an issue with this, and I realized I've been in denial. I seem to have everything except as much money as I'd like. I just felt in my body the *fear* I have, this wave of energy. I *keep money away*, just always push money away...I felt waves coming through my body. Part of me had a lot of resistance to saying that. And then it just came to me that I have been working with a false idea of spirituality, what I call the "white bread theory of spirituality," that spirituality is being pure and whole and very refined, keeping everything out. Then I just suddenly got that true spirituality is...

KEITH - Like a fruit cake with nuts. **(Laughter from the group)**

JOHN - Yeah. True spirituality is owning and connecting and being part of everyone and everything and not excluding *anything*. Spirituality is, like you were saying yesterday, saying *yes* to everything. It's saying *yes* to everyone, to all motivations, all desire; it's saying *yes* to everything. And then I just began saying *yes* to everything, and that energy opened up, and it's amazing.

SUZANNE - When you said, "It's not only money and abundance," all of a sudden I felt such an appreciation for all the *coincidences* in my life that *are* the universal supply.... They're *all over the place* for me.

AUDREY - I have a great appreciation for all the telepathic communications I'm receiving. It started when I heard somebody call my name, a woman's voice. I'm still experiencing an alchemy triggered with Keith's suggesting the doorway that he hadn't allowed previously. Now I feel a shifting throughout my being and throughout my environment, further connecting me with universal support. I know I am *completely connected with my environment.* I'm allowing it to affect change in me and open me up.

JOHN - What you see is what you get. What you see out there is what you're putting out on some level. Sometimes you create a separation between your loving spiritual life and the material world. Whatever you say comes true for you. Your words have power. You're manifesting this. There is no separation. What you see out there is your inner attitudes and beliefs mirrored outside. The physical world is profoundly spiritual. It's not anything *but* spiritual. *Everything* is spiritual.

LINDA - My back has been hurting for about two years. In this *dream out,* these angels were all there saying, "Let us in. Let us in. Let us in." And I'm saying, "Am I stopping you?" Apparently, I have been. Though I just *feel* their presence, they were talking to me, saying all different things. Some of the things were like, "We will help you. We'll help you attract those things that you're looking for in your life." The angels became everyone in the room. It was *really* nice. I felt very supported and appreciated by everyone.

REX - I was being told to *get on with it.* I asked, "What does that mean?" The response came, "Just keep moving, do the little steps." I realized there are all sorts of people around me who are ready and *moving...* They want that same thing. That brings the support and propels me right along.

LINDA - I got how we are in the process of creating abundance for all of us.

DEBRA - Want to work with me a little? Something came up about creation for me and what I remembered was Keith's creation of the *Gathering* and all of his work that resulted in the *Gathering*. What came was how this intention came forward and you held that energy, and other people joined you. All of you are holding that energy for the space of the *Gatherings*. When there's something out of alignment with that intention, you are aware of it and you pull it back into focus. Whether it is someone moving that was disturbing the group or the dogs barking or the location where you choose to have the *Gathering*. There's a refinement that takes place, in the creation you're choosing to create. In my life, for the last nine years, with four children, I have 100% trusted and relied on the universe to supply me and it always has. I have had experiences in that, with no income, with no idea where the next dollar's coming from. And now, as I'm in this next stage, it's like you with the *Gathering*. I want to say, "This is *my* experience." There is a refinement I want to take place in my creation of universal supply. I want to go to the grocery store and fill three carts. I want to get into a new car and have it start. And I want to drive to the gas station and put gas in. I want to come home to a beautiful home and sit in comfortable furniture. I want to see my kids go to the store and buy clothes they really love and go to school, proud, happy, and excited. Those are all material things, but they're part of the experience I want to have.

For a long time I felt that, if I was spiritual, I shouldn't need those things or they'd take away from my spiritual experience. All I had to do was *trust* the universe to supply for me, and it *always does*. It's been a continuous miracle for me, and I have *great* appreciation for everything I've experienced. And now I just want to open wider and I want to refine it. I want to take better care of me, and say it's okay to be comfortable. It's okay to be loving, *and* it's okay to have discernment.

KEITH - I had one question that just came up. Everything you just shared with us, have you made that exact, explicit, specific request to spirit? I found, personally, I wasn't requesting specifically enough what I wanted. But when I got detailed, clear within myself what I wanted, and asked wholeheartedly, whoosh, it came...a beautiful house, ease, going to Hawaii.... I'd never clearly asked for it before.

Have you requested it before; *that* clearly, *that* specifically, *that* openly? What you just said, have you done that before?

DEBRA - Well, I used to *teach* that.

KEITH - Right, so did I. **(Laughter from the group)** That wasn't the question. Did you personally, wholeheartedly, clearly, *specifically request* or say *exactly* what you just said to us? Have you done that before?

DEBRA - No, no. I don't think it was as laser like.

KEITH - Or as clean, clear, free of veils and obstructions, like opposing feelings, ambivalence, doubt and fear, for example. To me, in my life, that has made all the difference.

MICHAEL - That's what I experienced in this *dream out*, the same realization. I felt being supported on this planet. This planet is this amazing creation perfectly designed for *me* to do what *I* need to do. Everything is *here*. I started seeing in this *dream out* that when I *have asked*, when I've gotten very *clear* about *exactly* what it was I wanted and I asked *clearly* from within, that's what *shifted* it. That's always what shifts it. So I'm starting to look at where have I not been asking, where have I not been clear.

KEITH - I just asked for clarity and it came. I got that the reason I haven't, until now, been getting immediately, exactly, what I've been asking for, even with as much clarity as I had, is because it wasn't time. It wasn't yet time for me to do what my spirit came here to do. It was still time to learn, to go through suffering, victimhood, betrayal, all the other limited experiences. I saw that, as it is time, people immediately have the resources, time, energy and money to fund their dream, to fulfill their purpose in being here. I could see it wasn't time for me to fulfill my purpose yet. Being poor, struggling, confused, and angry was part of the deliberate spiritual design mechanism to keep my spirit from expressing itself fully before it was time. One of the reasons I really enjoy Allen as a spirit and soul partner, is he asks questions at the *Gathering* that I don't have ready answers for. It upsets me; it makes me feel a lot of emotions. I feel frustration. I feel anguish. I feel what he's feeling. What that does is stimulate me to search deeply for answers and move past the blocking feelings. His comments shake me up catalyzing me to ask deeper, go deeper about what we're presenting at the *Gathering*, and what I'm sharing. In fact, the last time we had a *Gathering* in this room, Allen and I were sitting here, and he said, "I know some of you know. I know some of you are experiencing oneness. I want to know what you know. I want to know what you're doing." He looked over at me and said, "I know that you're experiencing "oneness." I want to know how you're doing it."

It really shook me up because my only purpose in being here is to express my experience to be of some value to people. If I'm not successfully transmitting my experience, I get frustrated and decide to go deeper.

Part of it goes back to how the day started when Pat and others said that they experienced a visit from me during the night. It was actually higher self or God using my personage. This is the answer to what I've felt you and the others have been asking me, Allen, and what I've been asking myself. Spirit is asking me to go to a deeper level of myself, a level of clarity, sharing, and of openness about my experiences. I haven't been consciously withholding that. It just hasn't been time because I haven't been clear. For years, I've felt embarrassment about showing up in other people's visions. This phenomenon has happened to me my whole life. I asked for clarity, during the break, and I went back to the moment it started. It has to do with universal supply, with exactly what we're talking about, and that's why I'm bringing it up. Twenty some years ago, when St. Germain first contacted me, and I didn't order him out of my bedroom, we started talking. I was presented a package deal by St. Germain, Jesus, Sai Baba, and the nameless ones, these representations of my higher self. Every time I meet with them, it's basically to discuss this arrangement we have. Since people were mentioning the visitations this morning and I was feeling stirred up about it, I went back to the original time when my higher selves and I first discussed this agreement this lifetime. They said, "Look, here's the deal." The deal was, I allow myself to be available for *the* work, *the* awakening, *the* enlightenment. I allow myself to wholeheartedly surrender, to go along with whatever is needed for the plan, to allow all of my being, on every level, to be available to whoever wants it, whenever anyone wants to use it. In return, I get fully supplied and supported with everything that I need to prosper. That includes love, healing, and money. Let me tell you, they've kept their end of the bargain. It's a great deal. I joke about it, but I get paid well and in a timely manner.

The paycheck for me is total support on every level if I am totally available to life and the plan. And since the time I made this deal, I have had people who have experienced me coming to them in visions, dreams, and in physical form when they were conscious and awake. The *Gathering*s are a good example of the deal. I go where I'm directed to go, and I do what is indicated. I can do that now wholeheartedly because I've been supported wholeheartedly. I was whining and bitching, and now I've learned I just wasn't making my request for support clear enough. Now that I am, my wants are being fulfilled down to the finest detail.

On the last day of the *Gathering*, since they began, we have focused on "What is your dream?" We usually wait until the last day so that we can go to a deep level of knowing with it. The *dream out* is focused on, "What is my spirit really up to here? What's my dream, what's my purpose, what's my mission? Why am I really here this lifetime?" Frankly, people haven't been getting that much. They get whatever they get, but from my point of view, they get vague answers like "To share love, to share who I am." Well, of course, yes, obviously. But what, *specifically,* are you here to experience, express, explore, or embrace? That's why this specific detail thing is so critical. I'm seeing the connection; it just hit me. Everyone, for three years, has been getting "To share love." That may be a very nice *dream out,* but what I notice is no one gets any details, nothing specific about what exactly they're here to do. They are lacking details in terms of what forms and vehicles to express through, exact material support needed, what people to connect and coordinate with. What do I do tomorrow when I get up? What specific actions do I take? What do I do for money, time, resources? The connection, I see, is that *if we ask for exact, specific support, it will come.*

Spirit who comes out of the East

Come to me with the power of the rising sun

Let there be light in my world

Let there be light on the path I walk

Let me remember always you give me the gift of a new day

Never let me be burdened with the sorrow of not starting over.

A Native American blessing

Chapter Four

NATIVE SPIRITS

The Supernatural, Native Music, and Alchemy

IN THE UPPER RURAL DESERT HILLS ABOUT TWENTY miles from Reno, Nevada, there is a dwelling in a place of incomparable energy. Referred to as the Domes, the pair of geodesic structures is connected by a sunroom and crystal garden and bordered on one side by a beautiful creek. There is historical evidence that the site has served as a spiritual and ceremonial gathering place for over ten thousand years. At six thousand feet of elevation, in the foothills of the majestic Sierra Nevada range, the pine trees meet the sagebrush of the sloping desert floor.

Aspen trees line the banks of a nearby stream. Another mountain creek graces the back of the Domes, providing a constant flow of energy from the mountains.

Not surprisingly, the inspiring power of this site has attracted several prominent writers to spend time there tapping into the spirit and energy of the earth and her beauty. Gary Zukav, Arnold Patent, Sandy Ingerman, and Carolyn Myss are a few of those who have been attracted to this place in their spiritual journey of life.

Powerful *Gatherings* occur there, so we picked this as the place in which to showcase the *dream outs* on Native Spirits and the Supernatural. The supernatural energy is so strong there it would be virtually impossible not to be influenced by it. Upstairs in the loft overlooking the creek, sagebrush, pines, hills, and Sierra Nevada mountains, I wrote some of the most powerful material that has ever come to me. It was as though my pen was guided by a being or beings outside of myself. Some of the most profound wisdom ever to escape my pen issued forth there. Months later, I was reading passages from *The Seat of the Soul* by Gary Zukav. I was completely overwhelmed at how similar Gary's inspired book was to the writing I had done while at the Domes. I learned he had written there too. Were we receiving the same message from the same energy or beings or was it just a coincidence?

During a lunch break, Keith saw the Native Spirit guides at the grove of trees as the trail starts. They told him, "The gifts are coming." One particular gift from the guides is the energy, the sheer power of the place. We were there at the Domes to draw on this energy, their knowing and experience.

While on one of the two-hour lunch breaks at the October 1996 *Gathering* at the Domes, I went for a hike with a couple of women in the group. I was feeling a little lightheaded and was in a somewhat dreamlike state. It is becoming easier for me to get into that space now, especially with the influence of a tunnel of trees such as those which lined this trail. At that time, this feeling was relatively new to me and it was at once wonderful and a little bit scary.

I was looking at the trail in front of us as we hiked and the women talked. In the distance, I saw a fairly large-sized boulder, miraculously, suddenly move right into the pathway ahead then back to its original resting place! I had been asking to see a nature spirit, but I didn't expect it to show up in the form of a moving *rock*. Neither of my hiking partners had even seen it move. My first inclination was to dismiss it and believe I was only seeing things. Upon reflection though, I began to see it as much more than that. Maybe that boulder really *did* move. I had recently actually felt and *seen* a fern wave at me back at home in Seattle. I was still in the process of integrating that and was questioning whether or not it was simply a natural phenomenon caused by the breeze.

Feeling somewhat in awe but also a little bit playful and spunky at that point, I asked the two women to walk on ahead so I could be alone. After they had walked well past the boulder I had seen move, I decided to see if I could roll it into the center of the path. It was quite a struggle because the boulder probably weighed over three hundred pounds and, to all appearances, had been in that same spot for a hundred years or more. I was very satisfied with myself when I finally managed to roll it on its side then position it directly in the center of the trail. The trail was very narrow at that point, three or four feet wide. It would have been nearly impossible for the two women to walk down the trail without walking around the boulder. I felt like staying there to see the expressions on their faces when they came back down the trail and saw the huge rock which I had placed right in their path. Instead, I headed down the mountain myself, content to wait until they returned to tell us all the story of the miraculous moving rock. After a good laugh, I planned to admit to being the perpetrator of the prank.

The laugh or, should I say, the lesson was on me. They never saw the boulder! At first I thought they must be playing a trick on me, but they *never saw the boulder!* It was *impossible* to miss. The surprising lesson to me was that there are a lot of things we do not see, even when they are right in front of us. Did that rock move by itself when I saw it move on the way up the mountain? I say, "Yes." Did it move again when I struggled to place it directly in the path of the two women? "Yes." And yet, the two of them did not see it *either* time.

Up until this time I was quite skeptical about the possibility that nature spirits existed. I knew Keith talked about them quite often, but I dismissed it as some sort of experience reserved for the privileged, highly enlightened, or the crazy among us. As I opened to allowing even a slight possibility of their existence, a whole new world opened for me.

The next day, it was cold in the high desert. There was actually a thin layer of snow blanketing the desert and the scene had a surreal but beautiful feel to it. I was reflecting on the boulder experience and wondering if I was enlightened, going mad, or both, when I saw a sage bush dart away then back to its original spot! Later, and throughout the *Gathering* when looking out the huge picture window of the Domes, I sensed the compassionate and supportive Native Spirits watching from the bushes. Reality as I knew it had shifted. I still had trouble believing that fairies and devas existed, but no longer judged those who said they saw them.

In that spirit, we placed this chapter toward the front of the book even though it has the potential of scaring some people away. If you are one of those or *thought* you were, I have a message for you. Your reality is what you make it. If you're still reading this, you're certainly more enlightened, aware, or open than I was just over a year ago. Allow that anything is possible, and you will see new worlds every day. Keith tells us some true stories that might assist you to open to accepting some new realities:

THE SUPERNATURAL

KEITH - Does anyone remember the quotation from Edgar Mitchell, the Apollo astronaut? He said *"There is no such thing as the supernatural or the extraordinary. There is only the huge gap between what we* think *is natural and what* is *natural."* How many people would like to know more about or have more experiences in what they would normally consider extraordinary or supernatural? We could open some gateways if you want.

I recently had an interesting insight with a wonderful 84-year-old woman at whose house I stayed at during a *Gathering*. On the fourth day, we were eating breakfast together at her house, and she said "I would *love* to be able to see a nature spirit, gnome, fairy or angel. I would just *love* to." As soon as she said that, a little deva appeared right next to a small plant on her table. The creature was so bright, the intensity hurt my eyes. I said "Well...*there's* one." She stared and stared and could feel its presence but could not see it. Then the sprite said, “Ask her if she would tell people about me if she saw me.” So I asked her. She said, “Oh no, I couldn't.” For 50 years this woman has done spiritual work and has had the misfortune of being called a witch by skeptical acquaintances and friends. If she is not willing to *declare* it, *live* it, or tell anyone, then, in a way, she's really decided not to see it.

I realized when we ask from a place of speculation, of consideration, it does not work. Sometimes we might say “Okay, I want to *see* it first, *then* I'll decide what to do with it. I want an answer, *then* I'll think about acting on it.” I'm finally seeing it doesn't work this way. When you're ready to share, when you are ready to go with the magic, with the power, with seeing nature spirits and saying “I see this; this is real for me,” then you'll *see* it. I'm discovering when I'm ready to go *toward* an answer, toward clarity about *anything*, I *get* the clarity. If I ask, “Well, let me hear what my purpose is, *then* I'll think about it” or “Let me get some support, *then* I'll decide what to do with it,” it doesn't come. When I ask from a place of total willingness, total intention of going with it, it's there.

The other day I was reading a magazine on Arizona history. They had a fascinating article on the first European people who came to Arizona. There were about six waves of explorers. I don't remember what the order was, but there were Spanish conquistadors, a wave of early friars and monks, a wave of furriers and trappers (there are forests in Arizona, believe it or not), a wave of U.S. cavalry, and a wave of gold prospectors. They were all different and didn't communicate with each other because they were years apart. Every one of these waves went into territories never written or talked about or known to the European or to the East Coast consciousness. They all had diaries, and all of the accounts of what they saw were strikingly similar. Guess what they experienced in the deepest canyons of Arizona? They saw dinosaurs, jungles, and palm trees. They also witnessed the natives talking to cliffs and the cliffs talking back, and cliffs opening and closing at the natives' request. These first adventurers watched the cavalry come in, heard the natives chanting, and the canyons would close behind so there was no exit to the canyon. The soldiers would never get out. These first explorers also saw the natives chant and talk to the earth, and witnessed the earth swallowing up the intruding soldiers.

It reminded me, when I read it, of Admiral Byrd who was the first person to fly over the South Pole. As he flew over the South Pole, his radio contact was broadcast on live radio in Boston. Several hundred thousand people heard this. It was written up in one of the major Boston newspapers at the time. It was also written in Admiral Byrd's personal diary. Those pages have since disappeared; they've been ripped out of his notes in the Library of Congress. Thousands of people in Boston heard this on live radio. "Here we are, we're about to go over the South Pole." Guess what he saw? He saw dinosaurs, jungle, and tropical paradise. He reported it in a live radio broadcast to the American people. The next day, the U.S. government put out a notice to the papers and the rest of the world, saying Admiral Byrd was suffering from exhaustion, and had been hallucinating. That was the end of it.

I have explored the canyons of Arizona a lot. I bought a four-wheel drive so I can go into canyons, right up the riverbeds. The deeper I go into the more remote areas where very few hikers go, the easier and easier it gets to contact other dimensions, extraordinary beings, and supernatural events. There was one very wonderful canyon I used to go to. It was very magical there, and it wasn't very far from civilization. One day, a friend and I came back early, and we were resting and watching these people come up with their beer coolers, radios, and the works. They would come up to the entrance of the canyon, and someone in their party would inevitably twist an ankle, not too badly, but just so they didn't want to go on. They'd say, "Well, let's just stay here." So they just stayed there and partied. Later, my friend and I watched when another group went up. A little boy got poison ivy or cut himself or something. Every group that came in *stopped at that point.* As we watched over the years, we witnessed first hand over and over again that our favorite canyons, the ones in which it was most easy to reach magic, had protected entrances. The people who were not in harmony would not go in. Something would happen, and they would change their mind. They'd just plunk down and have their picnic there, but they wouldn't go into the canyon.

There is an easy, open, wild, natural aliveness, a flexibility, fluidity, new breadth of dimension, always available in the universe. When linear, logical, technically-minded people, go into an area of life, they start writing about it. It gets charted. It gets described. What happened in Arizona is that only the first wave of each of these explorations witnessed the dinosaurs and the jungle. Even the second wave didn't find them. The second wave of people would invalidate the first wave saying they must have been on peyote, hallucinating, or out of their minds. Only the first wave witnessed these things, but *each* first wave of these different cultures witnessed the same thing. Other people, more skeptical, went out to try to find these wonders, and they couldn't. The area was no longer *uncharted* territory. New people went in and told a story consistent with mainstream beliefs and collective consciousness to make it fit the Western model. Nobody could pierce the collective veil anymore. Well, it's time to do it now.

FRAN - In other words, it's all there but we just don't see it.

KEITH - Exactly. I had a lot of friends who went to Findhorn, the spiritual community in Scotland, when it first started. The first person in the community to see and talk to Pan was a guy named "Roc." The first thing Pan said to him was "Would you take a message to humanity? Tell them *we* never went anywhere. *You* left." It's true for *everything* we're exploring in the *Gathering*. The vibrations never *went* anywhere. Our natural state never went anywhere. *We* did. Our attention went somewhere else. This is a very playful, gentle way of reminding ourselves we have alternatives. We can allow our heart and our energy to flow, As the Kahunas say in Hawaii, "Where your attention flows, your life flows." Literally, where you focus and put your attention is what becomes your experience. In the canyons of Arizona, the less inhabited, charted, and hiked the canyons are, the easier it is to see and feel the flow of the greater dimensions of life.

STAN - So why does it get harder to see these dimensions when more and more people get there?

KEITH - To me, each wave of people brings in the limitations, paradigms, and beliefs of our collective consciousness. They have surrendered to the way things are supposed to be. They have traded spontaneity and aliveness for routine and drudgery. It doesn't *have* to be harder. I take friends to canyons who want to have these experiences, and the less traveled the canyons I go to are, the easier it is for them to start feeling and seeing in a fresh and extraordinary way.

I know a lot of people who are doing jobs they hate, living with people they don't like, and tolerating situations they don't like. These people ask why they're not supported, why they can't see the magic all around them. Well, *gee, duh.* If you were your higher self, would you support investing your time, attention, and energy in situations that are not right for you? You *are* your higher self. I'm saying this to myself too. I was asking for support in something that *wasn't making me happy*, something my heart wasn't into. I didn't get support from the universe for that. Gee. I have spent a lot of time in the past asking for support for a life my heart wasn't into, that wasn't making me happy. My higher self simply didn't support me in it. Guess what? Since it didn't support me, I got so frustrated and angry I made some changes. Now I can see how I've *never* been supported when I've asked for something that wasn't going to make me happy, that wasn't right, appropriate, and harmonious for me.

DREAM OUT: THE SUPERNATURAL

Would you like to do a *dream out* on *encounters with the supernatural or meetings with remarkable beings*? Shall we see what encounters of the third kind we've actually had? Take a moment and allow yourself to get into alignment, into attunement. Let that energy, that God current flow through you, that vibration you recognize as you. Allow any stray energy or attention to come home, to come into the present moment, into your body, into your being, with your breath, with your heartbeat. Just gather all of yourself, all of your spirit, and have all of yourself, all of your power present and available to go exploring. Allow your heart to guide you.

Allow yourself, if you want, to *open* to a time or place, an event or experience where you had a special encounter. This could have been a meeting with a person, angel, spiritual being, or some entity you have forgotten about, buried, veiled, or cloaked. Recall some significant encounter that was of great value, but you just haven't recalled it consciously. Open to seeing all of reality instead of what society tells you is real. Allow your heart to choose, for your intuition to take you or open you to a significant moment, event, meeting, encounter. Open to an exchange or interaction that is right, timely, or appropriate for you to remember or to re-experience. Allow yourself to open to the perfect, right, appropriate encounter. With whatever memory comes, allow the experience to evolve, emerge, and reveal itself in its own way, in its own time. Feel the vibration. Follow the river of life to your adventure. Allow your attention to flow to a time or place, event or experience where you had a very important encounter, a heart meeting with a soul, being, energy, person, an angel. Allow your heart to take you.

The silent *dream out* ensued for about twenty minutes. Then, as the *Gatherers* reclaimed their chairs, Keith interjected a little humor.

KEITH - All right. We have surveillance cameras, we have agents, we know you've been seen with these people, these beings. You've been spotted. We have it on tape. You may as well come clean. It's either *we* reveal it to the world or *you* do. How would you like to do it? It's not *if* it's revealed, it's *who* reveals it.

MARK - The only one I can remember so far is a relatively recent encounter with a nature spirit. I was sitting at the base of this huge maple tree where I go quite often to write. I asked to see a nature spirit, and there was a little miracle. I actually saw a fern waving at me. The wind was blowing things in different directions but this fern wasn't going in the same direction everything else was blowing. It was distinctly waving, giving me a message. That's what brought some of my magic back. I am realizing there really *are* things like this going on, and it is opening a lot of doors for me.

JOANNA - I am *always* having encounters where things are not what everybody else approves of, and it has to do with their judgment of me if I talk about it. I know it happens to me all the time, and there's one I keep in my conscious mind just to remind myself it *does* happen. This wasn't a conversation with somebody else; it was when my husband and I were asleep in Georgia and the window was open. I remember the alarm clock went off at 5:30 or 6:00, and I was taking my time to answer it. I got up to turn it off, and I felt a hand on my hand. I turned around and thought Ed had reached up and gotten it. I turned around and he was lying fast asleep in the bed. I said, "I thought you turned that off." He said, "I thought I did too but I must have dreamed it." This is just something that is not quite in the ordinary and it serves me to keep the channel a little bit open. I hold onto that because I have these all the time. I do see, in nature, trees and bushes moving. I live in a wooded area and I see this happening all the time. I see it and I forget about it because it just doesn't fit in. (**She laughs.**) It was a really enlightening *dream out*, probably the best one I've had so far or that I've been totally conscious for.

LINDA M. - As I reclaim the magic, it will unfold. We had a little talk, just me and these little gnomes. It's kind of personal actually. I just don't want to tell you, or I might start crying again. They laughed, and they said, "When you reclaim your power, you'll see what happens." In a way, it didn't have anything to do with me directly. It's about reclaiming the magic we have all lost. These beings are around, and they have messages for us.

CAROL - A couple of years ago, some good friends and I were doing some singing and *Jesus* came to me in a vision. I don't remember what the message was, but I remember thinking, "I'm Jewish. I'm not supposed to be seeing Jesus." It was real, and it was a really beautiful, beautiful feeling.

KEITH - How many people have seen, felt, or sensed angels, ascended beings, guides, gnomes, or fairies? Allow yourself to get really familiar with how *you* do it, how that space feels when *you* open to it. When we do the *dream out* and go to times, places, or experiences where you did have an encounter with other beings, notice especially what it *feels* like. Notice what you feel like, what the space feels like. There might be a smell. There might be a surreal aspect to things. Your body might feel a certain way. There's a sense that something's different, an electricity in the air, an emptiness, an openness. See what it feels like right before, during, and after you allow this to happen for you. As you become familiar with that space, you can invoke it or create it when you're out in the forest, in a quiet place, or some other special space. It's a zone that athletes, dancers, and gamblers get themselves into, and they know things happen in that space. It's the same with this.

When we do a *dream out*, it's to become acquainted with how it feels for you. It's not an emotional feeling necessarily. It's a broader sense of feeling the vibration, the frequency. Can anyone describe it in another way? I sense an opening, a gateway.

MARK - For me it feels a little like tunnel vision. Then all of a sudden I'm in a dreamlike state; a little light as if I'm floating. A good energy portal for me is a tunnel or canopy of trees, large bushes, or plants. The pure energy in nature, particularly in trees for me, provides entrances to other realms.

KEITH - I'd like to share, too, how amazing, miraculous, and loving the support is from the other side of the door. The other day, while walking in the snow, my knee hurt, I had so much going on. I was scared to go through the next gateway for me. I was up in the woods in the mountains. During every break, I have been outside and finding Native Spirits I could talk to. They said, "Look, we can *tell* you about it. *We went through*. It's scary, but we went through." They all told me their personal story. They said, "We can't walk through *for* you, but we can tell you what's on the other side, and what we went through to get there." These beings are wonderful. Jesus and St. Germain were there reminding me, "We've been through it." The support is amazing when you open to it. It's personalized; it's unending; and it's *wherever* you are. There is a lot of support from the beings who have gone through the door before you. That's *all* there to assist you. That's all they exist for.

I'll tell you another wild example. I was in Seattle staying in the house of a woman I'd never met before. She had lots of family pictures in the guest bedroom I stayed in, aunts, and uncles, children, and dogs. There was a woman in one of the pictures who just *glowed*. Every night in my room, I just stared at this photograph of Nelly. I started talking to the photograph, and her essence entered the room. Nelly is an ascended being. I asked the woman who owned the house who Nelly was, and she said Nelly was her grandmother. Nelly had given her this picture of herself years before. Just when I needed spiritual assistance, Nelly came right out of the picture. She was with me and is *still* with me. She has assisted me with the *Gatherings* ever since. The support and the available assistance is amazing. It is there wherever you are, whenever you need it, but it's on the other side of the door. You need to step through on your own.

AUDREY - I just got a funny message. For days on end last year, last Easter time, I was getting the song "When the Saints Go Marching In." It was all about those who have gone before me, and those exact words I was saying to everyone I knew. Those that have gone before you. They're there; they're waiting, returning to the *one heart*. Each passed through each other. I go and someone goes through me, and we're all returning to the *one heart*. So I started putting pictures around the house; saints, enlightened beings, ascended beings and anybody I could feel that kind of connection with because I wanted to walk with those who have gone before me; walk with the saints. That was my motto and still is.

The supernatural can also be conveyed in spirit through media such as music. By listening to the appropriate powerful music with the right intention, you can get in touch with your inner vital being. Your soul uses the music to slide through the veils. One such piece of Native American music is used in the *Gathering* to facilitate a dream out.

NATIVE AMERICAN MUSIC

KEITH - I have something I'd like to share with you for a few minutes. It's a piece of music, a sound, an energy, a vibration, that a fellow brought to the last San Francisco *Gathering.* It's partly of Native North American origin, but it's timeless to me, and I can understand it even though it's in another language. Luckily, it's not in English, so we can't misinterpret, over analyze, or invalidate the words. Somehow, I understand the meaning and get very strong transmissions from it. I'd like to share it with you and allow it to become an experience, an interaction, with the energy, the vibration. Afterwards, we'll allow some silence for you to *be* with it, say "Yes" to it, go where it takes you. Allow yourself to go with what it opens in you, the message, the transmission, enjoyment, or whatever it brings out for you. We'll then allow some time to have a *dream out*, an intuitive journey, an opening. Afterwards we'll share our experiences.

Keith played music which was awe inspiring. I believe he was as surprised as I was at the level of energy it brought to the group. We were all a bit overwhelmed.

DREAM OUT: NATIVE AMERICAN MUSIC

KEITH -That voice, that voice, wow. We're definitely going to be playing that more in the *Gatherings.* That *voice*, that vibration, that sound when he starts singing just feels to me as if it's coming from eternity and just connecting me right there. I recognize that. It's calling me home, home. *Finally*, a signal from home.

While the music was playing, I felt an irresistible inspiration to write down a message coming from the spirit of the music. It came on all of a sudden in a rush and this is what it said:

MARK - We are the spirits of your ancestors, the spirits who have come to share with you the divine, the source, the peace within that surpasses the understanding of your collective truths of illusion. Let us in. Let us come to you and guide you to the higher plane. We are with you always. We are with you in all ways. We bring you the dance of the universe, the dance and joy of the life of rivers, the life of the clouds and the life of fire. The volcano brings you our power, the raw power of the divine. Come dance with us in the universe. Come play with us in the divine light. You are our children, you are our fathers. You are us. We are all alive in this dance of the universe. Come back.

JANE - When that music started, I heard the words "get back my belly." I just felt like I had never appreciated what was in my stomach. What is in there is this primitive feeling, a primal understanding of sounds and smells and *dirt*. The way the dirt smells, the way the green grass smells. It was just wonderful to feel that **(crying)** and not to judge my body. It felt *so good*. So I'm holding this wonderful feeling and then the music changed, and I saw a jungle. Life was sprouting up in a *tremendous* variety of orchids, vines, and birds. Anyway, I was *there*. I was standing there looking out and there was this huge pathway out in front of me, and I sent birds out to scout to see what it was like. Then I started running around. It was like, "Oh, this is *creation*." I knew, on a primal level, that creation was what *we create* **(crying)**. All of us *created* this, and we started to feel it and then came this whoa, this sound, then everything *stopped*. It hurt. It was just like clamped fingers, like sandbags, the chit chat, all those things. *Everything stopped,* and it hurt so much. Then there were little twinkles of growth again, and it was releasing. Things then started growing again, and things *are* growing again. I want to be *in* my belly. I want to *feel* and to *smell* and to *hear*. I haven't heard enough yet of this kind of sound, this kind of music. Every time I do, I go back to this kind of place, and I want to be there. I choose to be there more and more and more. This talk stuff we do is so skimpy in comparison. It's not enough.

LINDA - I felt that rhythm as the power of the earthquake, the power of the volcano, and I felt myself as an outgrowth of the earth. I knew I wasn't *separate* walking on the earth, that I had actually sprung *from* the earth. There is no question of connection.

LISA - I had a powerful experience with it. It felt totally to me like *"I am"* music. I'm getting more adjusted to Native American music, so I can actually hear the heart of the Native American people and can identify with where they're coming from. A couple of years ago it seemed like really primitive stuff. I felt clearly this time the Native American people were speaking to me. I really felt these are my ancestors. I felt them, and I felt like dancing. I understood the drum-beats, the force behind them, the root music, the "*I am*" music, the courage of the noble identities of the idealized Native American, the good qualities in them. I could really understand *this* music very clearly. That is a quality and an ancestry I *am* going toward.

DAVID - A couple of things became clear to me while experiencing that music. One of them was feeling the difference between *dreaming out* on all the things wrong with me and, "Where did I lose it?" verses *dreaming out* on the *joy of being alive*, the greatest highs, the deep experiences. That was one key I felt was being shared by you, with us, yesterday. Now it feels like there's this *next step* which is getting completely *out of the linguistic*, completely out of even the experiential and into just *being*. There's some power that happens when we get out of the normal thinking part of our brain. I always wondered what that other part was thinking, all that quiet area in our brain. What's up with that? A way in for me has been music like this. This has been, for the last four or five years, something I've been playing with a lot. Probably the next production I do **[David is a film producer.]** will be a music production. I've never really taken any classes, but hearing this experience in my head, a lot of it seems very similar to the direction we'll see music going in the next ten or so years. We'll hear a lot of things that are so powerful they will just bring on moods. You know the ancient Greeks outlawed music because it was so powerful for people they would sometimes literally hallucinate. They had to regulate it as we regulate controlled substances.

KEITH - As the U.S. government regulated Native American music and ceremonies for so many years. I just realized I had been keeping a secret and didn't even know I was withholding it. For me, when I heard this music, it activated something that's primal and deep; a deep part of my core I had forgotten even existed. Something started moving; it's been activated. What I meant by the secret was I just realized my life has changed to a point where I can sit for hours outside or in my living room just feeling all these changes and openings. When this is occurring, I am being triggered and stimulated to move, grow, and transform. I will hear the sound of a bird. It just explodes things inside me, activating me more and more. Then I'll hear another sound like a truck or jet, any sound, and it catalyzes me further. I'll sit there for hours. I've never told anyone this. It felt antisocial or something. I now spend a lot of my time just being activated. Much is changing. All I want to do is let that happen.

AUDREY - That's what's been happening for me a lot. There's such a readiness. When I get into that place of being ready I'm all there. When I'm not *quite* in that place, a lot of you aren't there. When *I* get there, nothing is wrong because I *know* it's all going; it's all moving. Since the music is so powerful for everyone and I have spent a lot of time with this music, I'm putting out a request that we listen to the fourth and fifth track which are very powerful complements to what we just heard. Since the energy seems to be with us to not be so linguistic, although I want to honor the poetry and beauty of the language, it gets to be in the back seat.

LISA - That music really made me want to *act* it out. I didn't want to talk anymore. I wanted to *dance*. I wanted to tone. **(sing)** I wanted to move and scream and act it out rather than talk about it.

Keith played more of the music. As it was playing, the group members got up and freely expressed themselves in movement and dance.

KEITH - I have some words attributed to chief Seattle which touch my heart. This passage contains excerpts from a speech to the president of the United States after an offer had been made to purchase land occupied by the Natives:

"The great white chief in Washington sends word that he wishes to buy our land. But how can you buy or sell the sky? The warmth of the land? The idea is strange to us. If we do not own the freshness of the air and the sparkle of the water, how can you buy them from us?

Every part of this earth is sacred to my people. Every shining pine needle, every sandy shore, every mist in the dark woods, every meadow and humming insect. All are holy in the memory and experience of my people. We know the sap which courses through the trees as we know the blood that courses through our veins. We are part of the earth and it is part of us. The perfumed flowers are our sisters. The bear, the deer, the great eagle, these are all our brothers. The rocky crests, the juices in the meadow, the body heat of the pony, and man, all belong to the same family. The shining water that moves in the streams and rivers is not just water, but the blood of our ancestors. If we sell you our land, remember that it is sacred. Each ghostly reflection in the clear waters of the lakes tells of events and memories in the life of my people. The water's murmur is the voice of my father's father. The rivers are our brothers. They quench our thirst. They carry our canoes and feed our children. So you must give to the river the kindness you would give to any brother. The air is precious to us, the air shares its spirit with all the life it supports. The wind also gives our children the spirit of life.... You must keep the land apart and sacred, as a place where man can go to taste the wind that is sweetened by the meadow flowers. Will you teach your children what we have taught our children? That the earth is our mother? Whatever befalls the earth, befalls the sons of the earth.... The earth does not belong to man. Man belongs to earth. All things are connected like the blood that unites us all. Man did not weave the web of life, he is merely a strand in it. Whatever he does to the web, he does to himself. But one thing we do know which one day the white man may discover.... The earth is precious and to harm the earth is to heap contempt on its creator. Your destiny is a mystery to us. When the last red man has vanished with his wilderness and his memory is only a shadow of a cloud moving across the prairie, these shores and forests will still hold the spirits of my people for we love this earth as the newborn loves its mother's heartbeat. If we sell you our land, love it as we have loved it. Care for it as we have cared for it. As we are part of the land, you too are part of the land. And with all your strength, treat the beasts of this land as your brothers, for if all the beasts are gone, man will die from a great lonliness of spirit - all things are connected.

This message from the heart speaks to our need to tune-in to the environment while there is still time. While mainstream thought is slowly moving toward understanding the inter-

connectness of all things, a faster, deeper, and permanent change will be necessary. Changes like this are contagious and they have the power to bring about personal and world transformation. Keith and other gatherers call this kind of change "alchemy".

ALCHEMY

KEITH - What does *alchemy* mean to you?

STEVEN - What comes to me about alchemy is something that goes back to the time of The Middle Ages. An alchemist was someone who was gifted and did healings or was knowledgeable in herbs or the elements. They could magically change the composition or transform things so what people saw was really an illusion,

ANNE - Turning lead into gold.

CHRIS - Extracting the essence of what appears to be worthless.

INGE - Those who are against alchemy or transforming the world tend to nail people to a cross.

KEITH - In our society, we have lots of slang expressions for the alchemical space. It's called being *on a roll, in the groove, in the zone, the juice, your passion*. That's the alchemical space. We looked it up in the dictionary and it was very interesting. It said, "a blending of previously separate compounds into a new compound, a new creation." The reason I bring it up is because, to me, that's what's really going on in the *Gatherings*. There are people who say they don't get it, who sleep for four days, who go unconscious, and who spend time in altered states. Yet their lives are transformed at the same rate, in the same way as the people who can articulate every sharing session. There's something going on underneath, behind the surface. The other reason we use the word "alchemy" is it gets everyone's attention. If I said, "What is transformation?" people would become bored and feel, "Oh, I know that already," and not be as open.

To me, alchemy is *permanent* transformation. It is a metamorphosis, permanent change in the way your energy is showing up in the world. The old alchemists talked about changing lead into gold and other seemingly worthless things into something valuable. They were really talking about personal transformation, but the Inquisition and other political elements in the past were opposed to anything that would wake up or empower the general population. It wasn't safe to talk directly about alchemy. Part of the *Gathering,* to me, is realizing that the veils around alchemy are simply a remnant of the Dark Ages, a remnant of all those times in the past when we couldn't talk openly about our knowing, our spirit, our personal power, and our God within. The *Gathering* is about allowing ourselves to let alchemy come to us. It's a permanent shift in the way we speak, live, and where we allow ourselves to be.

I've noticed there's a shift in vibration, in frequency, that's going on. In the first *Gathering* and since then, I've been directed to go to certain vibrations, energies, or qualities within. It really doesn't matter so much what the qualities are except that they're energies, vibrations, qualities that we prefer, that we like. Every time you do that, allow yourself to enjoy it, bask in it, merge with it, integrate it, blend with it. Your vibration is there. My friends and I have found as we continue to do this, our everyday core vibration starts to change.

I want to encourage everyone to *enjoy* every moment and every vibration and quality. I had the thought the first six months I was doing this, that just feeling these wonderful times in childhood, these vibrations of happiness, joy, and playfulness, could not possibly be so powerful. I thought this can't be real; this can't do much; this is re-experiencing my childhood. That's nice, but how could it be so beneficial? What I discovered is that I started *waking up* in a state of childlike joy. I started ending the day in a state of childlike peace. I started playing with people out in the world from that state, that playfulness, that openness, that trust and innocence.

All of a sudden I discovered I was coming from a playful openness most of the day. When I would relax, I'd automatically return to these vibrations of well-being. That's what's happening here. What we do, what we explore, is not as important as allowing ourselves to really be *in* the joy. Be within it. Let it change you. Let it metamorphose you, biologically, energetically, spiritually, emotionally, physically, mentally. Just allow all that to shift. We're really shifting to a new vibration, you can get it on your radio dial. It's K-N-O-W. You've seen the bumper stickers by Nancy Reagan that say "Just say no." She just spelled it wrong. It should be, "Just say *know*." That vibration, that frequency, has *always* been there. I've found it is getting easier and easier to access it. After awhile, you just don't leave.

The mind and the Western collective consciousness has been in charge and done a good job of veiling the alchemical space. In the *Gatherings*, we play a little trick on the mind. Quite often, the mind *thinks* it knows what's going on, and that it's safe to let you be here. The mind will let you go through all of these techniques it thinks aren't going to work anyway, because it feels not much will happen. Meanwhile, there's something happening on a deeper level. It's called *alchemy*, vibrational alchemy. From my personal observations, that's what's *really* happening here. That's why laughter is such a powerful part of the *Gathering*

To me, it's like a sand castle you build at low tide so that when the tide comes in it washes away the *foundation* of the castle. While the mind is busy fitting every process and term we use into its intricate, technical belief system, the vibrational flow of pure primal life force is undermining the very foundation of our whole reality structure. I enjoy eroding the foundation of everything the mind has built in the third dimension. That's really the purpose of the *Gatherings* for me. It's to wash away the foundation. While the mind is watching its domain, thinking everything is okay, the castle is collapsing underneath it. That washing away is the *alchemy* happening, the vibrational shifts and changes go on just by being here with the *intention.*

DEBRA - Something's coming up for me, in talking about the mind. In my experience, when I go to battle with my mind, it's not a pleasant experience. Since it's my intention in this physical form to experience pleasure and joy, I would like to embrace my mind, and honor it for all it has done for me and to create an equal partnership that is honoring and respectful of my mind.

KEITH -That's really the spirit of the unveilings. It's honoring the mind for what it has done for us. There is an aspect where we are honoring the mind but also saying we're going to go ahead and feel good, and live. That's more the spirit of this alchemy. It's allowing the alchemy to take place.

LINDA - What you just said about the veils allowing us to honor the mind helps me, too. When we were having this discussion at break, one of the things I realized that I'm working on is elevating my mind so that it's in alignment with spirit. I want everything working in alignment, my heart, my mind, everything. So with the unveiling I can see how it plays into that elevation process.

JANET - What I like about the *Gatherings* is that all of us are seeing a large painting, but if we look really closely, we see a dot. As we pull away again, we see *more* of the picture. In having everyone represent their knowing, I'm starting to see the whole picture. It's amazing.

MICHAEL - I don't have much book learning about alchemy, but I gather that it was these ancient wizards who were turning lead into gold. What I got out of looking at the process the alchemists seem to be going through was that they never created the gold *outside* themselves. *They* became the gold in the process. That's what I know about alchemy.

KEITH - Alchemy is the caterpillar that goes into a cocoon and then comes out a butterfly; it's metamorphosis, a change that doesn't go backwards. It's a permanent, lasting transmutation. An alchemical change is a lasting one. Your very *nature* changes. It's a *permanent* transformation at the core.

DAVID - It's transformation on a more plausible level because we're coming from a locked-in position of our mind or ego.

PAT - It's taking the impossible and making it possible.

KEITH - It's a blending or mixing of polarities, dualities, things that have been kept apart, different, and then they begin to play. It's an alchemy of mind, body, and spirit. It's playful, spontaneous, irreverent creation. It's ignoring scientific law and the past. Does everyone get a *feel* for alchemy? Shall we see what your intuition has to say?

When we've done *dream out*s on alchemy, it's been very helpful because our soul talks to us, showing us that we *know* what alchemy is for us as individuals. The alchemy *dream out* takes you to a time or place where you experienced real transformation, metamorphosis, transmutation, radical change, a 180-degree shift. Who knows better about how to remind us how to get through our veils, than our own heart, our own soul? Your soul worked with your mind to create the veils. Your soul knows how to talk to you through and around the veils. That's why we use this process of going to your intuition, your knowingness, and allowing it to take you to the *experience* of alchemy or transformation. It's fail-safe. In that spirit, I'd like to suggest we do a *dream out* on alchemy. Allow it to give you a dynamic, customized, personalized, powerful experience, so you own it. It's easy to own because you *know*, because it's your own. A nice byproduct of knowing our experience is our own is we don't invalidate it; we don't discount it. We allow it to be real.

If you want, allow yourself to feel and enjoy God current flowing through you, that river of knowingness that *is* your center, is your core. If you have any attention or energy anywhere else, just invite all of your life force to the present moment. What I do is tell my attention I'm going on an adventure. It's going to be fun. I want all of me here. I invite all of my energy to be present. Allow your heart, your intuition, to guide you, to flow where it wants to go. Allow yourself to open to a time or place, an experience, or directly to a feeling, vibration, energy of alchemy. Open to a time when you *knew* how to delightfully, joyously, safely, playfully, allow things to change in your life, to undergo metamorphosis, to transform, to shift. Go to a time when it was fun and easy, playful, natural, joyous, harmonious, and choose a time when you *knew* the safety, excitement, and nurturing of allowing true alchemy in your life. Just allow your intuition to take you to the perfect times, places, energies, vibrations, that will open a gateway for you, a portal to experience the true nature of alchemy, a permanent evolutionary change, an easy and fun shift, an open flow. Allow it to unfold in your own way, in your own time. Allow your heart to open to the perfect place or vibration or energy for you, at this moment. Experience change as being exciting, fun, fulfilling, easy, joyful, safe. Allow your intuition to take you to the perfect time, place, experience, vibration of true alchemy. Just step into it. Merge with it. Let it affect you. Let it fill you.

After people have relaxed completely and gone "inside" to see what their heart had to tell them about alchemy, Keith rang the chimes and people came back from their exploratory inner journey and began to share.

DREAM OUT: ALCHEMY

CHRIS - I kind of played back my early childhood before nine years old, the first time I can remember. I remembered my first puppy and the magic of that. What's wonderful about this process is the puppy isn't there anymore. The little boy I was is gone. Those experiences, the sense of joy is right *here*, right in this very moment, this wonderful way to access. It's kind of like losing your mind to access the place of joy within that's *always* present. It brings you there, and you just have to hold onto it. It's always, *always* there. It doesn't depend on the puppy. It doesn't depend at all on that environment. It doesn't depend on mommy and daddy. It doesn't depend on *anything*.

DAVID - I have been coming to realize what I'm calling disasters in my life are really just transitions.

KEITH - We're not talking about positive thinking here. We're not trying to paint a rosy picture on disaster. We're getting more *honest* and real about what we know for sure. We're getting away from boxing it or framing it. Recently, I have noticed I can go to an open, happy vibration anytime. If I notice the situation starting to get heavy or conflicted and disharmonious in a supermarket, store, restaurant, in court, anywhere, I'll just take a moment and basically do a *dream out*. I get back into a space of relaxed receptivity, a vibration of fluid allowing, and all of a sudden, I find a way to do what wasn't possible two minutes ago. Almost out of nowhere somebody apologizes or says, "Oh, I know what you mean," or the situation just shifts. It's fun to apply that to any situation, bringing it into physical realities, such as relationships, money, sex, and my body.

CHRIS - It's not even so much like bringing it; it's accessing what's always, always there and allowing.

INGE - It's like a movie. It really works for me well to describe it that way. One of the most magical times for me was at Christmas when I was a child. The way my parents did Christmas was just outrageous. All of a sudden, the tree was lit, and my dad had the cord going from the bell on the tree into the dining room. At just the right time, he pulled on the string under the carpet and said, "Oh, the Christ child is here!" It wasn't Santa Claus; it was the Christ child. Then I'd go in, and the tree was lit up with candles. He went in first so he could take a picture of my face, and it was just like *wow!* There it was, the tree and all of these presents. Then I got many, many more visions during this *dream out* and it was just like going to the movies. When the real fun began was when the tragedy happened, and they kicked us out of my home town in Czechoslovakia. We were pushing cattle carts into Germany, and we lost *everything*. Then my life unfolded, the alchemy continued. I met my first husband and came to the States, and I really recognized this is where I am *supposed* to be.

PAT - I never left. It was much too good *here*. I've witnessed, experienced, participated, and shared with so much healing vibration that as I was trying to go somewhere, I discovered I don't *need* to go anywhere. I never closed my eyes. It was better than chocolate. What I got from it is I don't have to go away anymore. Alchemy is *here*.

SULANA - I experienced myself as the alchemist and as that which is being transformed. When you rang the bell, I didn't want to come back; it was really wonderful. I could feel it happening within my body. I felt the power of the flow and moving into spaces and sort of like a painter painting. What I'm discovering is...there *is* a space that isn't in the mind. It's a space I'm currently having difficulty putting into words because my mind isn't there.

DAVID - I had an experience of essentially going back to when I was teaching a workshop. All of a sudden, I was with a group of people who had an absolutely amazing white glow over them. In fact, I said at the time, "You'll never believe what's going on in here." It was one of these absolutely amazing things. What I was able to do in this *dream out* was get in touch with the fact that *that* is where I want to be. I want to be in the glow with that experience. Then I went to some other experiences where I knew I had a *heart* connection with the people I was dealing with and came away with a glow, a super glow.

JOHN - I had a wonderful experience with that *dream out*. First, I began recalling experiences of transformation. One was while driving up here on Friday. I had this tape on that has songs from *"A Course in Miracles."* I kept playing this one over and over again that goes "I am not a body. I am free. I am still as God created me." Even though I'd heard it before, it triggered me somehow. Then it triggered another memory of when a teacher I worked with confronted me about something I was doing. He confronted me so gently and lovingly; there was nothing but grace and *love* coming through. I recalled experiences I've had, in other workshops, where I was glowing the way David described. I revisited a powerful dream I had once. I found myself surrounded by heavy walls and was on some kind of death row where I was sentenced and I waswondering how to escape. I was feeling this amazing heaviness and fear. Suddenly, I looked around and behind me were two angels. I looked at them, and one of them said, "Well what are you doing here?" As soon as I looked at them, I woke up. I was out of the dream. I realized I didn't need to be there anymore. I'm feeling these alchemical memories as openings. Now that it's over, I have a pleasant openness and vibration.

AUDREY - I *am* experiencing alchemy. My awareness of *knowing* alchemy. I'm learning how I've always known and am now shifting my awareness of the changes that are occurring.

JANET - For me, it's very powerful to describe what happened. I was asking my divine presence to show me alchemy. I was expecting something I did in this lifetime and all of a sudden, I saw two wedding bands, and I said, "What is that?" Then I saw a wedding gown. Then I was in the womb, when I was actually still partly in spirit, and partly physical. The physical was down here. It was a little bit dark but I was coming through; my spirit was coming through a tunnel of light. And all the beings who work with me and who want to help me in this process were there. The *love* I felt and the *privilege* of being able to come into a body, of being given the *opportunity* to come into a body was *absolutely amazing*. What *joy* I felt. Who gave this to me? Wow, it was amazing. My *God!* I was actually feeling *joyful* about coming into the body. It was very enlightening to me because I haven't ever thought I wanted to be in my body. When I saw how I felt, how I *really* felt in my heart, it was like, *Wow!* It was amazing.

LINDA - What I got was a real feeling for how much I *love* change, how much I *love* alchemy. That *is* what I'm here on the planet for, to effect change in this world. To effect change in myself, to effect change in the people I come in contact with. I love it in all its aspects. I love it when it's painful. I love it when it's fun. I love it in all of those ways. It was very affirming to me, rediscovering why I'm here.

Only that day dawns to which we awaken.

Henry David Thoreau

Chapter Five

AT HOME IN JUBILEE COTTAGE

Living 100% and Your Soul's Purpose

TALLAHASSEE, FLORIDA, IS HOME TO A BEAUTIFUL southern colonial mansion which sits atop the highest of the seven hills in the area. Goodwood Plantation is replete with the charm, grace, and beauty of a large southern home right out of the movie "Gone With the Wind." A long gravel road, shaded by the lush dense trees, winds its way past old white cottages and guest houses to the main house.

Spanish moss hangs down from the magnificent oaks. The grandeur of the place is breathtaking. It's like taking a leap backward in time to when southern belles strolled the grounds with their lacy parasols, and horse drawn carriages delivered guests to lavish summer picnics.

While there, I could feel that energy and activity as though actually in it. I felt the caress of the warm breeze and heard the delighted squeals of children who have long since lived their lives and moved on. Closing my eyes near the reflecting pool by the greenhouse, I could feel the presence of the slaves as they scurried past carrying large, savory roasts from the cook house to one of the festive halls. The element of time disappeared for me as I relaxed on those grounds and became part of all that ever existed on that site.

As I first entered those timeless grounds, I was immediately struck with the feeling I had come home. I arrived late on an unusually crisp but clear Saturday morning. There was nobody walking around the grounds because the *Gathering* had already begun. This added to the feeling that I was in a dream or a time warp. I could envision, actually feel myself climbing in the huge oaks, some of which had branches so old and so large, they reached down and touched the brown earth.

A small path led me to Jubilee cottage, one of the white buildings adjacent to the main house, which was used as a meeting and dance hall in another era. I approached cautiously because, although the sign out front clearly identified it, there was a still hush in the air. I was stalling so I could take in every possible breath of the timeless air outside. I was afraid it might escape back through the portal of time, never to be experienced again. As I approached Jubilee cottage, the echoing laughter from past festivities on that site mingled with a low level of laughter from the present day gatherers. Then abruptly, as I opened the white paneled door, the loud clarity of the present-day laughter shook me out of my dreamlike trance. I found a seat among the assembled people in a building which had been the site of countless parties and celebrations, and the source of joy, ardent love, zeal, and enthusiasm, for more than a hundred years. I felt at home.

There was a *tremendous* amount of magic going on in Jubilee cottage all four days we were there. I experienced more coincidences (or synchronicity) there than I have in my entire life. We did not record the sessions, but it doesn't matter. In having accompanied Keith to thirteen *Gatherings* in a row, I have been witness to what I would have formerly called "incredible" events. I'm finding *everything* is within credibility. A theme will emerge and grow in one *Gathering,* then spontaneously reappear in the next one without either Keith or I ever having said anything about it. It's as though the *Gatherings* are moving forward and it doesn't seem to matter *who* shows up. The people who are there are supposed to be there. It is an appointment with destiny.

It doesn't really matter whether something was said in Austin, Phoenix, Seattle, Philadelphia, or anywhere else. There is a purpose and a continuity about this phenomenon defying time and space. There is a commonality to the themes in the *Gatherings* that transcends conventional thought.

Feeling at home in Jubilee cottage is what this entire book is about. It's about going inside to truth and living in our natural state, the state of love and *passion,* the source of our jubilee. The timeless interconnectedness of passionate events from my life became clear to me, at lunch break in Tallahassee, as I was being driven through a splendorous tree canopy road to a plantation in nearby Georgia. I became so entranced by the beauty and the energy of the tunnel of trees, that time stood still. I experienced a natural high I still haven't come down from yet. I had been in that space before, and am now beginning to go there more often and linger for longer periods of time.

That's how it is with passion. It has no beginning and it has no end. You get there by becoming so absorbed in *now* that the past and future merge into a vibration of the present so strong it transcends the physical. The way to passion is through *living 100%.* You can find your path or blueprint by asking, *"What is my soul's purpose?* Why am I *really* here? What is written on my divine blueprint?" The portal to knowing is open all the time. All you need to do is open the door and step through. It's there, on the other side of that doorway, that you'll find your passion, your source of jubilee, your *dream.* You've been there before. It's time to *stay* there, *live* there. The following are two connected themes experienced in Jubilee cottage, shared here through people from other *Gatherings.*

LIVING 100%

KEITH - One summer I worked on the Mr. Rogers' Neighborhood TV show. There was a photographer there with whom I hung out with in the evenings. He would take photographs of the most exciting plays of professional baseball games and dramatic car accidents. He'd get riveting footage, and we'd speed eighty miles an hour to the TV stations to get it developed and put on the eleven o'clock evening news. I would see him do amazing things with film. He showed me how he got these brilliant shots in poor lighting and terrible conditions. He did superlative camera work and photography. I was in film school for a couple of years already, and I said, "How can you do all these things?" He said, "Well, it's easy." I asked, "How come none of my professors and the professional filmmakers I have worked with showed me this?" He said, "Oh, they know. They just won't tell anyone. They don't want you to get better than them. They don't tell you everything. No one tells you everything."

About the same time I was reading an old, old book about martial arts in the Far East. It reported that holding back information has been a tradition in Tai Chi, Kung Fu, Aikido, and other martial arts for thousands of years. I asked several martial arts masters about this practice. A lot of them wouldn't even talk about it, but no one denied it. Some of them validated it. What the book said was it's a tradition in the Orient for masters to hold back the last crucial 5% of their technique, of their approach, of the way they really produce the results. It goes way back to when the emperors ruled China. The way they kept their power and prestige was to be the head of a school and the best. If their students got better than them, then they would no longer have a position. So none of their students ever surpassed them, masters would not pass on this last 5% of their knowledge until they were on their deathbed, and then only to one student.

It made me very sad and angry, not only that vital information was being withheld, in the Far East, but I found out withholding crucial knowledge was prevalent with Western people in other fields of endeavor as well. The more I heard about this, the more I ran into it. I saw it with art, painting, dance, and photography instructors. I saw them hold back, consciously or unconsciously. So the last couple of *Gatherings*, we've developed this theme into a *dream out*. Take a look at your life and see, consciously or unconsciously, where you are holding back your love, your reserve, your power, your joy, your *passion* from *yourself* and others. Without that last 5%, you're not giving 100%, and you are not living up to the potential your soul intends for you. If all of your knowing and power isn't present, alchemy doesn't occur.

Where have you withheld some of yourself from your friends, society, family, and loved ones? This is the same veil as diminishing yourself. Where are you diminishing yourself? Where are you playing disabled, stupid, incompetent, *normal*? Are you saying you're too old, not old enough? Allow your intuition to take you to the parts of your life, your power, love, wisdom, sharing, perception, courage, to see where you're diminishing yourself. Where are you withholding that wisdom, love, energy, from yourself as well as from others? See where you're ready to break the dam, drop the wall, let the waters flow freely. There is one fellow, in Tallahassee, who had such an awakening. He realized he'd held back that last 5% his whole life and never fully gave to anything in terms of love, sex, money, enthusiasm, play, rest, creativity, *anything*. So he started playing with it gently. What would it be like to give himself fully, to open himself fully, to love himself and open to others fully, receive fully, know fully, feel his power fully? What would it be like? Since then, *so* much has come into his life: energy, vitality, good health, love, friendship, opportunity, creativity, and self-esteem.

MARK - That has done a lot for me. To put it another way, living 95% of the truth...what *is* that? What's 95% of the truth? It's a *lie*. So what are you living all of the time? That's why it transformed him, and it has transformed me too. I realized I had been holding back the last piece. But it is the piece that *really matters*.

KEITH - I've watched the consciousness in the *Gathering* go toward allowing everything to be *felt* completely, *experienced* completely. Every workshop, therapy, or discipline I've ever been involved in always advocated that we should *fully* experience whatever it is we are experiencing at the moment. But it never happened much. There was not enough safety. There was too much judgment. There were too many boxes and constricting paradigms. I can see now that the consciousness is developing to allow us to find ways to experience everything fully, even judgment or guilt, and to *allow* it, embrace it. Once these aspects of life are allowed to express themselves 100%, then we reveal ourselves and tell the truth 100%. I can see that is what's going to complete *this* creation, lovingly. Then we can move onto the next adventure. My hit was to do a *dream out* and allow your intuition to direct you. Let it take you somewhere where you either are still withholding and are ready now to experience 100%, or to that vibration of when you *did* experience 100%. You can remember how great it felt, the transformation and the opening, when you revealed yourself fully, or told 100% of the truth. Just feel that vibration, the safety of it, the power of it, the joy of it, the movement in it.

Magic happens when you go that 100%. If *anything* that happens is experienced 100%, what occurs? It moves, changes, transforms. It is allowed to express itself fully; it comes full circle. It's *complete*. With chemistry, when you mix all of the ingredients but the last one, what happens? That's what we've been doing with our magic, our power, our creativity, our divinity. So again, it's your heart directing you. Your soul is not going to ask you to go talk to five hundred people or walk on hot coals, unless it's right for you. Your heart is going to direct you lovingly. Allow yourself to trust that your intuition is not going to overwhelm you. Your knowing will show you where you're *ready* to be full, to be whole, to show up 100%. Your intuition has got your best interest at heart. Shall we?

DREAM OUT: LIVING 100%

Allow your river of knowing to flow to a time or place, or directly to a vibration, when you experienced *all* the way, relaxed all the way, opened all the way. Allow your heart to choose the perfect time, place, or event where you experienced life at 100%.

A *dream out* followed, then people from the group began to share what they felt or experienced on their inner journey.

DAVID - I think I'm ready to show more of myself to others. I believe it would be good for me. I don't know for sure.

KEITH - Would you allow me to bring up something I've found very empowering for myself? Usually I just let it go, but I'm bringing it up because we're on the subject of allowing ourselves to move more fully into *being* now. As you shared you used the phrases: "I think," "I believe" and "I don't know." My experience of you, when you spoke, is that you were not coming from "I think" or "I believe," or "I don't know." This is what I do when I'm conversing with myself or with another person. I stop and go back and say to myself what I just said, but I say it more accurately, the way I was *really* experiencing it. Not only is it empowering; it brings tremendous power to what I'm saying. By leaving off the last five percent of certainty and clarity, we diminish the true power of what we are saying; we don't give it enough juice or energy to move ahead, to gel. So, would you like to try it out loud, just share what you just shared but more accurately. What are you really experiencing?

DAVID - I feel I'm going to begin expressing myself more....

KEITH - Is that right? That's a very common term. A lot of us use I "feel" from our consciousness training, therapy, or counseling background. It keeps a little bit of a buffer between us and our full power. Do you really "feel" it or do you *know* it? I know you feel it, but is there more?

DAVID - I *know* I'm ready to reveal more of myself to myself and to others.

KEITH - Feel the difference?

DAVID - I really do. It saves a lot of words. (**Everyone laughs.**)

KEITH - You can save centuries of experiencing and suffering... My whole life, even when I was a shipper unloading trucks, somebody would take me aside and ask, "What is it about you?" I played really dumb. I would freeze and I'd say, "I don't know what you're talking about." They would say, "Let me take you out for a beer" or "Let me buy you a cup of coffee. There's something about you. You're doing something. What is it? I feel different around you." By playing dumb, I've been pushing my power and self-acknowledgment away for 30 years, saying, "No, you're crazy I don't know what you're referring to." Now I realize it is time to stop.

STEVEN - I really resonated, in my *dream out* session, with what you said. A spirit guide came to me, a very proud Native American chief or medicine man. He was walking along the plains and had his ceremonial costume on, carrying a shield and a spear and was saying to me...let's go. I immediately got up and decided to commit myself 100% in all that I do.

DUNCAN - I found I rarely, if ever, live 100%. There were a few physical experiences where I've exhausted myself physically in hours of tribulation. I'm allowing 100% to come closer but I still feel 100% is something I rarely do, if ever.

KEITH - Did your intuition lead you to a time when you did?

DUNCAN - Only a couple of instances when I was physically exhausted swimming in the ocean rescuing my wife and a couple of other times when I was in peril of some sort and I was so exhausted when it was over that I knew that was all I had.

MICHELE - I went to several instances where I consciously knew I wasn't giving 100%, and I consciously withheld that 5%. Then I went to a time when I definitely gave 100%. It was the birth of my daughter and feeling power beyond anything I've ever felt before. I felt the awesome power of creation and total presence.

KEITH - I remember several major points in my life when I jumped into something new 100% like a kid. I recall the first time I discovered rebirthing, explored New York City, cut and healed my hand, fell wholeheartedly in love. What happened every time was, I was changed permanently. When I came out the other side, I was a new being.

NELSON - I experienced a lot on this *dream out* which showed me several things. I came to the realization that the trip to this *Gathering* was really a 100% effort. There were all the reasons in the world for me to not be here. I kept pushing the reasonable objections aside and allowed the universe to make the arrangements. There are a lot of things in my life right now where, with the extra 5% in place, they would all be completed. There is so much to complete, I'm scared of having it all completed. I'd be back to zero again. The escape to this *Gathering* was really avoiding those completions from occurring. But my issues are being completed now. I know that I will become complete in all those areas. It's all right there; I need to just close the door, mail the package, send the bill, tell the person "no," all that. It's exciting. The reason I'm so thrilled about it is there's nothing to be scared about. There are nothing but wonderful things to look forward to. Actually, it's going to be a new unfolding. If you're in this state of awareness, there's nothing but goodness and mercy and grace and love and peace and joy to experience. It's really exciting, very fulfilling.

DUNCAN - I didn't realize that not giving 100% is actually a veil.

KEITH - What a veil, huh? A cultural veil as well.

JOANNA - I went to a couple of areas. I get involved in new things sometimes, and I do them 100%. A few years ago, I was into photography, and I was into it 100%. I bought all the equipment, a dark room and I really put a lot of effort into it. It felt extremely fulfilling but it wasn't permanent. Now, I know that being in my awareness is a permanent thing, that I can do 100% all the time. I also realize If I'm not there 100%, even when I'm telling the truth, I'm not *really* telling the truth. You can't tell 95% of the truth. I realize there are some things I do now, in which I give myself fully; I'm more centered when I do them. One of them is when I teach my class. I know I give 100%, and I see amazing results. I am teaching advanced fashion design to twelve students right now, and I see that when I give all these disparate people the same project to do, they actually *all* complete it. It's not an easy project. I feel that a lot of that has to do with the fact that it's almost like there's a flowing energy coming out of my head and into them. They get it directly from me without the words. The words are for just a little clarification here or there. That's what giving 100% means to me.

To live at 100% more than just occasionally, it is important to check with our inner knowing and see what our soul is doing here on the planet. By discovering why we're here, we can begin to live daily in the vibration of *our* truth. Another theme that developed in Tallahassee was, "What is your soul's purpose?" Keith began:

DREAM OUT: WHAT IS YOUR SOUL'S PURPOSE?

KEITH - Want to check in to see what your soul has to tell you about why you are here, what you are here to do? Are you living the passion of your dreams? As you go inside, look to see if there's any botheration, any disturbance from any part of you that's caught up with what happened earlier this morning, an idea, thought, or activity; the past. Is there any part of you worrying about the future? Is there some part of your body tying up a part of your energy? When you start to notice these disturbances or feelings, could you allow yourself to experience them in their natural state, as energy, as movement? Allow that movement, that energy, to stay unqualified, uncategorized, unnamed, unlabeled. Just leave it as energy, movement, vibration, life, flow. Allow it to move, move through, move up, move out, whatever. Just allow it.

Allow yourself to resonate with it, for your energy field to recognize the energy of the feeling. Allow your energy and the energy of the feeling to greet each other, welcome each other, allow each other. Can you appreciate the energy in that feeling, that condition, that sensation: feel love for it, for the power, *your* power, for the life in it, *your* life? Do you acknowledge yourself for being here this morning, for being willing to feel, to be present, for allowing all you've allowed to be here?

Could you appreciate that in yourself? Could you feel love for yourself, for your heart, your openness, your willingness, for your life, love for *all* life in whatever form it shows up? Could you allow all energy, all form, all manifestation, all manner of all things to be, just as they are, right now? Could you say "yes" to life, in all of the ways it shows up each moment, this moment? Could you say "yes" to yourself in all of the ways *you* show up every moment, in this moment?

Right now, where do you want your attention, your energy, your focus? Do you want it on form or on a present energy? On an old thought or a present movement? An old rerun or life force? More *story* or more *essence*? Speculation or truth? What did your soul bring you here to do? What does your soul's blueprint look like? What does your heart long for? What is your soul's passion? What is the source of your jubilee? What's on the other side of that door keeping you from your passion? Just go deep inside.

The room became completely quiet for the duration of the *dream out*. After about twenty minutes, Keith softly roused the group from their still and quiet state with a soft ringing of the chimes. As people sat up to share, Keith provided a gentle reminder about speaking from the heart.

KEITH - I would like to put out an invitation to check in with our hearts, soul, spirit before we speak, share, or act. Just see if what we're sharing is what *we actually* came for, what *we really* want, not what's right or proper or what we agreed to. Choose words which are in alignment with what you really want to be and do, nurture and put into effect in your world. Does anyone care to speak, to share what energy wants to be expressed through you?

SUE - I was giving up and letting go, and I just wanted to understand what was going on in my life and in the world. My soul said, "Do you *really* want to know the truth?" I had to check in to find out if I really *wanted* to know. Up until last night, I wanted to know the truth as long as it agreed with what I wanted to hear. So, for the first time I let go of the truth needing to be the way I wanted it. Then I experienced the undoing of the way I've done life up to now. Because nothing's working. I've been trying hard to get it to work and it's not working. I went inside to feel my dream and what had been my joy. It wasn't there. I searched everywhere for it, and it wasn't there. So I asked "What's the point?" **(crying)**

I had to grieve over the life that I've known as mine and begin to let it go in ways I didn't know I was going to have to let go. I feel really good to be here today. I know we have come together...I know all of us are here letting go of *something.* I trust God so much now, which is in all of you. I know I will find the answer to the question, "What are we here for?" I feel I am here in a new way, to do something I've been waiting my whole life to do. It's a new day. It is the undoing. I've been really trying to make more structure and that isn't it. Today, I'm glad to have you guys here with me, to go through this.

DAVID - Happy new day. Happy birthday! **(Clapping and laughter from the group)** I'm glad you came today because your radiant smile and energy this morning was beautiful.

MARIE - What I saw in this *dream out* was my fear of my dreams coming true melting away. I saw myself *as a* child of innocence and purity, coming alive as I combined with my divine self. That was the piece on crossing the threshold, where I combined with who I was. So I asked my divine self to stay and to combine with me and to never leave me. The child inside of me started to laugh because the child was finally having fun. A surge of energy was flowing through me as I was writing this information about my blueprint; my divine self expanded throughout my physical body. It pulsated within me. I saw my magnetic pull of bringing in leaders from different teachings for transformation to come to me. And the setting of this place, our house of Eos, created an opportunity for combining many eclectic workshops in transformation. I lead people back to the womb, back to innocence and purity. I experience empowering others to feel and be that energy vibration of innocence and purity. In time, books are written, workshops are given all over the world in strategic spots to bring people to their pure essence. I work from the highest loving vibration of compassion and service. I'm a genetic engineer to share my knowing of regeneration. This is yet to be revealed in time.

I am to bring forth specific sacred knowledge and help others in the unveiling of their sacred knowledge of spiritual growth and understanding. I am a co-creator, and I teach the co-creative process through relationship, science and technology, art, music, and life experience. I am a giver of hope and courage to move gently and gracefully into change. I am a person who brings people together in community to co-create, to come together in union. I teach as I learn. I learn as I teach. I am an artist, and I express myself through words: written, spoken, and sung. I am a growing consciousness. I have a specific role: to support the sacred, to honor, to love, and to know *radical freedom* with *infinite responsibility*. I am to teach the essence of being. I am a visionary. *I am the faithful arrow that flies straight into destiny's dawning.*

JILL - When I originally came to *Gatherings*, I knew that I was at a major turning point, a transitional point in my life. It's very scary and fearful. And then I would beat myself up because it doesn't need to be that way. When Sue shared with me earlier this morning, it was very similar to what I've been feeling. She said one sentence: "The *Gatherings* are dead for me." I had to ask myself why it felt that way. It isn't the *Gatherings* that are dead to me. It is the part of *me* that I have been gathering all of this time that is dead to me. I have not yet re-assimilated all of my new parts where I'm comfortable in them. It has been a period of confusion about where I am, who I am, what I'm *really* up to. I only know, at this point, what I have *known* about myself in the *Gathering* has died, and it is gone. It feels good, but it also at the same time feels empty. There's a huge void I am looking at filling today. There's a *huge* part of me I want to refill with love. That's all there is for me, love. I want the kind of love now that's all encompassing, for all forms, for all beings, for all life. I'm ready, willing, and open to receive that now.

JANET - I decided when I went home last night to keep all my energy rather than share all that had happened during the day as I usually do. I gave myself permission to be with myself. That's the first time I have ever said consciously that I don't *need* to be with people. I don't *have* to be. I have not been able to set that boundary before. I have always given everything away. And then I don't know how to nurture myself. So it was great.

DEBRA - Before I went to sleep last night, I was doing a practiced mindful meditation. It's a tape that brings me totally into my body. I've been noticing how much I've been resisting being in my body. I tried to do the tape before I went to sleep, and I felt like I wanted to jump out of my skin. I was *not* going back in there. I went to sleep then woke up in the middle of the night and turned the tape back on, and I *was* fully in my body. Then I realized what Keith is saying when he says, "It's safe now." All of a sudden what it meant to me is that it's safe to be in my body, and to feel my energy fully in my body. Like everyone else, I had my energy *everywhere*, just bursting out, leaking and floating everywhere. Earlier, I thought about someone I'd been working with. She has tremendous personal energy but she has no idea how to manage it. All of a sudden I realized that is why I am in the place I'm in. I'm learning to manage my personal energy in my physical body, be fully present, be with others, join group consciousness and maintain my own energy.

SUE - You reminded me of a message I got last night that I'm supposed to deliver to you. I was being whispered to, "It's safe now. It's time to wake up." I just kept getting it: *"It's time to wake up!"*

SUSAN - One thing I wanted to share, from my knowingness, is that anything I ask for materializes. I started playing with this before I knew what the heck I was doing. I would have dream boards, go through magazines and pick things out. And the damnedest thing happened. In the company I worked for, I said, "I'd love to live in Arizona." Within two months, I was living there, doing exactly what I wanted, down to a tee. I asked for it with the intent, with the belief I would receive it. I also left it open like Marianne Williamson's book, *A Return to Love*....you get clear on your intentions. You get clear on "Is this ego or is this my true self? Is this what would make myself happy?" And then, ultimately, you still leave it in God's hands. Always leave it open, to know you'll get exactly what's right for you to get, when you need to get it and that it will unfold perfectly.

KEITH - I would go further to say that, in my experience, if you really want to *know*, you can go and look at that blueprint. You can see what, in fact, the God inside you is going to give to you because you wrote the plan together. That God is part of you.

SUSAN - That's what I'm here for. I want to go deeper. I want to....

KEITH - You don't have to wait for it to show up. You can go look at your personal life design and see when you're going to get what. I just had a hit. May I share? It has to do with what you shared earlier. It was neat. You said, "I *want* to do that." "Maybe I'll do that." What I've discovered is that part of what was blocking me was there were things I really wanted to experience that were unmentionable, that weren't okay, not only to ask for, but to *do.* They weren't spiritual enough; they were wrong, evil; they'd be judged. But they are part of my life plan, so now I do them wholeheartedly.

JANET - So how did you ask for that? Did you just say, "I want to see my divine blueprint?" or...

KEITH - I just didn't kick St. Germain out of my bedroom. I didn't block new transforming energy from coming in. That's when it started.

JANET - But what if we're not all visited. I mean, we are visited by beings, but what if we don't see them, or experience them in 3-D reality?

KEITH - If you sense them, talk to them. I'm just saying that I listened, I opened, I didn't reject that experience. That's just where it started. I said, "Yes."

JANET - My frustration has been, since I've been a little girl, I've been saying, "I want to *see*. I want to *see*. I want to *see*." In every possible way I could do it, including writing down what I want, including being very detailed, including praying, including crying, including *all* of it.

KEITH - May I ask you a question? When the door opens, however it opens, it might come through smell, sensing, feeling, a light, another person... when the door opens, when Jesus, God, grace comes to you, do you say, "Yes," no matter what the form?

JANET - Let me put it this way. I *thought* I said, "Yes." So, in all of my intentions, all of my longings, in all of my desire, that's the thing I cried about yesterday, I *want* to, I *really* want to. That's the thing I've been longing for all my life, in this lifetime.

KEITH - Can we play with this a little, do you mind? Would you demonstrate, for the group, *wanting* to say, "Yes"?

JANET - I know it's in the language.

KEITH - Okay. That's fine. You just demonstrated *wanting* to say yes. Now, would you demonstrate *saying,* "Yes."

JANET - "Yes!"

KEITH - Feel the difference? It's *that* simple. It really is. *Wanting* to do *anything* doesn't even exist; except in a theoretical realm of conceptual possibility. "*Yes*" *moves* the universe, it *opens* the door. Let's all sit here and *want* to open that door. **(Pointing to a door in the room)** This demonstration really helps me. Now would someone *open* the door? Go ahead. **(Someone opens it.)** See the difference? It's really *that simple*. I want to share that when I say, "Yes," It does bring up fear in me. I've been asked the same question for thirty years: "Why do you have these *extra*ordinary experiences and others don't?" And I'm starting to get clarity right now. The bottom line, when the shit hits the fan, when the terror hits my gut, I *still* say, "Yes" and I go through the door. In a similar moments, I watch my friends and others *not* go through the threshold into the new space.

JANET - But don't they think, at the moment, they *are* going through the door?

KEITH - Yeah, they *think* they are.

JANET - That's my point, my frustration. I could say, "Yes" to myself, "I *have* gone through the door," and yet I'm not experiencing any changes, or being in a new place.

KEITH - To me, that's the test. Are you *there*? If you're there, you went through the door. If you're not there, you didn't go through the door. My friend Lester used to say, "You only know what you can *do.* You only know what you can do at will, on command. If you can do it when you want to do it, when you decide to do it, at any time, then *you know* it's real. Otherwise it's all speculation. If you're *doing* it, you know. If you're *experiencing* it, you know. If you're *being* it, it's a *knowing."* Everything else is an idea, concept, or belief; not 'knowing.'

The reason I'm asking this way is because I *know* each of you are presented, daily, with the openings, the doors you want. On the other side of those doors is what you're seeking. If you say, "*Yes*" and open the door and walk through, you'll *have* what you desire. I *know* it's being presented to each of you daily. I can *see* it right now. It's just deciding you're going to say, "Yes," to any gateway, any time, any way that it appears. Often, the doors do not appear the way we *think* they're going to appear. They can be scary to see.

Most people say, "No. Not *that* form. Not *this* way." Gifts don't always show up in the package we expect. I realize I've been saying, "Yes," to the unmentionable and scary, since I can remember. To me it's like the story of Jesus spending his time with lepers, prostitutes and robbers. It all made sense to me. I've said "Yes" to things that were ugly, horrible, dangerous, and disease-ridden, because I was drawn there. I felt an excitement there. When I said, "Yes" to those things, I went through a door. I found magic on the other side of the door.

No door has *ever* appeared to me the way I *thought* it would. It's never been easy; it's always been scary. But my little child heart was so excited, it went through *anyway*. I've found you can't stand there immobile and get anywhere. Someone mentioned earlier he felt like he had one foot on one side of the river of life and one foot in the other. Here's the doorway. You've got one foot on one side and one foot on the other. You're over here wanting to see what's on the other side of the river, right? You can't *see* very much with a foot over in your old world and only one foot in the new. **(Keith illustrated by standing in the doorway stretching out his neck trying to see around the corner.)** You've got to take your foot out of the old world, the safe, familiar shore go with the flow, then you see the magic. Most people won't take the last foot out of the old world. Some will go to the doorway and look. **(straining to see around the door)** "I want to *see* what's in there." They can't see very much. You must go *through* the *door.* Then you can *experience* what is on the other side. What I've found is when you look through a doorway, a gateway, you *can't* see much. It's so bright, you can't see through the threshold. You have to go *through* to experience the new space.

People want others to describe the other side, guarantee them it will be safe. Well, hey, *I'm* here. That's the only guarantee I can give. On one occasion, I wouldn't go through a particular door. Then I had a car crash. My guides shook me up and told me to keep my end of the deal. I don't go through all of the gateways easily. My heart did say, "Yes," and so it happened. I would never have agreed to it, had I known, but part of my contract is I don't *want* to know what's going to happen. I'll just say, "Yes." That's the way I allow myself to go through the door. I'm having stuff going on now in my life that's terrifying me, and I'm still saying "Yes" to it because I *know* that "Yes" works. I know it from my own experience. saying "Yes" to everything is blowing all my old paradigms; I feel out of control 98% of the time. In my *feeling* world I am out of control. In my soul, in my knowing, I feel more peace than I've ever felt in my life. So that's where I want to put *my* attention. I feel them both, but the peace is so much stronger than the terror of out-of-control-ness.

MARK - I've had the same experience the last couple of weeks. I often get in touch with my inner God voice through my daily writing. I was recently struggling with the prospect of leaving my present job. As I was thinking more and more seriously about it, I wrote, "Okay, your foot is in the door and now you can see the light." The next day it was, "Okay, your knee is in the doorway." It was just like that every day and then on the day I went completely through, it asked, "How does it feel?" It's a *new world.* It's a *completely new world!* I look back now and find my struggle humorous. I was choosing to stand there struggling in the doorway instead of choosing the light.

DAVID - I've spent four years screwing around that damn door doing nothing. Because of circumstances over the last five days, I'm going *through* the door! If anyone wants to know what it's like, check with me next *Gathering*. I really appreciate your model. Thank you.

REX - I think it's really true: I am a verb. I'm getting a sense that God is a verb also. It's an action, a motion, a divine flow, a stream. There's a goal pulling me. When I feel myself falling into a space where I allow intuition to lead, it's like a vacuum *pulling* me in this direction. If I allow that, then the motion is supporting. It's like floating in a stream, a nice warm stream, I'm just being carried in the right direction. Every once in awhile I feel strong. I lift myself up in the canoe and put the paddle in the water and give it a big stroke, maybe two strokes. Then I settle back down in the stream of the flow.

Often, one discussion and *dream out* session will naturally flow right into one another. In this case, living 100% provides a perfect entry way for a discussion on going through the door:

GOING THROUGH THE DOOR

MICHAEL - I don't have conversations with ascended beings and so on, and yet I feel totally supported. I'm actually *doing* and *living* what came to me as my life purpose 10 years ago. It seemed, at the time, so outrageous and so impossible, like "*Forget it.*" But what I can see now is every step of the way I've been guided, trained, taught. Everything I've needed along the way has been given to me. Now I'm *doing* what I'm here for.

SHAWN - What about choice? Is the choice that we're supposed to have the choice to go through the door or not? Is that what this choice is all about? If it was choice, it would be a revolving door you could look around and come back.

KEITH - What does your heart really want to ask right now, Shawn?

SHAWN - I'm caught up with the problem that it isn't complicated enough. (**Laughter from the group.**) You're making it sound too easy, so what's wrong with it?

KEITH - You're right. It's not complicated enough. It's so simple.

SHAWN - So tomorrow the *dream out* is going to be "Let's go read our blueprints"? So what if you look at your blueprint, and it's dated 1974, and you should have been doing this a long time ago?

KEITH - That's not what people discover.

SHAWN - What if your blueprint is dated 2010, and it's not your time? What if you find out it's not your time? Do you hang out for 15 years? What if you're 86 years old and find out it's not your time? I'm afraid this is what could happen.

KEITH - Are those your fears? Would you like for me to answer the question from *my* experience? My experience, as well as the experience of those I know who have seen their blueprint, is that no one has seen those situations. They have not found a blueprint dated 2010 or 1974. I don't know anyone who has experienced that when they've looked at their blueprint. It's been a totally comprehensible, fulfilling, exciting, and enlightening experience.

SUZANNE - For me it's been a tremendous *relief.* Everything I have done in my life has made sense and has made it so *easy* for me to see the deliberate unfolding of my life. Now I understand. Since I've been opening up to my blueprint, I've gotten my joy back, because my inner knowing is that my spirit is on the right track.

KEITH - I'd like to say too, Shawn, that at the beginning, during the second *Gathering* ever, in Vermont, when everyone's personal blueprints started to show up, so did our cloaks and veils. I said, *"That was no 'Dream;' it was a nightmare!"* I called it the *nightmare* because we had so much fear and terror surface. Then during the third *Gathering*, someone talked about seeing their blueprint and how everything in their life made sense. I sat there and went into total resistance. I was terrified of just what you mentioned. I did not want to be betrayed again, let down, disappointed, lied to again. I didn't even want to open to the idea of what I'm saying right now because I did not want to be messed with again. I just couldn't take it.

I was in total resistance to doing an unveiling to the point of seeing my whole blueprint. One of my biggest issues was my (former) blindness because when I went blind at age twenty, I had twenty more years of pain. For two months I thought I was never going to be able to see again. Just the idea that that was all purposeful, deliberate, wise: "*No*!" I did not want to be fed any spiritual rationalization, positive thinking, "*No!*" Finally, after two or three months (and meanwhile I'm leading all the *Gatherings)*, it *was* time.

I sat down and decided to do an unveiling: "What's the beneficial purpose of my being blind and the twenty years of pain?" I saw my life plan and saw the blindness was part of it. I saw what it brought me, what I gained from it: a permanent connection to God and an ability to heal myself of anything. I saw what it gave me. Then I started letting *in* God, started letting *in* the grace and saw that all the suffering was worth it. The regret, the anger at God, the anger at myself, the sadness, and the pain of twenty years, all dissolved over the course of the next several hours. It took hours to leave because I had built up so much of a backlog.

The key, to me, is it isn't until you let in the *gift* on the other side of the veil that the whole experience becomes worthwhile and appreciated. I had understood conceptually the spiritual lesson of the blindness for twenty years. I could see intellectually the way it opened me to God; it healed my soul. I could understand all that, but I wasn't letting in the experience of grace, of joy, of peace. I wasn't letting the gift in. I just understood it. I was sharing it with everyone else, but not with *myself*. So it *wasn't* worth all that pain *until* I gave myself the gift experientially. And that's why I emphasize *feeling* the gift, letting the gift in, *dreaming out*, letting in your God current. The plan, the blueprint, was intellectually exciting and made sense, but it *wasn't worth* going through the whole experience until I fully received the purpose, the goodies, the *gift* of it. When you start letting in the gift you say, "Sure, twenty years of pain, no problem." I've got eternal bliss. I've got eternal peace. Now that is *worth it*.

AUDREY - I feel, I *know,* the coming of the *Gatherings* has helped trigger my awakening. It's the beginning of seeing my blueprint. I'm making all these connections in my life of being a caterpillar and becoming a butterfly. Just recently, I *knew* I had to revisit a terrifying experience from my past before I came to this *Gathering,* so I could *now* become the butterfly. One night, I revisited the place and the terror. Only this time I was safe. I'm going to be able to make the transformation because I know how to do it now, and I don't get terrified anymore.

I have an abundance of connections around the caterpillar and the butterfly in my life. These images are revealing themselves. I know, because I already did the transformation. I feel lucky. I've already gone through the doorway and terrified the shit out of myself. It was a revolving door and I've come back. Now I know, when the time is right, I'll be able to go through and not be terrified. Often, as I'm getting ready to go through a door, I'm terrified but whenever I actually go through it, I'm not afraid anymore. It's the moment before death.

KEITH - An example is right now, this last hour, a doorway has opened. It's there to go through if you choose. It's not any more complicated than "Yes" or "No."

SHAWN - Maybe formalized religions have complicated what is really just going through the next door.

KEITH - *Maybe*, yeah. Does anyone know the song, "Losing My Religion?"

SHAWN - I don't know the words to it, but I know the song. **(Loud laughter from the group)** In other words, I ain't singing it.

KEITH - It's been playing in my head for the last three days. It used to be on a TV music channel all the time, one of the most popular songs in the past three years. It's about what you just said, losing your religion, your dogma, your set ideas. That's the point of the song. It *speaks* to people's *soul*. People have no idea. They say, "I don't know what it's about," but they buy it and music channels are still playing it three years later. The song is *very* powerful. It's about losing enough of your religion to see the doorway to something new, fresh, more real, more alive. It's about abandoning your rigid belief system, especially your spiritual belief system.

SUZANNE - If we can ask for what we want and how we want it and we are petrified to go through the door, we can ask to have a pleasurable, enjoyable experience. Does it have to be terrifying?

JILL - For me, it isn't a fear of it hurting, it isn't even a fear. It's an excitement of the unknown. When a portal opens and I feel its presence, I want to consciously say, "Yes." I want to go through. I know from experience that when I've been conscious enough, I know when the doors have opened. To me it's like Lewis and Clark, it's like the explorers. There's an excitement pounding in my heart right now to go where I've never been before. I get palpitating really fast. It isn't a fear. It isn't anything connected with that for me. It's an excitement of the unknown that's just been opened to me to become a known, a new experience. It's exciting. I'm *really excited* right now.

AUDREY - Keith just described in his talk that when you've gone through enough doorways, you have a choice. I feel that is what we are doing at the *Gatherings,* too. We realize we have a choice to put our attention on our *knowing* instead of on our feelings, or to be able to do it simultaneously. In my knowing state, I'm completely serene and comfortable. I'm not affected emotionally.

JANET - You just reminded me. I said earlier today that I can't see my guides or any spiritual phenomena. But that's not accurate. At a Sedona workshop I went to, I was up on a mountain doing a ceremony. All of a sudden, I saw these huge supernatural beings and they reminded me of my Native American ancestry. I was a medicine woman, and I was *extremely* powerful. They reminded me how I had rebelled against them and said, "I don't want to have anything to do with you guys again because that lifetime was very painful." *It's interesting to see how easily we forget these things.*

Our deepest fear is not that we are inadequate.

Our deepest fear is that we are powerful beyond measure.

It is our light, not our darkness, that most frightens us.

We ask ourselves, who am I to be brilliant, gorgeous, talented and fabulous?

Actually who are you not to be?

You are a child of God.

Your playing small doesn't serve the world.

There's nothing enlightened about shrinking so

that other people won't feel insecure around you.

We were born to make manifest the glory of God that is within us.

It's not just in some of us. It's in everyone.

And as we let our own light shine,

we unconsciously give other people permission

to do the same.

Marianne Williamson

Chapter Six

LIGHTS IN THE DESERT

Equality and Light

MARIANNE WILLIAMSON CAME TO THE UNITY church in downtown Seattle in October of 1997 where I met her, in person, for the first time. She was in town to talk about her new book, *The Healing of America*. My attention was first drawn to her when someone in a *Gathering* read the passage on the adjacent page from *A Return to Love*. Nelson Mandela was so impressed with the wisdom and truth in those words that he quoted them aloud to millions of people listening across the world in his inaugural speech.

It is a bold assertion of equality and inner power that begins in our heart as each of us allows our own light to shine.

I went to see Marianne because she speaks such fundamental truth. I was drawn to her. Because of her, millions of people have, either directly or indirectly, been influenced to share some of their own light. I was also on a mission. I was hoping to somehow be able to actually get close enough to Marianne to ask her personal permission to use the quotation in this book. I knew there would be hundreds of people there, and my mind chatter told me not to bother because it was a waste of time. Though I should have been inspired beyond fear by the strength of the very words I was asking permission to use, I was actually petrified.

Despite my fear, I tuned in to my own light faintly flickering way down within, despite a host of excuses I had which were trying desperately to extinguish it. That voice told me what I was intending to do was far more powerful than my fear. I could be as scared or could struggle as much as I needed to, but I *was* to meet with Marianne, and the rest would fall into place as it should.

Before the lecture, I bought a copy of Marianne's book in the hallway foyer of the church and immediately opened it up to a quotation by Rumi I had already included in *this* book! It gave me a big "rush." I have discovered, and it's being strengthened more each day, that when I'm allowing my own light to truly shine, "coincidence" abounds. As though to place irrefutable evidence to keep me charging forward, a series of remarkable synchronistic events began to unfold, and I knew I was "in the groove."

I found a seat in a pew in the beautiful Unity church, which was quickly filling with eager people, and took the opportunity to look through a hymnal. That was convenient because I had just made a fruitless trip to the library a few days earlier to look up some of the words of Keith's, (and "coincidentally" my recently departed mom's) favorite song *In the Garden.* As I read it and sang the song silently to myself, I got another big "rush," so I knew I was on the right track. After a series of housekeeping announcements, the host introduced a musician who had been given his first opportunity to play his music in a church with Marianne years before. Kevin Benedict came forward and dedicated his song to Marianne. He said it was one of her favorites.

I was completely blown away! I had met Kevin a few months before after hearing some of his amazing, enlightened music. My favorite, *If You Were God,* was the one he played, to the accompaniment of my goose bumps. I have played and intensely enjoyed, playing that song almost every day for the previous three months. I have played the CD so much, I've been a nuisance with it. I played it at my last *Gathering,* and I want to play it for everyone who comes into my house. I'm inspired, and simply giddy with that song. I get a "rush" every time I hear it. If I still had *any* doubt this string of events was going to lead me to meet directly with Marianne, it was very soon put to rest.

Still reveling in the music of Kevin Benedict and marveling at the coincidences unfolding that night, I was in a euphoric daze by the time Marianne started to speak. She enthusiastically talked about *The Healing of America* by letting our individual lights shine. She said, "Speak to the *light* in people, and the *light* within them will respond." In her talk, she also quoted Jesus in the Bible as saying, "Remain awake with me *in the garden*." That was the name of the song I had been singing quietly to myself *just* a few minutes before!

After Marianne had talked for some time, there was a break. During that time, I felt compelled to go over and wait by the inside door to the left front of the church. It was a little awkward, because it was, after all, at the front of the church and right next to the stage. During the break, people were looking up there all the time. For a while, I was able to keep my fear of public scrutiny at bay because I could truly feel if I waited there long enough, she would come to *me*. The fear that I was actually "powerful beyond measure" caught up with me, and as I was bold enough to recognize it might really happen, I practically ran away from the area. I was still in terror of the success I knew would be coming with this book. I could feel this encounter with Marianne was one of the final steps ensuring the book would do well.

As I was sitting safely back in my pew in the middle of the church, Marianne came out and stood there, exactly where I had been standing and waiting nervously for her to emerge. I was instantly filled with remorse at not having listened to my intuition. People converged on her, and she talked with them and signed their books. What struck me as I was sitting there watching, was how sincere she was with people. She was a model of genuine equality, treating everyone as long-lost family. With that, I regained the nerve and composure to go wait in line. She was, however, already edging her way through the crowd to the stage. Part of me, an old part starting to atrophy from disuse, thought I had blown it. "I guess that's what I get for not listening to my intuition."

I had one more chance and was determined that nothing was going to stop me. After a session of questions and answers, Marianne was going to sign books for her fans. I was going to be in that line. As soon as the question session was over, I scrambled up the few stairs, nearly tripping, as I approached the raised platform where Marianne was sitting down at a table to sign books. Being fourth in line, I had little opportunity to practice what I would say. But I knew it didn't matter. I decided to go "inside" for strength and asked the universe to lead the way.

As I surrendered, the woman in front of me asked, pointing to a piece of paper she was holding in her hand, "Did you know Marianne wrote this?" It was a copy of the passage I had in my hand and was asking Marianne to allow me to use in the book! As I was already floating along on the "rush" inspired by all of the other coincidences of the night, that transported me into the stratosphere. I was in a blissful world of my own as I observed how wonderful Marianne was with the people for whom she was signing books. Complete strangers, full of love in their hearts, were allowing their lights to shine because she had opened the door with true equality.

I was very tentative as I approached Marianne and attempted to tell her a little about this book and asked her to sign a release form. I tried to explain that the night had been filled with wonderful synchronous events. I may not have said one coherent thing, but it didn't matter. This woman has spoken her truth and allowed her light to shine so brilliantly that it affected millions of people. She, as an *equal,* said, "I would be *honored* if you would include this in your book." She meant it. I'll never be the same. The word "equality" has since taken on a much deeper and more personal meaning for me.

Equality emerged as a theme at *The House of Eos*, the beautiful desert domicile discussed in chapter three, and the site of this *Gathering*. It is a place of energy, equality, and light. The house gracefully blends with its rural desert surroundings. As the *Gatherings* are in progress, it is not uncommon to see desert rabbits darting from the brush to the shade of a tall saguaro cactus, or mother quails with a trail of chicks, scurrying around in search for food. Lizards bask in the warm morning sun. Birds flutter and chirp around the fountain and provide a happy background for the gatherers. Neighborhood dogs wander freely in the desert adjacent to the house and will occasionally sit right outside the large picture glass window whining to come in. Sometimes, if a door is left open, they do come in and are sadly escorted out after lavish attention is laid upon them.

It is such a natural and serene setting, *The House of Eos* is the perfect place to capture the spirit of equality. Michael and Marie, who live there, are as much a part of the spirit of the house and equality as the surrounding desert's flora and fauna. They treat everyone as honored guests in their home and freely give of its energy. This *Gathering* began with the introductory material about the origin of the *Gathering* some three years before. There were a few unveilings and several *dream outs* to help people connect with their inner knowing on an experiential level. Very early on, the theme of personal light and equality emerged and remained strong throughout the four days. We have captured and shared the personal experiences people expressed from their hearts.

Keith begins with an analogy about fire and light: how we can warm others by igniting our fire within:

KEITH - From my point of view, what we are doing in the *Gatherings* is re-lighting fires. When I was a kid, I perked up when I heard a story about the early settlers in Plymouth, Massachusetts. When the fire would go out in their hearths, they would send a message out and someone would bring a lit coal to them. They had special leather pouches to carry burning coals and would immediately get on a horse to carry a hot coal to a house twenty miles away. It struck me, as a kid, how beautiful, important, and central it was to their lives. That is what everyone who is experiencing *Gatherings* is doing. We're carrying the light that we have, the fire that we've got going, and we're taking it to places and people who want to light the fire on their hearths again.

We're doing it in groups and one-on-one, wherever we can. My experience in the last process was of the heavenly angelic hosts. They allowed me to see an amazing new sight. I saw people allowing themselves to be re-energized and activated. They were accepting the seeds of knowing and receiving the flame of illumination. An interesting thing I've noticed is that people don't always feel the effects of activation right away. Many of the people who have later gotten the most out of the *Gatherings,* at the time didn't think *anything* happened. Some of them have come to four or five *Gatherings,* and they still didn't *think* anything happened. They went into altered states never got conscious pictures, ideas, or *anything*. Then, later, they call to tell me how much their lives has changed.

It isn't necessarily about getting images, realizations, or understandings at the time of the *dream outs*. Most of my insights come late at night, in the morning, in the shower, or when I'm taking a walk. Revelations come at unexpected times. Often, I won't notice I've shifted or changed until I'm in a situation that used to always go a certain way, and all of a sudden, there's a freedom that wasn't there before. A door opens that didn't open before. In fact, the week *after* the *Gathering* is when I notice what happened *during* it. I just really wanted to acknowledge and emphasize that it's not about knowing what's going on, understanding it, sharing it, or describing it. It's about *knowing* that it's happening and allowing it to unfold however and whenever it unfolds. So in that spirit, I would like to invite us to share in a new way.

Rather than share what we *think* happened, rather than describe it in words and concepts, especially *old* words and concepts and paradigms, let's open to something fresh and new. I *have* noticed in the *Gatherings*, at certain points, some people shift into a level of sharing, a place of sharing *from*, of talking *from*, that is *so* exquisite, *so* electric, it's nurturing. The sharing is from their wisdom, from the part of them that knows the gift they *really* came here to share with us. It's from the part of them that, whether they know it or not, got activated by, "What is your spirit here to do?" They start sharing *just* from that place, *just* knowing, *just* truth. It is usually one or two or three sentences. It changes my life when people share like that. It's what *I* came to hear.

I'm not saying let's make the other ways of sharing *wrong*, or not do them, or scream at each other if we do say, "I think," describe too much, or get emotional. There's a doorway open here, for speaking from a place of clarity, truth, and knowing. Sharing from the soul is not always welcomed by people. It's not surprising we don't share directly from our unveiled essence being, because it has not been time or been well received on the *planet* before. When we've tried, guess what we've gotten back? In the past, we've been criticized, rejected, and abandoned. Things have changed, though, on the planet. There has been a huge shift making it more okay to speak from the heart.

So, knowing all that, and knowing all those veils, *I* would enjoy, the rest of the day, if we might just take a moment before we share and see what it is, really, our *spirit* wants to express. What is that kernel of knowing, that gem of insight? Let's share heart to heart, spirit to spirit, knowing to knowing. Skip a lot of the prefaces, buffers, and other smoke screens to whatever degree you feel safe and comfortable. In speaking from our heart, there is amazing power to ignite, catalyze, and trigger *each other*, which is what we came to do. There are certain gifts still to be received and given here we haven't given or received yet. This is a way. So in that spirit, if someone feels moved to speak....

EQUALITY

RAY - As I told Keith when I first heard about this, what caught my ear and made my heart blissful was the *equality* aspect: *A Gathering of Equals*. This morning, I got a taste of what I was after. We were all in our hearts there for a while. The mind, which is not of the spirit, is full of inequalities, but when we come from the heart, we're all the same. I got a sense of the "organic-ness" you talk about, how it's really inevitable, what's happening. It started in the sixties. In 1966, I lived about three blocks from Haight-Ashbury, in San Francisco. When I heard "equal" and I heard "*Gathering,*" I knew it was the next step for me and for the process that's going on. What you're doing opens all of this energy that's coming, opens this path for it so each individual can find his/her own response and special way to go.

SULANA - I was attracted to *A Gathering of Equals*. The "equals" was the part that drew me also. In this intuitive journey, I went to "Where do you diminish your life?" With everybody, in groups and one-on-one, I hold a barrier. I was exploring why I did that, and I realized when each of you shares, I am in awe of your stories and your lights. They seem so much brighter than mine, so I shrink.

Throughout the years, people have asked me why I don't write a story about my life. They say, "Your life is so interesting." When I was sharing a part of my life, I thought, "There's nothing interesting about my life. Why would anybody want to hear about it?" As I was lying there thinking about it, I realized I've not valued anything about my life. Why have I done that?

Up until a few months ago, most of my life I've wanted to die. I have always wanted the choice to opt out when things got really bad. As I began to let that in, I was shocked because I began to feel the value of my life. In the glory of all of you sharing your light, I thought, "Gosh, that's in here, too, for me." My light is often hard to find when I'm alone. I have found such great wisdom, but when I come into this group, it's gone. But all of a sudden, I got it: I've been hiding. Every time I see *your* light, I am so in awe of it; I diminish mine. That's not equality. I don't want to *do* that anymore. It's just so important to let in the value of my light. I don't want to opt out anymore.

DEBRA - Yesterday, Carol said to me something about doing so many seminars and getting so high from each one and how many she's done. This morning I was thinking about the fire and the tending and people always keeping the fire lit so they had a source of heat and light. That is what the Gatherings do for me. It isn't about what I can *get* from here or even about what I can *give*. It's about being in a space that tends my fire, that feeds my spiritual growth, that fills my spiritual container. You can get it thousands of places. I choose here. The expectation I have from here is nothing other than to experience and fully feel my own fire in my own spirit and allow it a free place to play.

CAROL - I'd like to tell a story about a little candle whose flame was lit, and he got afraid. He said, "I'm not ready to be light." So it spoke to all of the other candles and they agreed. "Yeah, we're not ready." Then when the electricity went out, the woman who owned the house went to the closet to light the candles. They all said, "We're not ready to shine our light in the world. We haven't done this; we haven't done that." To make a long story short, of course, they *were* ready, even before they *felt* ready.

SULANA - They *were* candles after all.

MIA - We're all *equals*, we are all *totally*, *completely*, *absolutely equal,* and in my dream out, I had come to my true home, and everybody was celebrating my arrival. There wasn't some issue like I was some guru or that "She's *finally* made it." It was really incredible and beautiful. Beautiful like you would imagine heaven to be. That thing about the equals and the celebration and that you're arriving, we're *all* arriving. It's just amazing.

KEITH - I had a door open to an aspect of equality that taught me a great lesson and really meant a lot to me. I also got a lot of tips to use in the real world out of it. My intuition opened me to re-experience an interaction I saw a few years ago on television. There was a panel show on television with a young reporter. He was telling the audience about his first assignment ever with his newspaper. As he told it: Several months before, he was to cover Nelson Mandela's inaugural speech in South Africa, and it was a big deal. Most of the heads of state of the whole world were there. He was backstage before the inaugural speech, looking for the press room. In his search, he stumbled into a broom closet and opened several other wrong doors. He finally found a door that opened and wasn't a broom closet. He went in and saw Nelson Mandela there.

He excused himself and started to leave, but Mandela said, "No, it's all right, come in, come in, it's fine." Mandela was making himself a peanut butter and jelly sandwich before he was to address worldwide live television and national leaders from all over the world. He was about to step into the major governing role in this country that had put him in prison for twenty-seven years. He was making himself a peanut butter and jelly sandwich right before the most momentous event of his life. The reporter awkwardly introduced himself and Mandela said, "That's nice. Would you like a sandwich?" The reporter was so taken aback he uttered, "Yes," because he didn't know what else to say. They stood there quietly while Mandela made *him* a peanut butter and jelly sandwich, too, just minutes before he made his speech. They sat there and ate them together in silence.

As this reporter was telling the other reporters about this, he started to cry, which you're never supposed to do as a reporter on television. He couldn't help it. It was just beautiful. That's the power of being treated as an equal. This was months later. It was still affecting this fellow's life and it was affecting me sitting there watching. What I got from it was that *I* could learn what Nelson Mandela was doing. I could learn how to extend, or create, a space truly allowing people to feel equal, truly allowing people to feel completely accepted, okay, and equal in every way and able to come out. It could be silent and invisible. It wasn't one of these things where you talk someone into it. It could be extended as an expression of your energy. It's a vibration. It's a space.

LINDA - What I love about that is the humanness of Nelson Mandela making a peanut butter and jelly sandwich. So many times, with people who are great, other people forget they're human. They do things just like everyone else.

KEITH - What assisted me about that, too, was *I* make peanut butter and jelly sandwiches. Nelson Mandela makes peanut butter and jelly sandwiches. If he could forgive those people who tortured him for twenty-seven years, and now be their president, I can forgive those people who just said a few lousy things to me. It all has to do with equality.

DEBRA - That reminds me: I heard a definition by the Dalai Lama of forgiveness. He said, "Forgiveness is never allowing the injustice to happen again."

KEITH - It's deciding to have the injustice end now, not perpetuating it anymore. What I'm hearing throughout this *Gathering* is that a lot of people are in professions where they deal with clients or patients, but also have friends, mates, and people around them with whom they would like to have more equality or equal exchange going on. When my friend and I realized it was time to gather, we asked spirit, "What should we call this thing?" *The Dream - A Gathering of Equals* came up immediately. My first feeling of the *Gathering of Equals* was it was time for me to open to allowing myself to start to feel equal to the beings I considered higher, wiser, stronger, more evolved, and more courageous. I have had a number of very evolved beings, physical and non-physical, who have begged me to be their friends, their buddies, their equals. I just said, "No way." It was just unthinkable. I could not, then, accept myself as their equal. I now see what might be really fun is to do a *dream out* where we could allow our intuition to take us to a time, place, or part of our soul's experience where we truly know and have touched equality. Open to embracing the vibration of equality, so we not only can allow ourselves to bask in it, we can feel equal to others, and we can go out into the world in that space allowing others to feel equal to us. That same vibration works both ways, for us and for them. I know how to do it. I just need to recapture the feel of it. Ask for the guidance from God, from spirit. It's a lesson, a gift, that my higher self has been trying to give to me for thirty years...equality.

AUDREY - As soon as you talked about that, my energy instantly shifted into my knowing about how it feels when I meet somebody as an equal and they're right there with me and we're in it.

KEITH - I heard a story from Medicine Cloud who is one of my former teachers, now a friend. This was true of a lot of the Native American tribes from the plains and the tribe he was a member of. For many, many years, as an apprentice to becoming a medicine man, Medicine Cloud attended ceremonies, healings, medicine wheels, and sweats. In those, there was one particular person who was the medicine man overseeing all of the various ceremonies and rituals. Then, at a certain point, it was time for Medicine Cloud to apprentice, to learn more directly, one on one, the ways of the medicine man. This medicine man who had held that position for more than thirty years came over and said, "Let me introduce you to your teacher." He took Medicine to this older gentleman who, for thirty years, had sat in the corner and ground the herbs, prepared the sage, attended the fire, and brought in the feathers. He was the behind-the-scenes prop man. Medicine Cloud said, "Well, I don't understand. I wanted to learn from the *medicine* man." He said, "He *is* the medicine man. I am *his* assistant." So, sitting here at this *Gathering*, you might think *I* have the wand, because I am the facilitator—but I'm just the front, the prop boy.

SULANA - I wanted so much to give a gift to the group today. I was rehearsing a poem and I forgot the words, and I realized that wasn't going to be it. Then I started rehearsing a song and couldn't remember that either, so I realized that wasn't going to be it. On the break we had just before the *dream out,* I was walking right out here in the desert and this brilliant shiny light came at me. I moved, and it wasn't there, so I moved back and searched all around and found the light again, and I picked it up, and it was just this plain rock. The sunlight just hit the rock in the right way where it was almost blinding light.

The rock looked so plain, but it had a brilliant light.

JANET - You gave of your heart and that is a gift, a precious gift. Thank you. It healed something in me.

SHAWN - We were speaking before about feeling diminished, so I went back to a time where my ego made me feel *greater* than equal. It was one of the many times I was trapped in an elevator at the World Trade Center. The elevator was stuck, but the intercom was working so the main desk asked the people in the elevator, "What's the name of your company? We'll call your bosses and tell them you're all right." I was a systems analyst for a major bank, so I decided to let the secretaries and messengers go first. One by one, the secretaries and messengers told the guy at the main desk their company and their phone number. Then the desk would say, "They've heard of you. They know who you are. They're waiting for you." I was the last one to go. I told them, "Call my bank and tell them Jones is stuck in the elevator, so postpone the systems test." A minute later, over the intercom, "Hello, Jones. The bank said they have never heard of you." That taught me right.

JANET - For me, it was about owning the power. I saw golden light, a pyramid, and a Pharaoh. As soon as I started acknowledging that light, the joy was incredible. It was like connecting fully to who I am.

RAY - It's nice to see we're all getting exactly what we need.

AUDREY - I know it's impossible to get anything but your needs met.

MARIE - I have experienced a very interesting string of events in this *Gathering.* I keep getting the message to get physical, to be in my body, and to recognize the flow of energy in my body. I was told that I am one with the earth, and well grounded. All I need to do is to just acknowledge I am here in my body. I feel a sense of liberation knowing that. I feel an aliveness in all of my cells. I could trust myself. I can allow myself to be truly free. My intention for the whole *Gathering*, even though I haven't said it in words, is to let *my* light shine, to allow *our* light to shine, to allow fireworks to take place.

MARK - I received a message during this *dream out* and wrote it down. "You are the light in the mountains and the light filtering through the new green leaves of the forest trees. You are the light of a bright summer day, the two children holding hands and smiling at each other. You are the light and essence of light itself. You are the light of love and the love of light. You are the light of those gathered in love, the light of the world and a world of light. It is time to shine, for that's what you came here to do. You are the others, yourself, and everything. You are the light."

KEITH - To me, co-creation is when we allow our lights to shine *together*, when we play and create together with the fire of life, gracefully. Which means to apply it safely, gently, intuitively, with our hearts in charge, with God in charge. We don't have to freak out or shut down anymore. I'm tired of freaking out and shutting down. Is anyone else? Haven't we done it enough?

JANET - That's interesting because as you were speaking I was seeing we *are* co-creating. I really feel that on a very deep level. It's because we are being real, as real as we are allowing ourselves to be in the moment. I feel it. I can feel the energy shifts in here. To me this is not just another personal growth seminar because I can *feel it* on a very deep level. People's *lives* are changing. I may not go out there and feel I'm always centered or I'm always in touch with that feeling, but I *know* I'm changed. I *know* it to the core of my being. I'm very different than when we started on Saturday; very, very different.

MIA - We're creating this huge vortex, and it's awesome. It's opening up, and it continues to open up. It is very real. It's like the clearer we get, the more real it gets.

JANET - What I experienced when I first went into the *dream out* was a veil about sitting next to Keith because this is a visible position. I found myself, this morning, not wanting to be present in my body, just wanting to keep getting out. I've made a real effort to stay fully conscious and fully present and to really feel all of that stuff about being physical because I'm also going to be putting on a workshop, and that's bringing up a lot of veils too. When I went deeper, this incredible light just kept on coming. I remembered when I was the most conscious was always when I was having compassion for someone else. I remember when I worked in a hospital, and I was a physical therapy student. I was going to go see this woman who had a bed sore, a huge oozing bed sore. She was in her nineties, and she couldn't speak English. I had to communicate to her what I was going to do. She was crying. The message I got was to just touch her, just touch her. I went up to her and touched her. She immediately stopped crying, her face started beaming, and she lifted up her gown and showed me she had no breasts and she had a colostomy bag. She wanted me to know everything, but she couldn't speak it in a language I understood. But I connected with her through her eyes and through her heart. I remember getting a message to hold her, so I held her. She just kept patting me and saying, "My bella, my bella." She kept holding my face. Afterwards, she started singing. I was shown that, in my life, when I was really connected was when I was with someone else. It got me out of my own way. I was really connecting with me, because those people *are* me. So what I did was turn it around, and I saw it was about me, too, and to just let that be. It was very powerful. Now I feel a lot more comfortable sitting next to Keith, as an equal.

KEITH - There's a teacher named "Poonjaji." Does anyone know him? He tells a wonderful story that really helped me. He said, "What happens if you're in a dark room? It's really dark and then someone flips the lights on all of a sudden. How does it feel?" Disorienting, scary, painful. He said you don't even have to imagine it because it's what's happening *right now.* You've been in the darkness for eons, billions of years, and then the light switch comes on. How's it going to feel? He suggests you be gentle with yourself and realize *you have to get used to* the *light of truth,* your *own light,* your own clarity, *love, grace, divinity.* Be gentle with each other, too. Go easy.

I've seen people come from that place. The *Gathering* we had in the Nevada desert, was heart warming. I was really taken by how gentle and considerate people were, the loving way they did remind each other of their true selves. The humor in it was wonderful. People received the wake up calls as love. And people were receiving it as love for four days! It blew my mind. It was wonderful.

Someone in the Seattle *Gathering* shared about the first handicapped Olympics in Seattle. There was a one-hundred-yard race with ten contestants who were all physically handicapped. They had all trained for this for years. It was a big event, with people coming from all over the world, thousands of them filled the stadium. As the race started, the runners were accelerating when a young handicapped boy stumbled and fell, getting way behind. The other nine runners stopped. They all went back and picked him up, and they all went over the finish line together. The crowd stood up and gave them a five-minute standing ovation. Every time I think of that I realize *that's how we are evolving.* One day our hearts are just going to prevail over all the veils, and we'll just go with our hearts. It's already starting.

The following are the lyrics of the song, by Kevin Benedict, I mentioned at the beginning of this chapter. It is about connecting with and being gently reminded of the divinity within us all. Only as we begin to recognize the "power beyond measure" within each of us, do we begin to truly love ourselves. And it is only by loving ourselves and allowing *our* light to shine that we can express love for others and treat them as equals. If enough people do that, as Marianne Williamson, Nelson Mandela, Kevin Benedict, and the special Olympians have done, there will be millions of individual lights ignited around the world. The brilliance of that light will overshadow the need for words such as equality.

If You Were God

**If you were God, what would you do?
If you were omni-everything and nothing could surprise you
If you knew all the answers and asked the questions too
If you were God, what would you do?**

**If you could fly, If no star was out of reach
If no student could fail to learn the wisdom that you could teach
If you always could have sunshine and bikinis on the beach
If you could fly, well then, how high?**

**What if it said, "Made by me" on the back of all your toys?
And all your friends could all come out and play?
What if you had all the girls you want, or all the boys?
Do you think you'd get tired of it some day?**

If you were God, what would you do?
If you were all that ever is or was would you break yourself in two?
And then forget so you could say, sincerely, "Who are you?"
"Well, hi, I'm God. How do you do?"

You'd get to know each other for a lifetime, maybe more
And look at things from different points of view,
You'd set aside the future so you won't know what's in store
But keep the memory deep inside of you.

If you were God, what would you do?
Would you want to be surprised by something challenging and new?
If you could choose anything, would you choose to be you?
If I were God, that's what I'd do.

I'd spice up all my happiness with a little dash of pain
And make up lots of pretty things to see
Then I'd create endings...so we all could start again
Then I'd probably pop on down as me.

If we were God, what would we do?
Would we play at being separate so the wind could whistle through?
And would some of us get so caught up that we'd forget what's true?
If I were God, here's what I'd do.

I'd want to have some mystery, adventure, and surprise
Which I couldn't do if I knew everything
I'd want to see divinity through different colored eyes
And, of course, I'd want some silly songs to sing.

If you were God, what would you do?
Would you want to have eternity to change and grow and bloom?
And do you think eternity would be quite enough room
To do the things that God could do?
If you were God, if God were you.

We are the wise children

Children of Earth and Sky

Air and Water, Fire and Mountain

Come with us and we will play

Among the grassy banks of the river

On Mountain peaks,

And with the Shadows of the

Flickering Fire

Georgina Murata

Chapter Seven

REEDS IN THE STREAM

Freedom, A Sense of Play,* and *Open Portal

EVERYTHING YOU NEED TO KNOW ABOUT LIFE, YOU can learn from clouds and streams." This was a message from Medicine Cloud to Keith over twenty years ago. It was wonderful being back at the Domes in the foothills of Mount Rose. The grandeur and beauty of the Sierra Nevada mountain range, on the California-Nevada border provided easy access to the energy of nature. The adjacent stream played a key role in experiencing my second *Gathering* there. The Native Spirits were active. They came forth again to give us wonderful visions, memories, and inspiration.

These spirits opened "cracks in the world" to provide an entry way into another dimension, a dimension of pure joy at just being. What arose, almost immediately, was a degree of spontaneity, freedom, and playfulness which I had never experienced before.

I experienced a number of miracles there and made soul connections with people I'll be friends with forever, even if we never see each other again. I played a lot as did everyone who attended. We each played in our own way and yet it complemented the play of the others. I chose to spend a lot of time around the stream and in the hills where I witnessed for myself the magic which is available from clouds and streams. I learned, on a deep level, to appreciate magic in what I had formerly considered the ordinary.

Recently, I heard that the way you can tell the difference between truly spiritual beings and others is by how serious they are. Those who struggle in seriousness have not gotten the message yet. Those who are light-hearted and easy-going have found the other world. The laughter and spontaneous play in this *Gathering* transported us all to another level of existence. Keith began by talking about a group of people who reached a different level of existence in a very unique way:

KEITH - I'd like to share something about "L's" since there are so many people here whose name begins with "L," including *three* Lindas. One of the biggest rushes in my life was reading about the origin of the word "elder." The name came from the "L" race. They were a group of people who lived on this planet and went free, ascended. They discovered how to go free by making a perfect right angle shift. They were called the "L" race because they made a ninety-degree "L" shift out of three-dimensional reality. They became very wise when they became free of their human emotional conditioning. People looked to them for counseling and knowing. Thus, the term "L-race" became "elder," eventually, meaning someone who has wisdom.

Another gateway to freedom I discovered myself, in the reeds of a canyon stream. Have you ever seen reeds in a stream, bull rushes, cattails, any kind of reeds that are long and thin? A friend and I went into some reeds in a canyon, and just sat there for awhile and asked them, "What is this magical, special space all about?" We both got the same message. They said, "We're a gateway." Animals know that. Animals go there to heal. Reeds are a gateway because they shear the light; they refract it in a way which creates an opening; a crack in the world. Reeds offer a portal through which you can shift vibrational frequency, and enter other dimensions to explore, expand, heal, or just enjoy!

LYNETTE - Hearing about entering other worlds reminds me of a metaphor I once read about a butterfly. It was the most profound thing I have ever read. There was a pod of cocoons that were all together, talking about being in that cocoon in the dark. They were saying, "Let me know what it's like when you go out, when you break through the cocoon and change." The first one of them goes through the process of stretching out and breaking free and finally becomes a butterfly. Once a butterfly, this butterfly says to herself, "There's *no way* I can go back and describe what I'm feeling now to the caterpillars still in the cocoon. There is no way I could possibly share this wonder with them. It's one's own experience." It was profound for me.

SUE - So is that why you don't give us answers, Keith?

KEITH - I defer to the new butterfly.

LINDA L. - Here's another story about butterflies. I saw this on one of the nature shows. When the caterpillar is in the cocoon, it breaks the threads one at a time. It takes forever in caterpillar time to get out of this cocoon. It is during the process of leaving the cocoon when much of the metamorphosis takes place. It's growing wings and forming the new body *as* it leaves. Scientists decided to try and help the caterpillar get out of the cocoon by poking a little pin hole in it. Every cocoon they tampered with produced a deformed butterfly.

KEITH - A big realization I had a couple of days ago was that I looked at all the ways I've tried to become safe, happy, free, and loved. All of these approaches were at the suggestion of society, my cultural programming. I saw, very clearly, that none of these strategies have ever really worked. Maintaining my earlier approach to life took tremendous energy, effort, manipulation, and control. Then I saw the whole struggle hasn't paid off for me. I just decided, "I'm done with it." If these control strategies produced some solid results, some real happiness, or some of what they were supposed to produce, that would be one thing. But the truth is, in my life, it hasn't happened.

This realization has really accelerated my willingness and excitement to surrender, and to quit protecting myself and having walls. I started pulling back my energy from the beliefs and behaviors I thought would make me safe and fulfilled, but have not. I'm no longer empowering and energizing things which I *know* don't work.

That's why I can be so relaxed now. I don't *want* to do anything I *know* won't work. My friend Lester really helped me. He said, "You know all those techniques, those spiritual practices, especially the ancient ones? Go to the leaders of those disciplines and ask them, 'How many of your students have gone free?' *They'll* tell you: 'Zero.' The people who teach it will admit it. So why would you want to do something that hasn't worked for thousands of years, for *anybody*? Why would you want to do that?" I never forgot that. It was a great gift and now I'm applying it to my life.

So quietly, at a pace that feels compassionate, graceful, and gentle to myself, I'm withdrawing my energy from the *cult*, the cult of Western *cult*ure, the cult of tribal collective consciousness, and the cult of spiritual discipline, technique, and tradition. I feel strong enough, clear enough, and courageous enough to do it now. As I speak, I'm doing it right now. It's exciting.

SUE - About a week ago, I found a place in me that felt free for the first time. I'm letting that expand. That hasn't happened before.

KEITH - This is one of the reasons I had a funeral and a wake for the form and the *techniques* of the *Gathering.*

SAM - He's going to reveal that there's the "inner circle" of the *Gathering*. You'll get a special membership card entitling you to freedom in joining the inner circle. **(Laughter from the group)**

KEITH - There are a lot of people who are having a lot of fun and a totally fresh start to their life. It's really fun. Everything has changed in their lives and in their hearts.

LINDA L. - I have a sense that the people who show up for the *Gathering* are *already* free. They have already come to the point where they *know* what freedom is and actually want *more*. When I first came to the *Gathering*, I had already been on a path of freedom. I see that when I come to *Gatherings,* I go through my little judgment program the first day. I think I have everybody figured out. And then slowly, as the *Gathering* goes on, someone will surprise me, and I'll open up and allow myself to feel and share. As I begin show up, the freedom starts to grow, and I start to realize we can have what we want to have in our life.

HELAINE - Keith, what did you mean about having a funeral and a wake for the old *Gathering* and yet you're still passing out the same brochures?

KEITH - Helaine is being a literalist again. Actually, Helaine, all of your questions are really good questions.

HELAINE - I know I can go to my knowing to get an answer. But *my* knowing could be different than what *your* knowing is.

KEITH - Well, I'd be really interested in hearing what your knowing has to say about this. To me, it all makes sense.

HELAINE - My knowing sense is that there is a loose structure that still exists, but underneath that there is a greater freedom to adapt and to create what was not, perhaps, imagined before.

KEITH - You express yourself so well. That's my experience, my knowing. Rather than "structure" though, I would say there's an underlying flow, an undercurrent. It's the current that flows through streams and clouds and birds and bees, everything. That current, if you allow it to flow, will tell you where to go and everything you need to know.

HELAINE - I know you feel it this minute, this second.

KEITH - I'm *in* it. Feel it? Where does all water flow eventually? To the ocean. Would you like to go discover where you're actually *already free,* but you haven't realized it yet? In India they tell great stories about monkeys and parrots that don't leave when their owners open the door of their cages. I know it's the same with us. I know the door is open to all of these areas I haven't yet explored, and I have been sitting there in my own self-imposed confines.

LINDA K. - The same thing happened with some of the slaves in the South. They were suddenly free to go, but they didn't know what to do or where to go when they were set free.

HELAINE - Not going free when you can applies to the way they train elephants with chains. They use really big chains when they're younger, then later they put on very light chains, because the elephants don't even try to leave. They could easily snap the chain.

SAM - I heard about a rhinoceros that was raised in a very small pen. In later years, they gave him a bigger pen and moved him into it. The rhinoceros continued to make a little tiny circle track within the large pen.

KEITH - On the other side, I got a big kick out of East Europeans. As soon as the East Europeans saw that the Germans were free, and watched these Germans walk through the Berlin Wall of the Iron Curtain, they just started walking right past their own soldiers, right through the wall, right in front of them. In Hungary, Czechoslovakia, Poland, and Romania, they just walked. The soldiers didn't do a thing. I was watching the fall of the Berlin Wall on television. The day I was watching was the day they gave East Germans a twenty-four-hour pass to cross through the border to West Berlin for a day. In East Germany, a Western reporter was interviewing people as they came back. He asked them, while tapping his fist on the actual wall itself, "When do you believe the actual Berlin Wall will come down? One East German said, "It's gone!" The reporter then said, condescendingly, "No, you don't understand. When will the actual *physical* wall be torn down? When will this concrete barrier be gone?" The East German, sweetly said, "No, *you* don't understand. It is *already* gone!" It was very moving. That's where *we* are right now. The Iron Curtain has dropped. The wall is gone. Let's let our souls show us the next step.

Keith lead a quiet *dream out* on freedom then people shared what their soul had to say:

DREAM OUT: FREEDOM

MARK - In this *dream out*, I went to a lot of places where I felt stuck, and, in every area, the absence of freedom was an illusion. Wherever I *thought* I didn't have freedom, I actually *did*, in every single area. In the one place that felt stuck, I took *conscious* control so I can go forward and change it. It was fun seeing how much freedom there really is; everywhere.

KEITH - I've discovered phantom jails, phantom prisons, and phantom walls. They are still there, but now I know they are phantoms. They have no power of their own, only the power I have given them.

HELAINE - I found an area of freedom that I'm working on. I'm not being radically honest in every moment. I was concerned I'd lose some of my freedom in a relationship if I was more honestly and fully myself. I decided that I am strong enough now that I can be more real, open, and spontaneously me with others. I want the freedom to be me, to be just a natural omnipresent condition in my universe.

SAM - I went back to some of the decisions I've made. Twenty years ago I was on a spiritual path. One night, I was walking through sage brush and the whole landscape lit up. I was walking with light, from the source. Momentarily, the sun was shining through a gap in the mountains, illuminating; then it was gone. I saw a caravan completing a long journey. It feels now like the old journey is pretty well over, and it's time to start living. Hurray!

LINDA L. - I was feeling a lack of freedom. I proceeded to do an unveiling, but it wasn't working, so I thought, "I wonder what would happen if I just let love in? What if I put my attention on what it would feel like to just let love in?" Then everything shifted, and I started feeling this energy. When I let go, I went on this adventure, like the Celestine Prophecy revisited. Mark and Keith were there, and we had this mission. We had this really exciting thing to do and, we were in this place where there was all this *light*. It was really bright. It wasn't anything specific, but it was like we knew we had our mission to accomplish, and we each had our things to do and we were synchronizing. "Let me do this and you go do that. Then we'll get back together again and see what happens." It was really cool, and then I let go and went off on another adventure. I'm just getting a fleeting glimpse that there's something very big going on here.

AUDREY - I experienced a thousand butterflies taking to the skies. To me, that means the lifting of a veil.

HELAINE - I just got the feeling that this dome is our cocoon.

LINDA L - And we're asking each other, "Come back and tell me what it's like." There will be an explosive sound from fluttering wings.

MARK - Has anyone seen the book in which all the caterpillars form this huge, living pile? They are crawling all over each other trying to get to the top. It's such an effort to get to the top of this pile of struggling caterpillars. One of them decides, "It's really not for me" and, of course, becomes a butterfly and flies away.

LINDA L. - I saw a mime do a really cool thing one time. He was feeling the boundaries of the box he was in, and then he *finally* gets out of this box and starts to stretch and finds another box.

When you have true freedom, it becomes natural to play. I have noticed a very high correlation between the amount of laughter in a *Gathering* and the amount of truth people are willing to share. Laughter and play are portals to the soul. This *Gathering* was full of spontaneity and play. Naturally, it emerged as a topic to explore experientially.

A SENSE OF PLAY

KEITH - One thing that has really helped me is to be a lot more playful about all of these spiritual and other formerly serious issues. It really allows more answers to come. I don't mean that facetiously, and it's not positive thinking. It is literally allowing your vibration to get lighter so your body and spirit can move.

CHRIS - I can't quote it directly, but Ramana says something like,

"There will come a time when you will awaken from the stream of misidentification and you will *laugh.* That time is now. That place is here." As the awakening takes place, it all becomes clear. It is not an intellectual understanding, but a direct experience of one's true nature. From that perspective, it's kind of a joke. We have limited ourselves in so many ways and *forgotten.*

SUE - I've begun to play. I've done it a couple of times recently. Once, a friend and I went camping and played. It was so much fun. I hadn't played like that for probably thirty years. It was wonderful. And the other day, I began playing with someone. We didn't need anything, just our imaginations, and we'd go out and see wondrous things. "Look at that rock. It's a dragon." We'd climb and ride the dragon. There we were, two grown women riding this rock as though it were a dragon. "Yeah!" It's great when I can open that and let it out.

KEITH - It might be fun to do a *dream out* and allow ourselves to go to a time when we knew how to play. The vibration is different than *trying* to play or trying to be light. Let's go to that sprite energy called play.

HELAINE - It's really connecting with your aliveness, just another way to get there.

LAURICE - This is so odd, we're re-learning to play. When did I really forget?

KEITH - A door will open when you consciously experience when you forgot how to play.

LINDA L. - Shall we *play*? I just had a realization that "play" is exploring.

HELAINE - Not knowing what treasures you'll uncover.

KEITH - Okay, let's see what happens when we go back to a sense of play, to the vibration of true playfulness. I remember when I was a child, we would make snow angels all the way up the side of the mountain. As the sun changed, it would bring the angels out in all their brilliance. After hanging out with our snow angels for awhile, I'd be in the company of twenty or thirty real angels who would float overhead and sing softly to me.

Keith guided the group through a *dream out* on playfulness as a portal to inner knowingness.

DREAM OUT: PLAY

SUE - A quality I re-experienced was "spunkiness." It feels very much like sovereignty. I was spunky and creative. I knew how to take a plank and make it a horse and ride around on it. I felt the power of that, and I knew my world. I knew how to do that. It felt so wonderful.

KEITH - I was always aware that there was "our" kid's world, and there was "their" world, the adult world. We knew exactly where our world was and how much territory it covered. We had our own secrets. They were really two distinctly different worlds.

MARK - Most of my *dream out* was about very recent activities with my kids, like going to a grocery store and riding on a shopping cart. Actually, I do that with the kids or without them. It's fun. I get a tremendous joy from playing with my children. Right *now* is the childhood of my life and *this* is where the magic is.

HELAINE - I know I played. Growing up, I played by Lincoln Park in Chicago every day after school. It stretches seven miles along the lake. That was my playground. I would usually play with the boys. We would roller skate, ride bikes, and make forts. As I got older, we would climb the roofs of buildings together and play with pen knives. I had a great childhood that way; riding bikes down mountains, and sledding in the snow. I had a great time. I realized, too, I decided I would have to be in a relationship with someone who had the same attitude toward play. I also see the reason why I'd like grandchildren is to have some playmates, so I can experience what Mark is experiencing with his children. When my kids were young, I used to race them through the supermarket aisles with the shopping cart. I've always had fun with my kids. They're older now, but we really do have fun. I remember about five years ago, when my daughter was in her twenties, she and I were skipping down the streets in San Francisco, swinging our arms and looking like I don't know what. But we didn't care. We were having a really good time.

Then I recalled my grandfather who was a playful person. He'd help me on with my jacket, only he'd hold the end of the sleeve closed so I would never quite be able to get it on. Then he'd play a little joke, "Oh, you've got a spot over here" and when I looked down, he'd tap me on the face and make funny noises. He was a fun guy, and he lived to be eighty-five. He was a good role model for me. Then I thought about why it is I like play. It's because playing is free, creative, and you can be absorbed in it.

LINDA L. - I have a new motorcycle waiting for me when I get home. My experience about playing is I *never* stopped playing, even in my pain and misery. When I became an adult, it was in the late sixties. I started smoking pot and playing again, so I had a second round of creating whatever world I wanted and playing in that reality.

LAURICE - I was about nineteen years old when I started learning to *not* play. What a gift it is for you to be able to play as an adult and transcend the "adult world" where we're supposed to be responsible and serious.

LINDA L. - I knew when I was nineteen years old that I was on a spiritual quest. My friends started doing heroine, cocaine, and speed. I never had *any* interest in those drugs. I wanted the true experience.

KEITH - I have a friend, Rob, who is twenty years old. I have a two-for-one coupon book, so we often go to fancy, five-star restaurants. Once, while we were waiting for a meal, he started playing with his food, taking the glass, plate, and spoons and building pyramids. Then when we got the food, he built a pyramid out of the food. He was totally oblivious to where he was, and it was just wonderful to watch. Half the people enjoyed his creative playfulness, but the other half were appalled. The restaurant staff loved it.

HELAINE - Being totally playful is something good, it's being super present in yourself and not anything outside of you.

The *dream out* on *play* created an opening of awareness for the gatherers. There was a sense of a gateway to another reality right in the dome where we were gathered. Though I couldn't

actually see it with my eyes, I had a strong feeling that there was a three-dimensional physical opening or portal to another world. Keith began talking about such portals:

OPEN PORTAL

KEITH - I took a shamanic journey at lunch. Isn't *every* walk a shamanic journey, really? Isn't every time you *play* a shamanic journey? Several people have asked me what the gift is that the Native Spirits have for us. On my walk, I was asking spirit for guidance, and who really helped me were the Nature Spirits living in what I call this "valley of energy," the corridor of energy flow down from the mountains, through this canyon, and out to the open desert. What they told me was that assistance could only come from beings who have gone through the same transition that I am going through in life and have made it to the other side. When they were transitioning, they felt the same fears of not making it that I feel now. The Native Spirits said, "We've been through all this. We can tell you with authenticity because we are not like someone who is there lecturing or stating in a book that there's heaven or there's enlightenment. We're not talking about an idea, a concept, or a wish. We're *here*, home, heaven. The only source who is going to feel safe or real for you to listen to is someone who has personally experienced what they are speaking about. We're offering our assistance because we've been through it and we know, from our own experience. The 'other side' everybody speaks of exists. We're here! Ask *us* instead of going to books, ideas, and people for whom it's still a theory, a hope, wish, speculation, or belief. We'll help you. That's the gift of this place."

Now I know that's why we're having the *Gathering* here on this ancient sacred site. There's an actual hand or bridge being extended. The Native Spirits here have very recently gone through the passage we're going through right now. The gift they are extending is a bridge to the other side. They are offering their help in whatever way we are willing to receive it. They are providing a bridge to help us across the creek. We have one foot on one side of the creek, and one foot on the other, and we're afraid to take the last foot off the old bank. It's impossible to know what the new world is like when your other foot is still on the old shore.

MARK - I remember what I was getting was the gift; *We* are the Native Spirits. There's assistance in these others, reaching out to help us, but the reason they're reaching out to help us is because we're crossing the creek. We're between worlds right now. They're helping us to help ourselves.

KEITH - As scary as it might be, as uncomfortable as it might be to acknowledge, we are *in* the stream. That's *why* it feels uncomfortable. We are in midstream. Where we're going is not created yet. The forms are not here; the expression is not available yet. The vehicles are not here yet, because we're creating them. The forms will coalesce as we need them, as we allow them and invoke them. The Native Spirits are assisting us to do that. Right now the vortex, the gateway, is open for the vibration and form of this new expression to come through.

MARK - I went to the creek. I put my foot over to the other side.

KEITH - How did it feel when you did that?

MARK - It felt good. It was my "play."

KEITH - How did it feel when you touched the other side? In your body, in your being, could you feel it come up through your legs? Do you feel it right now?

MARK - Yes. It is a feeling of vitality.

KEITH - See what's happening to his aura, his energy field right now? Can you feel it? When you acknowledge, and speak your truth about what you're experiencing, it gives it reality. "In the beginning was the word and the word was made flesh." When you speak your word, it becomes real. Then you can inhabit it and live there. There is a gateway that's opened, a crack in the world for each of you. Do you want to see what happens when you speak into it?

LAURICE - I just remembered that in the *dream out* we did on "play" I became a bird, and I was swooping around and following this other bird and that was a lot of fun.

KEITH - So how did that feel, flying?

LAURICE - Oh, I love flying.

KEITH - So there's your entrance.

LAURICE - So, in a sense, this is like everything else. Go to what has passion, and there's truth for you.

ALLEN - My whole time here has been about letting things in and letting things out, so I can touch and be touched. I want to rediscover life and passion. That part of play is what's happening for me. The other thing that came to me in the last two hours, was the significance the drumming has for me. Sound, musical vibration, transports me. I know it's a door for me.

LINDA T. - Mine was the intense laughter from the depth of my being. There was nothing else, it was all me; present and having a really great time.

KEITH - That's great. So laughter was your bridge. When I take a walk, go into someone's home, or go into a supermarket, I look for my entry point, for the portal, the opening for magic. It can be someone's face. It can be anything. Our playfulness in these last two hours has caused a fluidness here. Where there is movement, where there is passion, there is an opening for you.

HELAINE - It's not what visually attracts you, it's where your heart or intuition leads you, right?

KEITH - It can be visual; it can be experiential; it can be sound. It can show up in any of those ways. So what happened that was new or fresh or really caught your attention the last few hours? What was charged, exciting, riveting, electric? Whatever has juice and aliveness for you will build a permanent bridge to your fuller self.

A twenty minute *dream out* followed, then individuals begin to share their experiences.

DREAM OUT: OPEN PORTAL

LINDA L. - The crack in the world that I experienced had to do with all of you. I feel connected wit everything. I feel connected with all of you in a way I've never felt it in a *Gathering* or anything. I feel okay with myself now and something has shifted for me that has to do with being in my body. I came back into my body. I feel really comfortable. I feel okay with everything that's going on, everybody here, and all the issues. Whatever you want to do is okay with me. Whatever I want to do is okay with me. That's not a feeling I've experienced a whole lot in my life. It feels really good to me.

LINDA T. - What came through to me was being fully present and connected. That is my bridge.

LINDA L. - Just to pick up from that, for just a second, what I saw is that you *are* totally present. And that's my connection to you. That's what provides the bridge, the connection.

SUE - I felt really disconnected from the group and went outside. When I was outside, I made a decision I could be safe in here, so I came back in. I just said, "I want to be safe in there." I walked in and I *was*. All I need to do is choose it, decide it. It's very easy.

MARK - I started to cross the stream over here again, in my consciousness, and I stepped to the other side. As I did, a strong hand grabbed my wrist and pulled me up. I felt completely light, lighter than air. I was brought into a circle of native beings. They weren't applauding, but I felt the energy of applause. "Welcome back, wise one" is the essence of what they were saying. There was a lot of discussion. They wanted to know all about what I'd been experiencing because, though they were the guides, they wanted to hear about how I *felt* things. So we had a long discussion. Then I took off.

I left them and was instantly in Costa Rica. There was a huge ravine. I was a hawk, squawking and flying straight down for the rapids in the raging river far below. I took a sharp turn and, still soaring, followed the river through the jungle, and came out at the ocean. On the beach was the same group again. I came back to them, and they were applauding because I had come back so soon. It was as though we had re-established a bond. It had been thousands of years since I had come back last time, and this time it was just a few seconds. I came back to them as a hawk and more of the same kind of things happened. What they were telling me was they need us, too. They need us to live. It's a mutually beneficial relationship. They want to be our guides; they *live* to be our guides, and we're not allowing them to be.

Then, I became a jaguar, running up the volcano. I jumped into the volcano. The next sensation I had was that I had become the rain. There was the same group of beings again, and I was falling as rain on them. They were rejoicing, "He's back again!" The connection had been re-established. They are more available now, and they want us to use them. Our guides will be there to help us, but we're there to help them, too. It was all visually graphic. I was *seeing* this. It was beautiful.

LINDA - Do you have a sense for what it is we are here to help them do?

MARK - I got a strong sense of the oneness and unity of everything. Use the resources that are here. That makes them live, and it make *us* live.

LINDA L.- I saw this old, ancient, native man who was in this space we're in now, but the dome, the group, and everything was superimposed into another space. I saw it in its original state. The old native was walking in a circle and rattling and chanting as he was walking. I asked him what he was doing and he said, "I'm holding this space; I'm holding the door open. I'm holding the vibration of this space." He said, "You're not the first ones." Then his arm came up and it was like a window pointing up. I looked up in that direction and there were all these people, thousands of people, walking up the mountain. It was a river of beings ascending to the summit. I said, "Wow, where are they going?" He said, "They don't know where they're going, they're making it up as they go." Then I started chanting his chant.

MARK - I left out a part because it didn't seem like it mattered, but when the native circle opened the first time, there was also superimposed a, *different* group from another place and period of history, occupying the same space and time. They were Druids from ancient England. They were simultaneously present giving me the sense there was a lot more going on than what I was seeing. It was something much deeper, and timeless.

LINDA L. - I've been thinking all day about the idea we are so afraid to take the next step. We're afraid if take the next step, there will be nobody living there. But, when we finally do, we'll find there's a whole civilization living there, waiting for us.

KEITH - I was watching the river in Reno this morning. Medicine Cloud, who's very much here, told me over twenty years ago, "Don't let it get complicated. You can learn everything you need to know about life from clouds and streams; everything. All life moves and flows in the same way." I was watching the river, and I saw it like I'd never seen it before. I watched how it flows over, under, around, and through all obstacles on its way back home to the ocean. Rain drops on these mountains. Where does it end up, no matter what, eventually? In the ocean and then back to the sky. There is no way a rain drop is not going to end up in the ocean. It might hit a tree, stagnate, freeze, go around things, under things; even dams can't stop it. Eventually, water goes under the dam, over the dam, or evaporates and drops as rain on the other side. Water gets around everything. Our spirit is like water. It inevitably finds it's way back to the ocean of oneness.

Don't worry about saving these songs!

And if one of our instruments breaks,

It doesn't matter.

We have fallen into the place

where everything is music.

Rumi

Chapter Eight

DESERT SONG

Lust Lock, Being Present, and Who am I?

WHEN THE BIRDS BURST INTO SONG IN THE HIGH desert in May, north of Phoenix, Arizona, they did so with all of their being. Not one of them seemed at all concerned about what the others might think or that the intense sun had caused the mercury to surpass the hundred-degree mark. They just sang. They sang because that's what they do. The joyous chorus of birds provided a sonorous accompaniment to our workshop throughout all four days of this *Gathering.*

The birds were a constant reminder to me that there is an easier way of being. Though I'd noticed their presence while in Phoenix during the month of February, the birds in May seemed more numerous and active. Flocks of them fluttered from bush to bush with a loud, happy, scattered melody. Hundreds of individuals were singing a variety of songs.

I ate my lunches in the protection of the shade of the saguaro cacti while the quail scurried by, the owls slept in their cactus burrows, and the doves cooed to their mates. I was inspired by their lack of struggle and their natural ability to just *be*.

KEITH - All that is needed to bring about the full expression of your unique spirit is to sing *your* song, sing what's in your heart. It doesn't matter what form it takes. It doesn't matter if it's that you sew really well or if you can fix cars. If we combine the energy of *everyone* doing their thing, being in their vibration, singing their song, that synergy is going to bring about the transformation of the planet. The divine plan unfolds by each of us sharing our own *unique* energy and spirit. Alchemy occurs when each of us expresses what makes our heart sing. It's not a vocation, occupation, or identity, but the things we *love* to do. By speaking it, dancing it, singing it; the unfolding of our essence will bring about harmonious changes on the planet. Let the life force flow.

The birds in the desert do not struggle to sing. Neither do we need to struggle to fulfill our life's purpose and to live as carefree as the birds. We already have everything we need in order to sing our song. Struggles and problems arise when we can't see what we already have. That is what is referred to in the *Gatherings* as a "lust lock."

LUST LOCK

KEITH - What does "lust lock" mean to you? Someone tell us what "lust" is.

GROUP - A wanting…fervent…being totally attached to something. Wanting but never getting.

KEITH - It's wanting and never allowing yourself to have. That's why it's a lock. That's why it stops people, like people who lust after money, power, prestige, fame. Do they ever get enough? Have you ever known people who lust after food? Do they ever get enough? It doesn't matter if they have chocolate cake or chocolate *everything* for four days. There are people who have sex four or five times a day, but they still want more. There are people who have eight or ten locks on their door for security, an alarm, watch dog, and a gun. Do they ever feel safe enough?

SHAWN - That's a lock lock. **(Laughter)**

KEITH - So what is really going on there?

LINDA M. - A wanting but *never* really getting. A searching but *never* really finding.

KEITH - Can you remember a time in your life when you were in lust for something for awhile? Feel what it felt like. What happened when you got more of whatever it was you were lusting for? Were you satisfied? The reason they call it a "lock" is because, by its very nature, people stay in the desire and the want. They never really allow themselves to have it fulfilled. People who lust after power never let themselves *feel* powerful; they never feel the vibration of the power. So they keep lusting after it, wanting more and more. They never allow themselves to embrace their true powerful nature and *live* in the vibration.

When a person is in a lust lock, there's no way of ever being filled because they're not letting it in. They're not actually experiencing it. Some people lust after money. Do they ever have enough money? Are they ever satisfied if they never allow themselves to experience being fulfilled? They don't let it in. A while back, I went to a class to learn to do Reiki healing treatments. When I did Reiki with someone for the first time, Medicine Cloud showed up in spirit form in my treatment room. He's a Hopi Medicine man who lives in Arizona. The first thing he said to me was "Keith, you and your friends have gotten really good at *letting go,* but you're lousy at *letting in.*"

He said, "You've learned how to release, to let go, to move on, but you haven't learned to let in power, love, and fulfillment. If you continue letting go without learning to let it, you'll end up in tremendous fear; you will feel only a void, nothingness, the abyss. You might even make a religion out of the void like some people have. How many people have been in the syndrome where you keep letting go of things, and keep getting more terrified?" As he explained, you end up in deep emptiness when you don't learn to let in the richness of life, spirit, essence. When you truly let go, and you're letting in, you'll be filled immediately with the abundance of life.

There's really no such thing as letting go into the void. It's not true reality. The only true letting go is into the richness, the fullness of life. If you haven't opened your heart, opened your being, to receiving, if you're not feeling worthy...need I list the reasons we don't do it? If you haven't allowed this receiving, then spiritual growth becomes totally terrifying. You are letting go of your identity, your images of yourself, old securities, and you're not letting in anything new to take its place. Medicine Cloud said, "Your only job, Keith, for the rest of your lifetime, is to 'let in.'" And, as many of you know, I'm still learning how to "let in."

For me, that's part of why I value the *Gatherings*. It is my intent to feel safe enough to open and to learn from others, and to receive. I'm learning in the *Gatherings* to let in support, resources, wisdom, fun, admiration, and appreciation.

SHAWN - In electronics, that's called a duplex channel. It allows flow in both directions at the same time.

KEITH - Also, in chemistry, there is a permeable membrane that allows things to flow both ways.

LINDA M. - Oh man, I'm getting scared. There's going to be a test. I can tell. **(Laughter)**

KEITH - Just "let it in." In India, what the sages do is assist people to open their chakras, their energy centers, so they learn to receive. It's not enough to just have it available. It needs to be received, embraced. I love the phrase, "We're like fish in the ocean, begging for water." A place I noticed this phenomenon it is with comedians. When they're interviewed, a lot of the old classic comedians, now in their eighties and nineties, admit they're still craving more applause. They say, "I just don't feel appreciated; I don't feel love. This is the one way I can feel appreciation and love, to go out there and make someone laugh." I was thinking, "My God, these guys have been successful for sixty or seventy years and everyone loves them." But they're not feeling it. They haven't let it in.

So, if you will, open to an area in your life where you haven't let yourself receive. Open to where you are already surrounded by love and appreciation, but and not recognizing that it's there. I was reading a book about radical honesty and in it the author suggests a lot of different ways you can speak your truth to people in your life. I kept saying to myself, "I can't say that." Earlier in my life, I couldn't speak really honestly because I couldn't handle the anger, emotions, movement, or the connection that would occur if I opened things up with the truth. I couldn't deal with any of those repercussions in the past. I really surprised myself because then I went to the present moment and realized, "Wait, I *can* handle that now." I discovered all of these outdated veils that weren't appropriate or valid anymore. I then recognized that I've now become strong enough to handle anything that comes up if I speak the truth, whether it is anger, sadness, fear, harmony, intimacy, or love. I have been really out of touch. I am not current with how strong I've become in terms of allowing radical aliveness in my life.

That was a lust lock because I was wanting strength, wanting to be strong enough to tell the truth. I'd had that strength and ability for years and didn't even know it. It's the same for me and others with love, universal supply, peace, and joy. So the approach is to allow your intuition to show you where you already have the qualities or desires you seek. This could be wisdom, compassion, innocence, playfulness, or psychic ability. These are qualities we may have but are still seeking because we *think* we don't have them. We haven't allowed ourselves to see it, feel it, let it in, and be filled by it. There is a veil filter over acknowledging and owning your present status.

How about enlightenment? I have a friend who has been to India over twenty times. Every time he goes, he visits four or five gurus; a lot of them truly authentic, enlightened beings. But why does he keep going back? He's never let himself receive the space, the vibration, the experience he has right there all around him. Some of the most fun teachers I know, like Poonjaji, speak about this. "You're already free! You just haven't let yourself realize it. There's really nothing left to do but be." What they're trying to do is talk us through our lust lock, our lusting for freedom, for love, for our divinity. Every book is doing the same thing. They're trying to *talk* people through it. In the *Gatherings*, we have learned a different way. We ask our spirits, our *souls,* to show us the way through that veil. Let it show you where you already have the freedom, the joy, the power, and the enlightenment you seek. It knows the way to sneak by the lust lock; those old defenses that aren't needed anymore. Would you like to see what you already know, what you already are, what you already have?

DREAM OUT: LUST LOCK

If you want to, allow your attention to go to something you're still seeking and desiring. It's best if you're really honest with yourself. In what experience do you not feel completely fulfilled? What don't you feel you have enough of? What is it you're still looking for? What do you desire, crave? Is it love, joy, peace, certainty, security, safety, power, creativity, enlightenment? Allow yourself to honestly look at what you really want or need to feel fulfilled and happy. When you start to get a sense of those things you still feel you're lacking, could you allow your soul to speak to you, to show you, in whatever way it can, the actual treasure house of abundance you *already* have? Allow your soul, in whatever way it can, to show you the truth. Allow your spirit to open you to a time or place, to a vibration, or to an experience. Open your beingness to the abundance you *already* possess. Allow it to unfold, in your own way, in your own time. Allow your soul to find a way to assist you to receive. What qualities are all around you and are not being felt? What states of being have you already achieved by your very nature, that you're not allowing yourself to enjoy? Is there *any* good reason for keeping yourself from having love and joy?

After a long session of quiet introspection, Keith called people out of their meditation to share their insights.

LINDA M. - I went to feelings like times when I've asked for things I've wanted. I felt the vibration of having them, enjoying them. I felt when I was twenty, and I started to receive a lot of free trips.

KEITH - I felt this river of energy, power, and love; trying to flow, but the only way it could flow was through an opening the size of a garden hose. Then I relaxed and let my channel to receive expand.

CHRISTOPHER - I had an experience that I *am* this river of love and all those things, and yet there I am trying to get into it. I could see it. It's all in here, but there's me outside looking at it and trying to get in.

KEITH - For me, ever since I heard about the lust locks, I've been able to notice them when they try to kick in and rob me of appreciating something. I see it at the supermarket, in the bank, with friends. I have started noticing when I'm not letting in. It's fun because every time you notice it, you can take your power back from the lust lock. And then you begin enjoying the bounty of life all around you.

AUDREY - I notice that I have a general purpose lust lock. I explored a lot of things I don't let in. I could feel the lust lock. I'm retraining myself to let in. I need a little tweaking and I'm there, enjoying my experiences again. The most powerful awareness, to me, is that everything is here right now. I spent a lot of time *dreaming out* this awareness. I am in the feeling of support in this room right now. It's total comfort, total love, total play. I feel like letting all this in. I said, at the beginning of the *Gathering*, that I wanted to say "Yes" completely while letting go. This is exactly it. It's letting go of the "I can't."

KEITH - I just had a flashback from my past of an embarrassing time when I was in love with this person, and I didn't feel I was able to be with her enough. I'd be with her all weekend, and I'd spend the whole time saying, "I don't see you enough." She'd say, "We're together here right now." I'd say, "But there are always all of these other people around." She'd say, "There's no one here; we have the whole weekend alone together." I'd say, "But I don't see you enough." I'd just go on and on. I can see I wasn't letting in even that moment, let alone the whole weekend. I was in the "I don't see you enough" lock.

I know an old spiritual joke about a couple during a flood. Their house is flooded, and they're on the roof. They pray to God for help, and a row boat comes along, and they say, "No, no, no, we don't need your help. God's going to save us." A motor boat comes along, and they say, "No, no, no, we don't need your help. God is going to save us." A helicopter comes along, and they refuse that too. Finally, they drown. They get to heaven, and when they see God they ask, "Where were you when we called?" God said, "I came *three* times." They didn't recognize it. I watch myself push what I want away for one reason or another. It's not in the package I ordered, or in a form I can recognize, or something else keeps me from noticing and receiving it.

AUDREY - I see where I do it. Sometimes I'll be having an experience, connecting with somebody or something I've always wanted to connect with, but then I will run away from them or it. From now on, I'm going to invite it in.

KEITH - I had a friend in Boston named Gigs. He had the knowing that he could have a car any time he wanted one. He would prove it to people every day. He didn't have his own car, but he'd always come up with one. He wouldn't steal it; he would just walk into a restaurant, café, bar, or park and start talking to someone. He'd come back with their car keys. He did this for two years. We went bird watching, to the ocean, and on all kinds of adventures together and neither of us had a car. People would trust him and give him their car keys. He'd always return the keys at the end of the day or the next morning. It only took him five minutes to find someone who would lend him a car.

CHUCK - It's clear to me that the lock is whatever is inside us that constricts. I know I've had some very powerful loving experiences, not to mention here this weekend, throughout my life. How can I not feel loved? And yet it happens. I get this constriction and get into an intense jealousy pattern of people who I see having the love I want. That's really the issue I've been feeling, especially these last few months. When I let it go, I'm so much more in love anyway. It feels a lot better to be open to the flow.

KEITH - Concerning love, I had this friend, Lester, who would counsel couples who were having difficulties in their love affairs and relationships. He had an interesting perspective on this. He told me, "It's amazing. Each of us whose very essence is infinite love, can't allow ourselves to experience our own lovingness except through one person at a time. And that one person has to look a certain way, say certain words, do everything just right, or we won't even let in *their* love. We've constricted infinite love into one little situation, and everything has to be just so, or we won't even feel love in that situation."

As with the couples in Keith's story, everything is really all there if we will let it in. The doorway is open. Everything is available here and now, the only reality there is. When you're truly present, you are through the door.

BEING PRESENT

JILL - All of a sudden at four o'clock this morning, I sat straight up in bed and felt the essence of who I am. I discovered what I have resisted and separated myself from. I was exhilarated. What came to me, and what I'm offering today, is that I have been gifted from about the age of four with an essence of being a mother. I have been in denial of that energy but now I'm open to receiving.

KEITH - I go to my soul, to spirit, to God, and I want to know, "Where is all this leading? What's going to happen?" Spirit has been telling me, "Look, all you need to know is where you are right now. Once you get there, feel the vibration you're in, and then allow yourself to move in the direction you want to move. Be fully where you are in each moment, and you'll start moving. Experience fully where you are right now, then you'll naturally move to the next moment. All you need to know is where you are. Open to your intuition, follow it, and feel where you are, enjoy where you are. Then you'll move to the *next* moment. All you need to do is allow yourself to move to the next step, then the next step, then the next step. Along the way, all your dreams will come true; everything you've ever wanted to experience will unfold. Let your heart guide you to *just* the next step. You get there by being where you are now and opening and letting in the complete experience."

One of the things that has really helped me to get myself out of the lock-in situation is to realize I was trying to jump over the present moment. I was trying to jump over my next step, what was right in front of me to feel, to experience, to let in. Sometimes what's in the present to feel is the energy I usually label anger, fear, or sadness. These feelings are there, but what's also there is this gift, this beauty, this amazing thing called the aliveness, the electricity of the present moment. I have always wanted to jump over it. What has really helped me is to go to spirit through a *dream out*, and open to experiencing the present moment.

I was looking at that word, "present." And the question came to me, "What's the gift of the present?" The *present* is the present of the present. Your *presence* is the present of the present. It's no accident this one word has these two meanings. When I am overwhelmed, or locked, or stuck, I just decide to let myself *receive*, rather than look at,

"What do I have to get through? What's here that I'm resisting? What do I have to feel? What do I have to unveil? What do I have to break through?" That was my approach for most of my life. Of course, I resist that approach. I'm tired of doing it. It's painful. It's scary. What do I have to feel that I don't want to feel? All of that is within a particular paradigm or belief system. What I'm seeing is that the paradigm itself is a lock-in. I don't want to play that way anymore.

Let in the present. Enjoy the present. In that comes the gift of the present. In your presence is a way out, an acceptance of where you are. Things just start moving. It feels to me like a physical conveyor belt starts moving with me on it. My life starts moving. It's a river that somehow had stopped and all of a sudden it starts moving. I'm on a boat floating down the river Styx out of the Greek myths. It's the river that passes through eternal time and space. It passes through all dimensions, separations, and veils. When that river starts moving, I start moving. Where I move to is the next moment. In the next moment is a whole new perspective, a whole new life.

A friend sent me a quotation from a Seneca Indian, "I live each day as a whole separate life." By not living in the past, expecting the next moment to resemble the previous moment, each moment can be fresh. So the way I've been moving is to simply say, "I open to the gift of the present." In comes the most unexpected, amazing, joyful, peaceful gifts; things so wondrous that it's surprising. It's fantastic.

When you're in the present, your life design gets energized. Your life plan gets funded. When you're 100% present, all of the connections and synchronicities take place that are necessary for your whole life's purpose to unfold. Your blueprint is there, your own unique, signature vibration is there.

DREAM OUT: BEING PRESENT

So, if you like, take a moment to tune into your own unique vibration. Go to the stream of consciousness, the awareness, that you know in your heart is you. Allow that energy to ripple through your body. Allow the radiance of your own being, to move through and loosen your tightened muscles, loosen your emotions, loosen the walls. Allow the ocean of light to send pulsating waves of light into your heart. Let it flow all over your body. The wave comes in and starts at your feet, this warm, life-giving energy just flows through your body, through your cells, just washing, soothing, nurturing, relaxing. Just allow life, the wave of grace that is life, to flow. Once you start to feel yourself moving with the ebb and flow of the ocean of life, just be open to all energies and all emotion. Begin to say "Yes" to it all. Allow yourself to open to this particular moment, the present, right here, right now. Feel who you are, where you are right now. Welcome the present moment. Allow it to bring you your gift, that perfect gift which is exactly what you need. Now we're in the next moment. Could you open to this moment, right now? This moment might show up as color, vibration, feeling, or image. Whatever shows up, say, "Yes" to it. It's a gift to you, this moment that's perfect, right now Open to this moment, let the gift of this one in, in whatever shape or energy that gift is showing up. Now we're in the next moment...and the next....

During a fifteen or twenty minute *dream out*, people relaxed completely and asked spirit to take them to the vibration of being truly present. As people returned to their conscious awareness, Keith signaled the others with the chimes, and the sharing began.

JUDY - The gift for me in the present moment is the present moment.

LINDA - Mine was an opening to a sea.

KEITH - Mine was clarity...about everything.

MARIANNE - I had a recognition to just be.

CHUCK - Mine felt more like dissolving in the present.

ANTON - Merging.

AUDREY - I got clarity about my presence.

MICHAEL - Mine is appreciation. I say, "Thank you," for bringing me calm. Michael's soul has wanted to come out for a long time. I love you, Michael's soul.

JILL - I had an extreme sense of just opening. Lying on the floor was just an invitation to me to open to whatever was in the present. For those of you who have not been to a *Gathering* with me, I have never lay down in a *dream out* before. So this is a big step for me. And I *felt* myself truly opening to the present.

MARK - Mine was allowing love in instead of running from it and denying it.

SULANA - Mine was letting go of the past. I let go of yesterday, so I'll have to have a whole fresh new life today. What will that be? It feels fresh!

CAROLYN - I received a strong message that the past and future are not more than a thought. The present moment is the only thing that is real.

ANTON - Michael's sharing reminded me of a song. **(singing softly)** "Bright morning stars are rising....Some have gone to the valley singing..."

WHO AM I?

KEITH - That song reminds me of something I've wanted to suggest as a *dream out* for two and a half years, but it never felt quite right. It's about the greatest gift I have ever received. It happened for me in Phoenix after about six months of *Gatherings*. At the time I was hiding behind St. Germain a lot saying "St. Germain told me to say this. St. Germain told me to say that." That way if anyone got angry, it would be directed at him. What happened was that someone very lovingly asked, "Well, Keith, what exactly *is* your relationship with St. Germain?" It wasn't at all confrontational; it was genuine interest. Their soul wanted to know because they had heard me talk so much about St. Germain. I went into absolute, pure terror. That wasn't really the question I heard. The question I heard was, "Who are *you*?"

I had such fear come up people said it was one of the best physical demonstrations of cloaking they had ever seen. Steel plates closed in layers around me. I could see them. Then, very sweetly, another person asked, "Could that be a cloak?" and I said, "Yes." Then they said, also very lovingly, "Would you like to de-cloak that, unveil that?" I said, "No!" I was terrified. It was clear that in that moment I had a choice, and the timing was important. I *knew* that moment wasn't the right time. The freedom to say "No" was an amazing gift from the group and from myself to myself. We took a break and moved on to a different subject. But I certainly didn't forget it. Every evening when I felt strong enough for the next three months, I would ask, "What is my relationship with St. Germain?" I was terrified by asking because I knew what was right underneath that question. If I discover my relationship with this energy, this being I called St. Germain, then I would discover myself. I tried off and on for three months, and I just got the best sleep I've ever had. **(Laughter)**

I'd ask that question, then go totally unconscious. But finally, one night, I felt the answer coming. It came simply and I said, "This is it. I can tell." I felt a deep calm come over me. I started to realize how unnecessary the struggle of this whole pursuit of personal growth is, this struggle in finding out who you actually are. That was a new experience for me. It wasn't a new idea, but it was a new experience: I could actually be going *toward* something exciting and attractive; it could be *fun* to wake up. It felt fun that night. It felt like a treasure hunt. The treasure was something my soul had wanted forever and ever. I even knew I was going to find it. I could feel it coming.

"Who am I?" is what I asked. Usually when I tell this story, I stop right here. Usually I just say, "And I found out who I am." But what feels new right now for me, is to invite all of us, together, to ask that question. Every spiritual teacher I've ever had has said, "There's only one question. There is only one answer. There's only one experience that means anything. That's the experience of knowing who you are." A couple of days ago, I knew it was time to *dream out* on this question when somebody asked, "Who am I?" Then she said, "I know I'm something beyond just a mother, a daughter, or friend."

It may or may not be time for you right now to ask this question. In my experience, it's a very, very powerful and liberating question. I've never lost that experience and vibration of who, or what, I really am. I had known what I was, but I had kept it away. I had never let myself experience it. I had been in wanting. It was a definite lust lock. I had never allowed myself to fully receive it. I had actually been coming from the place of who I am, all the time. But I had not let myself fully embody the moment, own it, enjoy it.

JANET - I've explored many different avenues, many different healing groups, and I'm really drawn to this because it's what I'm about. The quote I have on my flier is, "You cannot *teach* people anything. You can only help them to discover for themselves, *That's who I am*." I love that because each of us has such *wisdom* and such *power*. We sometimes need to be reminded of that. That's part of why I like sharing. I feel you bring that through, Keith, because you have the intention of that. That energy carries into the energy of the group.

DREAM OUT: WHO AM I?

KEITH -This is an invitation, if you want to ask, "Who am I?" If you'd like, take a moment to curl up with the unique vibration that's you. Gather yourself. Then in your own way, in your own time, ask your soul, "Who am I?"

A silent *dream out* follows then the group members share their messages.

PAT - My consciousness is me. I have no beginning, no middle, no end. I am older than life, younger than eternity.

LINDA C. - When you said, "to get in touch with this awareness that is you," something inside of me lit up because I knew what makes me "me" is my awareness; the individuality of my way of perceiving and my way of being. It was really wonderful because I could remember all the times in my whole life when I felt that awareness. When I was around one year old I can remember being totally conscious of my selfness, just knowing, "This is me." I was aware of what was going on, and I was aware that I was aware. I just stayed there. Then I looked at the labels I put on that awareness of who I am or the labels others have put on me. One thing I got really clearly is how intense I am, how strongly and deeply I feel. I do everything passionately. What I've heard all my life is, "You come on too strong." So I've tried to stifle it. It never works. I was just letting myself be. I actually love relating to the world. I love being passionate. It adds so much to my experience of life.

JILL - The first time I felt the essence of God was about twenty years ago. Last night I stepped into heaven, and for one brief moment, I was held close and felt the sunshine of life itself.

KEITH - Each time someone really shares from their knowing, their heart, from their spontaneous, raw self, it jolts me. In a nice way it shakes me. My soul starts to come to attention. That's what I come for and what I'm getting today. This morning to me, has gotten brighter and brighter, richer and richer.

SUSAN - I'd like to share something really powerful for me. A big veil for me has been being married for fourteen years and not expressing to other men in my life how I feel about them. This has resulted in a lot of repressed feelings I've been unwilling to share. It is about what I'm allowed to do and what's "proper." The message that came to me today is, "The only thing that matters is love. Share, express, and be who you are, and once you are in that vibration, nothing else matters. When you're coming from your heart, you're speaking truth. That's what really matters." The message was really clear. "Be who you are." It's so true. If we can come from the heart, there's absolutely nothing wrong with expressing ourselves with whomever, however, whenever we feel the desire. That is the only way we can really touch another person. It manifests in nothing but beautiful love.

MICHAEL - I was having a conversation with my soul and asking, "How do you stay in the now, how can you keep the now, now?" I received a loud shout back, "Allow now! ...now...allow." Then I was playing again, "Who am I?" I saw a duality I had set up and decided to allow the two to become one. What I experienced was a burst of energy.

JANET - I feel called to sing right now... "Alleluia God is on high...each heart is one with god....so others may be bright with your love." Thanks to each and every one of you for helping me to find this joy. God knows your whispers. God knows your truth. **(She breaks down, so overcome with joy she was sobbing)** Thank you. It's so powerful, that bridge to God and wisdom. I couldn't resist the love any longer. I made a contract, like you did Keith. The power is too strong to contain any longer. I have to sing in my healing work; I had to sing just now. In this *dream out*, I was surrounded by angels and the angels said, "It's not *us* that wants you to sing; it's *God!*" **(While**

Janet was singing in a beautiful, truly heavenly soprano voice and as she talked afterwards, people in the room alternately received surges of energy, almost as though they had been electrified. (This is the "rush" I have discussed earlier.) "God has commanded you to sing. That love needs to come through." Thank you all for letting me share my gift of song. **(Crying)** This is what I've always *longed* for.

Let us take a ship

To an unknown island

Where we will leave our hatred behind

And arrive home

With nothing but pure love

In our hearts.

Georgina Murata

Chapter Nine

FELLOWSHIP FARM

GRACE AND LOVE

FORTY FIVE MILES NORTHWEST OF PHILADELPHIA, in western Montgomery County, is a retreat center called *Fellowship Farm*. The grounds were purchased in 1951, two decades after the formation of what was to become incorporated as the non-profit organization, *Fellowship House*. It is one of the oldest education retreats of its kind in the nation, and its focus is to promote peace and understanding between all people.

The spirit of *Fellowship Farm* has affected each of us in profound ways. Martin Luther King, Jr., talked about it in his autobiography, *Stride Toward Freedom. "One Sunday, I traveled to Philadelphia to hear a sermon by Dr. Mordecai Johnson, president of Howard University. He was there to preach for Fellowship House...and spoke of the life and teachings of Mahatma Ghandi.*

His message was so profound and electrifying that I left the meeting and bought a half a dozen books on Ghandi's works...I discovered the method of social reform that I had been seeking for so many months...I came to feel that this was the only morally and practically sound method open to oppressed people in their struggle for freedom."

Country dirt roads and paths wind through the lush meadows and groves on this rustic, 120-acre site near Pottstown. The building in which we had the *Gathering* was adjacent to a large pond full of lively frogs which croaked day and night. Late spring brought out brilliant reds, pinks, yellows, and purples, as the rhododendrons and other plants blossomed in their glory. The sweet fragrance of spring in the air was another reminder to me of what a gift it was to be there. I visited the surrounding woods at every opportunity. I experienced the timelessness and spacelessness of communing with nature. This was the first time I had spent time in nature on the East Coast, but it felt as though I had come back home.

In this place, grace and love abounded; in the air, in the pond, and in the buzzing of the bees all around us. It was no wonder, then, that grace became a predominant theme during the *Gathering*. My personal growth continued, as I opened up to new parts of myself that had long been forgotten. I had a new trust that my fears were unwarranted and loving myself enough to speak my truth would open new gateways.

The evolution of the *Gatherings* continued, and I observed a trend toward spontaneity and playfulness. These themes became more prevalent as the structure of the *Gathering* gave way to pure essence. The portal or entry way to pure essence is through being completely present. Communing with nature facilitates this state of being for me. Keith began with his relatively newfound willingness to embrace this state of being fully present.

KEITH - I had an experience in being fully present when a plant woke me up in my own back yard. It was a bottle brush plant that sent a seed pod across the yard to kiss me as I was admiring how beautiful it was. I became so present in the magical two hours which followed that many desires were fulfilled, answers came, and all kinds of miraculous events occurred. The magic happened simply because I really showed up. Until the power and clarity of this experience, I had never seen a personal, immediate, and practical benefit in being present. I knew being present was spiritually correct. I knew if you were present, you cut yourself less often. I knew when you are more alert, you get in fewer car accidents. I knew when you are attentive, you say fewer stupid things and don't lose your keys, but I had never really gotten the exciting, creative possibilities of staying present. That day, I was present for two hours and for the next two days, every major issue at the time resolved in my life. I see how it's in our own best interest to be present for our life. Magic happens in every moment we are fully present. I realized that, in the past, it was too painful for me to show up. When I showed up in the present moment, what was waiting for me was sadness, fear, anger, betrayal, depression, and heaviness. When you really show up, *everything* is present, including everything you have ever done and haven't fully experienced. Emotions you don't want to experience *can* show up.

Now, through the assistance of the *Gathering*, I have learned how to deal with emotions *as* they show up. If you can stay current, and feel your feelings as they appear, you can remain present and conscious. When you're present in your *knowing*, the veils all lift. The difficulties go away. As long as we're being present and conscious, everything is handled harmoniously. It wasn't *pleasant* to be fully present until now. There was too much physical and emotional pain. Now that it's exciting to be present, I *want* to be. The present is alive. God is here. I'm eternal. I'm fully safe. Everything heals here. It's practical, and it's exciting. It's better than any drug, any spiritual practice. It's everything you ever wanted. And it's always available.

That's really the purpose of all of these tools we're using in the *Gathering*. Being accurate and honest is a *rush*. It connects you. You get in alignment with who you really are and speak from there. What I find exciting is that all you need to do is deal with the present moment. If you leave it in the next moment, just get present again. If you tell yourself, "Well, I don't know how to," then ask, "Did I ever know how to?" Allow your soul to show you that you *do* know how to get present again. Then you're back!

SYLVIA - When you said all of your problems were taken care of, did you mean without any action on your part?

KEITH - Yes, that's how powerful being present is.

SYLVIA - I'm having a hard time with this. I'm thinking about this toxic waste site near my home.

KEITH - Well, you're *thinking.* There is a sign where we used to meet in New York City that says, "Don't even *think* of parking here!" We've changed it to, "Don't even *think* of thinking here." Everything will feel hard if you think about it. After awhile, being completely in the present becomes second nature. It is the pathway to your happiness and bliss. What I recommend is, don't believe anything I'm saying. Try it out. Get your own personal, direct evidence. After a little while, you *know.* It doesn't take long to really like it. It sure beats the competition. It's easy. It's fun. It's asking yourself to always be in vibrations that are the most wonderful ones your soul has ever experienced since the beginning of time: grace, trust, courage, intimacy, mutuality, sovereignty, universal supply, power, and playfulness.

SYLVIA - Is going to the vibration, of the time you felt the way you prefer, the receiving part?

KEITH - *If* you let it in. *When* you let it in. One thing we have a tendency to do in this culture is to witness, observe, and watch events and experiences. A lot of people are merely spectators in life. It's like walking by a beautiful rhododendron and saying to someone, "Look at this beautiful rhododendron," and they say, "Oh, yeah, yeah. I love rhododendrons." They don't even *look* at this flower, let alone smell it or touch it. That's what people do a lot, even during a *dream out.* They'll say, "That was a really neat memory. I remember that." But they don't let it *in.* They don't *feel* it. They don't *merge* with it. They don't let the alchemy happen.

You have to let yourself be affected by it, ruined by it, discombobulated by it. You have to *change.* Let your vibration change. Then you become *alive.* Then things happen. Almost every powerful movie has a scene about this. There's always a pivotal scene where someone delivers to the heroine or hero the same basic message. It doesn't matter whether the film is about love, war, or someone's adventure in the creative or business world. Some strong character tells the heroine or hero the way life is according to that person. That person will tell them popular belief is all "bull." "There's nothing but right here and the right now. And right now, you know what you have to do in your heart. Do it." The imperative is usually to trust the love, take a chance, jump off the cliff, tell the truth, or some other form of surrendering to the flow and power of life. Then the heroine or hero "goes for it." The crowd applauds. That's the basic plot of most good movies.

There is one key aspect which has assisted me in getting myself to enter into the dynamic magic of life. I've used therapy, counseling, vision quests, yoga, massage, acupuncture, rebirthing and meditation my whole life with myself and with others. I've noticed that some people come for thirty or forty sessions and then heal or release. Other people come to *one* session and heal or release. Others come for a hundred and *don't* shift at all. I kept asking, "What's really happening here?" I knew it wasn't the technique, the needles, the herbs, or the facilitation. There was something else going on. What I noticed was, that right before people heal, release, or have a realization, their whole body and their whole being relaxes. They drop their guard. They let go of their death grip on holding life a certain way. They surrender.

People want aliveness and love. In my experience, people will do practically anything for it. They'll do sweat lodges, walk on coals, or do silent vision quests with no food or water. Some people bury themselves up to their neck and stay in the woods for four days. A lot of us have tried some of those approaches. I also have a lot of friends who are what I call "spiritual casualties." They got really scared at one point and quit opening all together. They never really discovered what's inside their deepest level of knowing.

The key ingredient I have seen is safety. People relax, shift, heal, and come back to life when they feel it is safe to let their guard down and let their energy flow freely. The way we assist people to feel core safety is by going to a level of our knowing where we see our personal blueprint. At that level of consciousness, we know how we put the veils in place, the lust locks, the fear, and the programming. We are going to the place where we put it together, where we programmed in all our veils and illusions. What better place to go, than our own soul, to undo our programming, in the most gentle way?

Going directly to our soul is the easiest and most fun way. I noticed that people will do all of these different spiritual quests, but they don't *enjoy* them. I have made a career out of being a good coaxer, encouraging people to take the leap or take a chance. People will push through their comfort zone because they want what's on the other side. The last six years before the *Gathering*, I was asking myself, "Why do we have to go through things we don't want to? Why do we have to continually experience undesirable states, to get to a natural, desirable state of being that's so good. We want to go where we're loved, secure, safe, playful, alive. We are still willing to go through anything to get to a good state of being. But I didn't understand why we needed to.

One day, I got my answer..."You don't have to." You can go *directly* home. That was the night grace came in, the awareness came in, and I started moving toward the oneness, toward my natural state, toward God. I let that river of knowing carry me right through the veils. I saw clearly that all of the veils, all of the thoughts, all of the beliefs, had power. You gave them your power. But at a certain point, you finally developed so much inner awareness and aliveness, strength, and clarity, you can tell a the difference between programming and fact. Look at stage fright as an example. A lot of very successful comedians and actors still get "butterflies." They have learned that is a phantom fear. After awhile, you begin to realize *all* fears are phantom fears. Anything telling you you are not whole, wonderful, and safe, is a lie. As you get more clarity in your knowing, in a very tangible way, you can tell the difference between truth and a veil. It's because you're living in the real vibration. That's the purpose of the *Gathering.* It's here so we can assist each other in feeling real love, real security, real connection. Truth has a feeling to it, a vibration. Let it in. When you do, and you can tell the difference between what's real and unreal, just respond to the real. Don't respond to what's not real anymore.

It's fun, a new way of being totally and radically honest with yourself and with life. Unless people come at you from their hearts and are real, where's the obligation to respond? Simply don't respond to lies, phantoms, and garbage anymore. Just quit doing it. People *know* what's going on. They'll say they don't. They'll protest, but after they're done yelling at you, crying, blaming, and feeling betrayed, they *know* what's going on. They either *want* realness, or they don't. I learned this with myself. There's still a part that lingers in unreal crap. I say, "Thank you, but no thanks. I've given already." I've given for forty-nine years, at work, at home, from my body, my aliveness, my fun. No more. I'm not giving anymore. It hasn't worked. It hasn't paid off. If it worked, even every now and then, that would be one thing, but it never has. This is the essence of what we're doing here at the *Gathering.*

One of the most gentle and universally appealing of *dream outs* at the *Gathering* is the one on grace. Just hearing the word "grace" seems to open doorways for people to a place of serenity. The energy of its vibration disarms veils. It signifies a total trust in the universe, a gift. When in a state of grace, people open to what they really are. Keith began the discussion.

GRACE

KEITH - Let's open to the vibration of grace. Allow grace to enter your life. What is grace, to you? I had been sending my mother love for years and years. She's in a nursing home and a mental hospital where they're giving her electroshock treatments. She had eight of them last week. She's done rebirthing, *est*, psychotherapy, hypnotherapy, and every anti-depressant drug that exists, including experimental ones that almost killed her. Nothing has worked. She was still angry, depressed, and suicidal. So I had a lot of strong feelings about this. Even after sending her all of that love, I still felt guilty, frustrated, and sad that I couldn't assist her in some way. Then, in a *Gathering*, we were, as a group, focusing on grace and we did a *dream out.* What I discovered was, grace is the energy, the vibration, the feeling, the space, that intercedes when nothing else will work. Grace appears when you can't even imagine any solution, any resolution, anything. There is still grace. I realized that grace is an expansion of love. It's an aspect of love that can get through to people even if they're blocking out love. My mother has blocked out God's love, my father's love, my love; she has not wanted anyone's love. In a crisis or emergency, even when a person is already injured or dead, grace can literally bring that person back to wholeness or life. I've seen it. That's grace to me.

I saw how grace had come to work miracles and magic throughout my life, when it didn't seem like anything metaphysical or material could help. God and the universe still had an alchemy, still had a transformation that I couldn't even think up. Grace resolved the situation and brought peace and harmony. My attention went to my mother as I was in a state of grace. I realized I had been sending her love since my father died, and she went into this suicidal depression. She's terrified of God; she's terrified of love. She doesn't feel she deserves love. What came to me was I've been sending love to someone who can't receive love. That felt like an impossible situation.

But there is something you *can* call upon. When everything is hopeless, when you can't see any solution, there's grace. Being in the knowingness of what grace is, I started to hold her in that vibration of grace. I started holding her, in my consciousness, in that vibration and about two weeks later she called me, and she had met a young priest she started talking to. She's started meeting this twenty-year-old priest two or three times a week and talks to him about God and love. She's let God in and she's preparing herself to meet God. Before grace came in, you couldn't even mention God, or love, or a priest from the Catholic Church to her for her whole life. It's very powerful. And whether we call it grace or something else; I have found, when you surrender your ideas of love, alchemy, magic, metaphysics, of *anything*; that opens the space for grace to come in and play. There's a harmony underneath it all. There's a connection that, if you allow it, will come in and harmonize *any* situation.

One of the things we've done in *Gatherings* is go to our own personal experience, that quality, that energy, existing when you surrender everything else, when you allow the universe, God, source, to come in. Would you like to go to that space? Grace ignores all belief systems and logical structure. It ignores the past and the future, cause and effect. Grace is pure and natural. It is pure gift. It's a very, very powerful force. What is grace to you? Does everyone have a sense of it?

AMY - I feel grace as a gift. There's no reason for it, and it comes. Sometimes I feel it at home when my husband, for no reason, kisses me. Right away my pretense says, "What was that for?" Then I stop and realize, it was just a kiss. I didn't do anything to deserve or earn it. My mother would do it, too. Late at night, we'd be watching TV, and she'd come out and just say something nice to us and give us a kiss.

SUZANNE - To me, it's the experience of just essence, and no mind.

KEITH - One veil I had was there is a quota of grace; I could only receive a certain amount of it. I didn't want to use up the quota, so I didn't ask for it very often. I thought it would really only operate when I'm in a crisis or an emergency.

KATE - To me, grace is when I really feel oneness.

DARLINE - Grace, to me, is the unexpected. It is also a certain feeling I get, a deep feeling from my heart.

DREAM OUT: GRACE

KEITH - Would you like to visit a state of grace, however your soul can get you there? Let it undo you. Let it in. Allow yourself to get in touch with when you already allowed grace in your life. Allow your intuition to show you where you already know how to receive exactly what you want. Let it show you. Feel for it. You'll find it. You already know how to do it. Allow, invoke, give permission. Appreciate yourself, your knowing, your power, your magic.

Once you get a sense for your own way, your own vibration, re-experience and remember what it feels like. Start to get the *feel* of it. Get the feel for your own experience of grace, divine intervention, the ability to get things moving, to open up a locked-in situation. Just get the feel of it, not the particulars, not the form it takes, not the details, but the *feel* of it, the flow of it, the knack of it, the energy, space, vibration. Allow yourself to enjoy feeling that. Allow yourself to be conscious of it. Just enjoy it. Own it. Right now. You know how to do that. You know how it feels. Let that feeling flow through you. Celebrate it. Allow it to be part of what you know. If you want, if it feels right, could you allow your intuition to guide you to a situation or condition...it could be a physical condition...it could be social situation, some issue, topic, situation, condition, in your life that you would like to move or transform. Allow your intuition to guide you to the right one that's locked in, that's stuck, fixed, paralyzed, diseased, or hasn't moved. Rather than try to understand, label, evaluate, or even describe it, just let your intuition take you. Allow the vibration of grace, of flow. Use the knack that you have for allowing. Allow that energy, that vibration to begin to resonate into the situation. Imbue the situation with the energy of grace and flow, opening to divine intervention.

Allow yourself to tune in to your own unique vibration, quality, or state you know of as the real you. Open to your heart, open your soul. Allow your spirit complete freedom in however it can assist you. Allow your soul to go to a vibration or an experience that will open a gateway for you to really let in, celebrate, and live, in a state of grace. Allow it to unfold, in your own way, in your own time....Really touch that state of grace. Enter into it.

Twenty minutes of quiet meditation time followed; then people began to share their individual experiences.

SYLVIA - I always know, afterwards, when I've been in a state of grace. Like when I fainted skiing on the downhill side of a ski slope. Nobody skied into me, and I was passed out for five minutes. I was in a state of grace. I knew it afterwards.

KEITH - You know, you've been in a state of grace since you've arrived at the *Gathering.* No skiers have run into you. **(Laughter)**

MARGARET - I feel in a state of grace when I'm with my grandchildren. They jump into my arms and there is such a tremendous love. And also watching, sharing their wonderment and love of the world. It's beautiful. They see the wonders I've forgotten.

AMY - Spirit gave me a remembrance of a state of grace when the hospital staff placed my daughter in my arms at my breasts and said, "Feed your daughter." I was giving her life-sustaining health and receiving love.

RANDY - I entered into the energy of grace by connecting with beings who love me for who I am, without any judgments. They simply love me for who I am. I flew with that feeling for awhile, and then I surrendered into the universal flow.

VENITA - I went and spent time with dolphins and humpback whales. I received light into my body and, after awhile, I came back to "reality." I said, "Okay, I need for you to show me how to do this..." Then I heard, "Just *be* here, and let us *show* you."

CLAUDIA - I find that I can allow myself to be put into a state of grace by remembering it has sustained me in times of intense turmoil.

Then I stopped feeling down.

DARLINE - Different times of feeling grace came to me, but the most important one came in again. It was the part of a song that goes, "God's grace will take me home." That part of the song zeroed in on me. Though the other things that came to me were important, that was the thing I really needed to know.

CAMILLE - If grace means my purest intention is present, I was in grace several times when people had accidents on our road. With no other thought than to help them, I went and did whatever was necessary.

KATE - I witnessed grace this past week, watching at the corner stoplight, two cars had an accident that was very, very severe and both of the people in those cars walked away untouched. It was literally impossible. In addition to that, there was an ambulance waiting at the corner, just in case.

VENITA - Grace is just so ordinary, and yet it's so miraculous.

KEITH - I heard a true story about a very famous rabbi who other rabbis and scholars had come to for his whole life, to study with him because he was so wise. He was getting along in years and they knew he didn't have much longer on the planet, so they held one big, final conference. They had to keep moving it to bigger and bigger venues because so many people wanted to come and hear this wise man at what was probably his last public appearance. So rabbis and scholars across the world assembled. There were thousands of them in this auditorium waiting for him. He finally got introduced, came out in long, black robes, and he looked at the audience and started to dance. He twirled and swirled around and around for twenty minutes. He used the entire stage, spiraling to and fro, back and forth. Then he went up to the microphone and said, "I trust that I've answered all your questions." Then he left the stage.

CHRIS - Grace is what's left after you surrender. It's an ocean liner. The captain is in charge of everything, so you just throw your baggage in and you're taken care of.

ANNE - I dropped my load. The garbage truck came in and dumped me out. I was in there kicking the stuff around with both feet and arms. Somebody came along and said, "Enough of this." And I said, "No, this is *fun*." As soon as I allowed it to be fun, everything turned into a muddy river. I was really comfortable floating downstream except I became worried because that muddy stream might lead to the ocean. Who knows what would happen to those problems in that big old ocean?

KEITH - They would be gone, lost, disappear. Oh, my, what a loss!

Love was another theme which developed in this *Gathering*. There was genuine warmth and understanding between people. It seemed natural, then, that love emerged as a dominant theme. Inspired by the energy of the group, Keith began to share:

LOVE

KEITH - I had an amazing experience recently with love. We were doing a *dream out* on alchemy and what came to me was that I had always held that freedom and relationships were separate, conflicting things. I wasn't planning on doing this at all, but I found myself experiencing the vibration of sovereignty and the vibration of love in a relationship blending together in complete harmony. It was obvious that they go together. I suddenly knew freedom and real love in a relationship with another being go hand-in-hand as one. I had never experienced that before. That was a few months ago, and since then, I've been attracting people who already know this reality in their lives. We don't even have to discuss it. The harmony of freedom and intimate connection is taken for granted, assumed. No issues have needed to be negotiated or agreed upon. There's been no need or notion of compromise, sacrifice, or conflict. Since the moment I realized these things are one and the same, that is what I've been attracting.

DON - In a state of unconditional love, there are really no conditions. The other person can be who they are, and I can be who I am.

RENEE - What I've been experiencing and playing with for awhile is, *I'm* my own lover. Everyone I meet is my lover. Before I could realize that, *I* had to get there with myself first.

KEITH - It's cool that you bring this up because at lunch break I did a *dream out,* and I asked for clarity on where it would be fun for us all to explore given where we are today. Something new came up, a suggestion from spirit that we do *dream outs* on three unique, seemingly different, vibrations. Do three in a row, then allow them to feed and nurture each other. The three that were suggested were sovereignty, self-love, and universal supply. They're all totally connected. They all enhance each other. The self-love was suggested with the words, "Everything else is for naught, unless you feel worthy of receiving. You can open up to all the vibration, all the energy you want, and if you don't feel deserving and worthy and open to embracing and owning it, you won't stay there."

I know what comes up for me is I feel I'll lose love if my heart causes hurt feelings or conflict with another person. But as I've gotten more and more accustomed to feeling self-love, God's love, spiritual love, it's obvious to me the most loving thing to do, with myself and with another person, is to express my truth. The most loving act is to say where I am, to be 100% honest. That's never been obvious to me before.

DON - "To thine own self be true."

LINDA - On the receiving end, it's a tremendous relief to know what the person *really* wants. It's a tremendous feeling of, "Oh good. I don't have to attend to that. I don't need to play in the negative energy of falsehood."

KEITH - Even if it's news you don't want to hear, it's a relief. "Great, now I know, and I can do what I have to do."

FRAN - I have a really close friend, and one of the reasons we've been friends so many years is that when we're talking, she'll say, "Fran, I can't listen to you anymore." It's wonderful, because she will always tell me when that is true, and I can always say it to her when it's true. And we can still be friends.

JAY - I wrote a little poem I'd like to share with you. It's called *Merge with the Lover."*

Once there was a person
who sought to merge with a lover.
Yet the lover would never be still and proper.
So the person continued to look.
Then, quite by chance, the person met the lover,
Bliss abounded—in and out.
And then it happened. The person turned inside out.
Whereas the person was on the inside looking out for a lover
now the person was on the outside and the lover was inside.
With the lover inside, there was no more seeking.
For everywhere the lover looked, there was the lover looking back.

DREAM OUT: SELF AND UNCONDITIONAL LOVE

KEITH - Shall we see what our knowing, our intuition, our heart has to tell us? Go to a time when you knew the nature of real love, a time of self-love, a time of free unconditional love, when you experienced it, received it, gave it. Your heart knows where to take you. Allow yourself to open to a time or place, or directly to the vibration of true self-love, true self-acceptance, worthiness, deserving, or a time when you gave yourself the experience of unconditional love with another being. Reconnect with that vibration in a way that's so strong you'll be able to live from that vibration. Allow your intuition to take you to the perfect time, place, and vibration, to open you to whatever is right for you to experience at this time on your journey. Just be open, allow.

A *dream out* meditative time followed, then people began to share their experiences with the others.

FRAN - At the end of the *dream out*, I had this image of a Tibetan relic. It is part of a mantra meaning the jewel and the lotus. And I said to myself, "Okay, that's me." I am tempted to say, "That's what we are," but I'll say, "That's who I am."

DELL - I didn't want to quit. I wanted to stay there. It was such a nice vibrational harmony.

DUNCAN - In that *dream out* and the one previously, I found I didn't need to *go* anywhere. Right now is the most powerful sovereignty I've ever felt. Right now is the most self-love I've ever felt. There's no place that compares to the way I feel right now. I don't have to hunt for it. It's right here.

CAROL - I felt that, too. It's always here in my heart. When I do need to go outside for it, I think about my little granddaughter who's going to be three next month. The unconditional love I feel, and I receive from her, the little things that happen. There is nothing in the world like it.

DUNCAN - What you said keyed something in me. I have a grandson who's two-and-a-half, and because of a tangled marriage, I don't see him very much. I got to play with him for about an hour the other day, and when it was done, he just kind of looked at me and said, "I love you." There was no preparation for that. Nobody was talking about it or anything. He just turned around, caught my eye, and looked at me, and said, "I love you." I have been in a spin ever since.

KEITH - There's a term for that. It's called "disarming."

DUNCAN - I don't know where it came from. I was totally unprepared. I was wide open and it hit me like a ton of bricks. That kind of love knocks you over. There's nothing you can do to fend it off. It goes right through.

DELL - My feeling is this is the most self-love I have ever experienced. And I know it's getting bigger and better, and it's going to keep on going. That's the joy of the vibration I've been feeling much of today.

NELSON - In this *dream out*, I was first trying to see the place where I was able to express unconditional love. I want to love unconditionally. The answer I got back was, "You *are* doing it." And I said, "*How* am I doing it?" It said, "Your gift to help people heal, that's unconditional. You're not requiring anything of anybody. You're just giving to them." That was really comforting and affirming because I feel I want to be in the right place at the right time to serve others.

DELL - I just thought of something from the Abraham material. **(channeled messages)** "Most of us think we want someone to love us when what we really want is someone to flow love to."

DUNCAN - I had an image at the end of that *dream out*, of a beautiful woman's face, and she was smiling. I knew there was nothing I could tell her she didn't already know. Then I knew there was nothing she could tell me that *I* didn't know.

Out beyond ideas of wrongdoing and rightdoing,

there is a field. I'll meet you there.

When the soul lies down on that grass,

the world is too full to talk about.

Ideas, language, even the phrase *each other*

doesn't make any sense.

Rumi

Chapter Ten

THE MESSAGE OF THE VOLCANO

The Message of the Volcano, Sovereignty, and The Future

COSTA RICA IS A LAND OF PRIMAL LIFE FORCE. Bordered by Nicaragua and Panama, it is a peaceful land with serene people who have no need or desire for a military. The people there devote their energies toward *internal* peace which "trickles up" and translates into an unparalleled international harmony with the rest of the world.

Pura Vida, or "pure life" in English, is a common phrase used throughout the country, and its message resonates throughout the land. It is used daily in conversation to remind the people there is a peaceful way of living, and it is here, now, in *this* moment. They are awake to the importance of keeping the spirit of *Pura Vida* alive in a world of turmoil and fear.

Costa Rica is a country of matchless beauty and aliveness. Adjoining the Pacific Ocean on one side and the warm aquamarine Caribbean on the other, it is full of natural power and wonders. Its dense tropical rain forests cover the land, and its beautiful waterfalls and rivers wind their way majestically from the mountain ranges and active volcanoes to the Pacific Ocean and the Caribbean Coast.

Almost a third of Costa Rica's territory is set aside as national parks and wildlife, and as biological, forest, and natural reserves. Much of the country's natural resources are dedicated toward culture and education. The Costa Ricans cherish their ecology and want to preserve the environment far into the future. There is a lot to preserve. The rich diversity of the territory and the lush tropical rain forests are home to more than 9,000 species of flowering plants, over 800 species of birds, over 200 species of mammals, and more species of butterflies than on the entire African continent.

Within an hour's drive of the capital city, San Jose, down small, winding rural roads, through dense tropical forest is a tiny town named La Garita. It is reported to be one of the most ideal climates in the world, and the temperature remains between 75-78 degrees with low humidity. The hotel and meeting place for the *Gathering* is nestled in lush tropical forest and adjacent to a beautiful stream. The cabana in which the *Gathering* was held has open screened windows and is surrounded by jungle on three sides. The wild sounds of the birds and various other camouflaged, though vocal, creatures are a constant reminder of the vibrant life energy of the country.

There was primal life force surrounding us. The fragrant scents of the wild flowering plants, the roaring vibration of the river, and the teeming jungle life carried our attention and energy away. Though our bodies were in the cabana, our spirits were soaring through the lush river valleys, splashing in the mighty waterfalls, and hanging from the tops of the highest trees with the colorful toucans, the skittering iguanas, and the furry, languorous sloths. We found so much energy in the paradise around us it became difficult to focus inward. The rushing stream was so close that much of the time I could barely hear Keith or the others as they shared. Consequently, much of the amazing transformation that occurred in Keith and me, as well as in many of the others, happened *after* the *Gathering*. We used the old *Gathering* as a portal to the new one, the return to primal life force.

Every morning of the *Gathering* in Costa Rica, I got up early to sit on a large boulder in the stream. I wrote down the messages I received from nature, the trees, the stream, the wildlife, and the volcano. In my notes I wrote that I was to "Take the spirit and the wisdom of the trees, as well as *Pura Vida,* to the rest of the world." This *Gathering* was an ancient appointment we had made in the past and was to serve as a pivotal point for humanity and the planet.

For days before we went to the volcano, I received the message to go to the mountain. When we were on the bus and still half an hour away, I could already feel the vibration of the volcano named Arenal. It put me into a trance, a primal state of pure beingness. That night and the next day, the volcano spoke to me even above the thundering sound of the torrential rain. It told me it was time to stop depending upon the way things *appear* through the five senses. I was to learn to feel the essence of things. I had a rather intense personal experience with the volcano. The main message I received was, "Everything is happening for a reason. You are here is to help maintain the stream of harmony between all things."

Much of what happened as a result of the portal opened in the *Gathering* occurred *after* the *Gathering*. So it is those things on which we focus this chapter. (The painting on the front jacket cover of this book was inspired by a couple of different vivid *dream outs* I had in which I was soaring, as a majestic bird of prey, through an opening. Entitled *The Soaring of Spirit,* it captures the essence of crossing through the portal toward the primal life force of the volcano.

As I began to assimilate and live in the vibration of the message I received from the volcano, Keith was having a profound awakening of his own. He received a message about touching the fire and spirit of primal life force. Keith begins:

THE MESSAGE OF THE VOLCANO

THE COLISEUM

In Costa Rica, I spent two days exploring the magic and mystery of the area with a friend. One day, after an inner calling had been urging me to go to the volcano, my friend and I went to a restaurant. Unsolicited, the owner came over to us and said, "You two look like you really want to get to *know* the volcano." Then he gave us directions to a secret path. I went up into the fog and found myself standing on a live, moving lava flow, and had the opportunity to merge with the beingness and life force of the volcano. When the fog later lifted, I discovered I'd been right near the crater of the volcano. It was quite dramatic.

Shortly after I returned, the Spirit of the Volcano visited me on Christmas and New Year's Eve. Much like in the story of Scrooge when the Spirits of Christmas Past, Present, and Future took him to watch various parts of his life, the Spirit of the Volcano came to show me around. It took me to when I had felt a primal life force and aliveness within myself. It took me to a time when I was about 19 years old. I was in Europe, exploring Western civilization, and the culture felt quite dead to me. European society had the appearance of life and happiness. But my heart was telling me there was not much real aliveness or happiness left at the core of European culture. At the end of this journey in Europe, I went to a 2,000-year-old Roman coliseum still being used in Southern France.

There were still bullfights in this old coliseum, which had been used for gladiator contests, circuses, and other forms of Roman public entertainment. As I sat within this coliseum, I was aware I was sitting in an example of man-made architecture that had lasted 2,000 years. It was very beautiful and symmetrical, and I experienced a sense of harmony and strength in the structure. I watched the French people enjoying the sun, the weather, and each other. The pageantry and the color were very, very enjoyable...until the bulls came into the ring. I looked at this beautiful inspired edifice that had lasted 2,000 years and these people who had come from a civilization more ancient than that. I watched all of their energy being focused on killing this bull, killing the aliveness in this vital, beautiful creature. Very slowly, spear by spear, the life force was drained from the bull. In the end, I watched three bulls die.

The Spirit of the Volcano was showing me the experience of these bulls dying, so I could watch this ancient, human civilization focus all its energies on killing the spirit of one creature. I re-experienced the decisions I'd made sitting there in that coliseum. I could even hear the words, as a young boy 19 years old, "I can't be part of this. This is not me. I won't be part of this." I had gone to Europe to see my roots. I was going to a great American university studying philosophy, psychology, and filmmaking. I was educating myself and learning from society in order to find my place within Western civilization. That's why I had gone to Europe, to visit as much as I could of the history and origins of the knowledge, wisdom, structures, ideas, principles, and traditions of this society I was trying to fit into. At that moment, I made the decision, "I cannot fit into this culture. There is no place for me in this society as it is. I won't do it. I can't do it. My spirit won't let me. My heart won't allow it. It's impossible."

It wasn't a judgment or really even a decision. It was a recognition that my spirit didn't fit. It was a recognition that my mission, my purpose, my destiny, was *not* to fit into this culture. My destiny was to open to a new culture, to be part of a movement or an impulse to allow a new sensitivity, a new society, a whole new direction, a whole new vein of expression to take place on the earth. I knew I wasn't born to, or intended to, be part of this old tradition.

It was really an insight, a realization, of what already was very self-evident at that point. It wasn't that I judged it and decided not to be part of it. It's that I suddenly saw it for what it was, and recognized, "I don't belong here. This is not my culture. This is not my home."

At that moment, what I experienced was a sense of my true destiny, my true nature. I wasn't yet at the point of being able to express, identify, or describe it, but I did know I needed to go in an entirely different direction. My spirit was here to express itself and evolve totally outside of the established human culture I'd grown up in.

Just a few weeks later, I lost my eyesight, and I went into a deep depression and despondency. I was completely blind for two months before I could see again. I realized I had to withdraw, and I went so deeply inside I literally withdrew into darkness. I know now that I withdrew from society so I could sort things out within myself and find a place to begin again, a place to put my energies, trust, and power, to something other than the culture I had been brought up in. I realized, sitting there in that coliseum, that everything I had been taught about the Roman Empire, the Greeks, and all of our Western European civilization was not what it appeared to be. I'd been fed so many lies that everything felt untrue. I had been told that Western civilization embodied the qualities of love, compassion, humanity, equality, fraternity, and liberty. But I realized if Western civilization truly had heart and wisdom, it could not and would not be doing what it was doing. It could not support the building of a 2,000-year-old structure, and continuously use it to destroy spirit, to kill primal life force in free beings.

I realized, in my youthful innocence, that society was actually structured toward the killing of spirit. I was also starting to experience this destruction of spirit in my college classes, as well as in the societies of Europe I was visiting. I was beginning to realize there probably was nowhere on Earth where civilization, society, and human culture were actually expressing the qualities they pretended to. The words that came to me were, "I'm out of here. I'm dropping out. I need to go somewhere totally different—somewhere this culture doesn't even know about—somewhere invisible to this culture. I need to because I can tell, in essence, this civilization is a killer of souls."

I knew I was in danger. This society that purports to raise and nurture the human spirit, is actually a *killer* of the human spirit. For my spirit to survive, I needed to become invisible to this culture, so it would not know I harbor this light within my chest, within my soul. I had a pilot light, a knowing, an awareness. I needed to protect it by hiding.

So I went blind, for if I became blind, if I became powerless, quit making films, quit communicating, quit being seen out there in the world, I'd be safe. I can feel right now that the divine purpose in this was for me to withdraw until I found my sovereignty, until I found God.

I decided to start talking to God, to see if s/he really existed. Sure enough, s/he does, within me. We spoke and made an agreement. My part was that I would not complain. Instead, I would go deeper. I would look behind the appearances of life and the circumstances I was complaining about. I would look underneath the way I was experiencing things, and keep looking deeper and deeper until I found the truth, until I found a reality that was more fundamental than what was showing up on the surface of human experience. I would continue to go deeper until I found the core reality of life itself. Within hours of talking to God and making this deal, events started to unfold which allowed me to get my eyesight back.

I can see right now the agreement I made was that I wouldn't waste my energy and attention complaining and trying to rearrange the furniture on the Titanic. From my point of view, human culture, at that point, was the Titanic. It was going down. It was rotten to the core. It was missing heart and without heart, it couldn't survive. I knew it was eventually doomed. It was going down because it did not have and was not interested in getting heart. It had convinced everyone that it valued compassion, equality, mutuality, freedom, and human rights, but it didn't. It was really out to kill those qualities, to kill the human spirit, the primal life force in people.

The agreement I made was that I would not accept the polluted waters on the surface. I would look deeper and discover the pure spring, the pure flow of energy, love, connection, grace, and God, that flowed deep within every individual person and every single expression on the planet. I would not complain, and I would not stop. I would not accept anything except that purity, which means finding the beingness and oneness behind all forms of life, and the knowing behind all beliefs and ideas.

That's what the *Gatherings* are about. We look behind the appearance of everything, under the surface of life, to see what is really happening to our souls. We meet to collect that information, to gather that knowing. One of the first indications to me of my soul's purpose, of the importance of my aliveness, came to me as a young person in that coliseum. That's why the spirit of the Volcano took me there.

RETURN TO PRIMAL LIFE FORCE

The whole trip to Costa Rica and the autumn *Gatherings* of 1996 were about sovereignty. To me, sovereignty is the importance of owning and knowing you are source. It's being able to generate your own energy, all the love you need, all the power you need, all the health, wisdom, clarity, and attention you desire. We need to open up to the river of infinity. Grounded firmly in sovereignty, we have the clarity to keep our life pure, real, honest, and in alignment with exactly what our soul is here to express, and we have the courage to go out and speak, share, and communicate our truth.

Maya Angelou, who read poetry at Clinton's last presidential inauguration, appeared recently on a TV talk show. She said she felt the most important quality in the human spirit, was courage. Courage, derived from the French word for "heart," or *coeur,* means "of heart, being full of heart." She said that without courage, we don't have the energy, stamina, power, or strength to go out and communicate what our spirit came here to do. Without enough courage, we won't act.

So courage is a vital quality, because without it, nothing else will get expressed. Her words hit me strongly. I realized in order for us to have heart, in order to have *coeur*-age, to be full of heart, to have our heart full of energy, knowing, strength, security, certainty, God, we need to open up to the fire in our belly, to the fire in the center of the earth, to that energy that melts all resistance, to that energy that melts the granite heart.

I realized that the collective human condition of the planet was heartless. Our hearts had gotten so closed to feeling real connection to life, love, and spirit, that our collective heart on the planet had become so crystallized, closed and armored, that it was literally as hard as granite.

Our hearts have closed down. To open them again takes a force which is pristine, powerful, and pure, outside the whole realm of our our intellect, outside all past paradigms. We need raw primal naiveté, an innocence of past beliefs. Primal life force has no human ideas, limitations, paradigms, and concepts. It just *is*. It's the is-ness of the universe, the raw movement of the universe people often call God. We need to connect with that again, and connect with it in such a way we not only embrace it and feed from it, but *become* it again, actually merge with it. We need to allow divine alchemy and merge with that energy so we become oneness, power, that primal, undifferentiated, undivided, unqualified, unlimited, raw, pure movement, that river of life, that is God. As we open to it, all the remaining structures, ideas, and paradigms are going to be transformed at the foundation.

I saw a video in recent years of a volcano in Hawaii. It was a volcano I had visited several times, on the Big Island. As this volcano was erupting a several years ago, the lava swept down the side of the mountain and went right through a village. There was nothing humans could do. There was no viable scientific technology or know-how to stop the power of this lava flow, this expression of the Spirit of the Volcano, of the Goddess, Pele. The energy and heart in this five-foot-tall lava flow, the expression of this spirit, was intense. As the lava got close to human structures and buildings, it demolished them, disintegrated them. The heat would explode the cement, wood and bamboo foundation of buildings before it even touched them. The power of the energy and heat of the lava disintegrated the foundation of these human structures. The structures fell, crashed, burned, and literally got covered over by the lava. Once the lava had gone from the mountain to the sea, there was absolutely no trace of the village or that humans had ever been there. All signs of the human world was totally covered up, totally destroyed. The human structures could not hold up because they weren't as real, as substantial, as the energy of Pele, as the energy of the volcano. That's why the Spirit of Pele dominated. The human paradigms, ideas, and concepts, are no match for the raw, creative, primal force of God, of our true selves.

The volcano is telling us that only by tapping into this primal, creative/destructive energy (as something new and fresh is created, what was there before naturally disintegrates) and allowing this energy to move within us and disintegrate the very foundations of what we think is real, will our rigid belief structures dissolve and collapse. All we need to do is tap back into this aliveness, this power within us, within spirit, within every living thing.

The Volcano also reminded me of what the Spirit of the Wild Stallion said to me, in an Arizona canyon, "You humans want to reconnect with your primal life spirit, excitement, aliveness, your passion for life. But the way you approach it—sequential, methodical, linear— precludes, prevents you from achieving it. The very way that you approach and attempt to light your fire to reach the oneness, gets in the way of actually ever finding it. You have to open to this energy directly, not through your old paradigm." This freeing energy doesn't exist within the bubble, within the box in which we currently exist. You need to go directly to the source, to the well from which life springs forth. Once you get to that source, you need to allow your life expression to flow in a new way, in a free way.

It's only that fundamental energy, that pure spring flow, that can wash away and dissolve the foundation of your current survival belief structure. The energy has to be from outside of the current paradigm. It has to be direct, raw, pure, spontaneous, and innocent. The value of opening people in the *Gatherings* to innocence, trust, flow, spontaneity, intuition, and heart, is that only in this fresh, innocent, open new way, can you find the unadulterated spring, the well. If we approach it through any of our belief systems, any of our logical systematic techniques, and between methodologies, principles, it'll miss the mark. And we'll never find it.

My current focus in the *Gatherings* is to assist myself and others to open to ways of reconnecting with moments of innocent aliveness in this lifetime. We need to go directly to the vibration of raw, creative primal force. Where we're going, what we're looking for, can't be found on any current map. The way there is uncharted, because the very finding of it changes, transforms, alchemizes our universe, our lives, to such an extent no previous map or chart or paradigm is any longer relevant. So by its very nature, the way home remains uncharted, unmapped. There's no methodology, technique, philosophy, or structured approach that can ever remain valid for any period of time. This space, once achieved, once embodied, once lived, is so free, transformative, and creative, that it keeps everything constantly changing, including *your* very nature.

As St. Germain, Sai Baba and my other "friends" have been telling me lately, the new guideline for the *Gatherings* is, "*Just* the juice. *Just* the electricity." If whatever is happening in the moment looks right, sounds right, smells right, but it doesn't feel right, then it's not real. It's not what we should be doing. It's not what's right to be doing. The key is: in this moment, for you personally, is there juice? Is there electricity? Is there aliveness? Is there passion? Is there heart? If not, you're not in the right place. Let it go. Move on. Keep flowing.

COSTA RICA

The Spirit of the Volcano also took me to each of the significant experiences of primal life forces I had just encountered in Costa Rica. It took me to experiencing the aliveness of the crocodile, sloth, wild birds, toucans, the roar of the jaguar, the roar of the volcano. It took me to the heat, movement, aliveness, and exuberance of the lava flow, the wild storms, rain, tide, waves and surf of the ocean, the virgin forests, and the unbridled growth of all living things there. I once again felt all these beings, all this energy.

The Spirit took me to the toucans, the very colorful birds that were in a cage where we had the *Gathering* for four days. When I expressed concern for the caged birds, the hotel caretakers explained that this was a small cage, but they would soon be building a huge cage around the whole tree, so these birds would have a large tree to fly around in. But the birds talked to me, and told me they didn't want a big cage. They said their spirit needed to be *free*, and no cage would ever be big enough. They asked me with their eyes, just like every animal has asked me in every zoo I've ever been to, "Why? Why are you doing this? Why would *any* being do this? Why would any free being ever cage another being? Why would any free spirit ever imprison another free spirit? Why would a being with heart, ever drive a dagger of imprisonment into the heart of another being?" As the toucans asked me this, I became so troubled, I couldn't go near the cage anymore.

As I felt this, I reached an inevitible conclusion. It was the exact recognition I had come to thirty years earlier in the Roman coliseum in southern France. It was so clear. The realization blazing in my gut was, "Well, no free beings *would* ever imprison another free being. No being listening to their heart would ever kill the spirit of another being."

It was quite obvious to me that a culture that would cage animals, this human culture on our planet, had a heart made of granite. I knew I needed to go more deeply, more fundamentally, to a level where heart is expressing itself in human affairs, and to find a way to tap into that vibration of real love, real compassion, real passion, real divine spirit in such a way that is so strong, and so powerful, it will literally melt the creations of human programming and human structure. I knew I must discover a connection powerful enough to melt the need for people taking other people's energy, the need to imprison or control others, the need for approval from others, and the need to kill other spirits in order to feel secure.

I realized what I can do is assist myself and others to light the pilot light within, to help people to reconnect with God by getting in touch with nature, loved ones, pets, plants, and art. Intuition can assist us in reconnecting with true aliveness, to start the fires burning again within. It's then we can become strong enough to touch God and to *become* that energy. We can touch that eternal cosmic energy, live from that energy, and draw from it, for all our affection, approval, supply, certainty, and security. It is only then, we can be sovereign and independent enough of this heartless society to tell the truth to the granite heart. We'll melt the granite by expressing true love. We're not out to make the granite heart wrong, not out to judge it, but to melt it, to gently offer it a warmth, and then a fire, that is so attractive, the granite will melt. The prisons, cages, and steel bars, that we have put around our hearts, will melt away. This energy will transform our collective granite heart so it can return to its original state as free-flowing love and primal life force.

The Spirit of the Volcano allowed me to experience moments I touched true primal life force, and moments where I saw what was missing in our culture. I know it will take the authentic re-igniting of this pilot light, and the authentic stoking of the fires within each of us, to bring about genuine sovereignty before we'll have the courage and the heart to go out and love with our true spirit. When we can do that, we will melt the granite heart. We will melt the prisons of the human spirit in all forms on the planet. The place to start is within ourselves, and we're gathering together to do that.

The Spirit of the Volcano showed me the way to connect with this primal life force is to connect directly with undomesticated, unbridled, unfettered wild animals and plants, whose spirits are not broken, who still live freely. When traveling in Costa Rica, we saw virgin forests, wild mushrooms, wild fungus—every family of the plant kingdom, expressing itself freely. We felt their energy, their spirit. We encountered wild, curious crocodiles and iguanas. There were basilisk lizards which have so much energy they can literally run across the surface of the water. With their speed and their large webbed feet, they actually scurry across the surface without breaking through the water.

We witnessed free-living wild birds dramatically displaying their plumage and the beauty for which they are caged, caught, or killed. We met those birds in captivity and in the wild, so we could feel the difference. We saw mammals, the sloth and tabor, and we even heard a jaguar in the wild. We saw as much variety of free beings as one could encounter, as well as tempestuous storms, wind, rivers, and beaches in their raw state—unprotected, uncontrolled, untouched by human control and manipulation.

We also encountered the mineral kingdom; rock in the volcano, rock that was moving, granite that had melted and was free to create new form, free from its solidified, crystallized, rigid state. The energy of the volcano frees rock to change form to move, to allow alchemy and transformation. That's the power of this force. The force the volcano is inviting us to open to an energy within ourselves so powerful, so fundamental, that it allows rock, the most solid, condensed form of matter, to change form. There's no form of matter that can resist the melting energy, the transformative power, of the volcano.

On the surface, life takes on the appearance of form, like rocks, plants, animals, people, and buildings. What's actually creating these forms is the energy. Once we become the universal energy and allow ourselves to flow with it as it flows through everything, to express and create, then we have true sovereignty. We have certainty, and knowing of what we are, of who we are.

Our paradigm needs to shift away from identifying with human personality, even the idea of being human, of being a body, of being a separate spirit. As our identity shifts from form to essence, we begin to feel total security and certainty of who we are, and begin to recognize our eternalness and absolute safety. When we have that sense of absolute safety, that's when we are sovereign over our own realm. That's when we're sovereign over our own energy, our own survival, and we are no longer at the mercy of the elements, weather, temperature, shelter, food, the earth. That's when we're no longer at the mercy of other humans—needing their approval, their love, their protection, their agreement. That's when we do not need to control or resist other humans any longer. That's when we no further need to give any attention to anything other than our own internal impulse, our own internal desire for expression, our own soul's dream. When we are self-generating, our spirit can flow unhindered, for there's nothing drawing its attention anywhere other than to fulfill its own purpose, because we know we are the sovereign source of our own energy, our own power, and even our own love. It's not necessary for us to withhold, alter, disguise, or veil our spirit and our dream for fear of upsetting or changing somebody else's world, ideas, or safety. Only as long as we're sovereign over our own universe, our own survival, and our own love, fullness, connection to God and spirit, can we express ourselves freely.

Sovereignty plays a key role in the flow of the *Gatherings*. As people open up their hearts and become more sovereign, an equality and oneness emerges and facilitates the entry into new portals. The following is a discussion of sovereignty from a recent *Gathering*.

SOVEREIGNTY

KEITH - What does the word sovereignty mean to you?

GROUP - Squatter's rights...King or Queen of your own dominion...freedom...a star among a whole bunch of other stars but separate...self-determination...mastery...self-empowerment... self-generation.

KEITH - We've found sovereignty to be a very powerful quality or vibration to connect with experientially. It's a sense of connected authority, a sense of self. In the *Gatherings* what others and I are doing is reclaiming the territory we gave away to veils, other people, beliefs, or fear. It's allowing yourself to be sovereign over your dream, over what is rightfully yours, what's always been yours but disappeared when you abdicated it. It's allowing you to move back to your natural space, your natural state, ownership, being in charge as opposed to being unconscious, veiled, in fear.

It has also become very helpful for a lot of us to explore playing together as sovereign equals. What do you do if you are *not* sovereign over your own energy? You try to get it from others, they try to control them. If you're not generating your own energy and love, God, spirit, and support, you try to get it from other people. Then you have civilization and war, beliefs, countries, religions, dogma, *Gatherings.* **(Good laugh from the group)** Sovereignty is allowing yourself to be your own source of energy and love so you can begin to *exchange* energy and love, as sovereign equals as opposed to stealing or bartering for energy, attention, approval. Sovereignty begets freedom. What the *Gathering* has meant for me is we don't get together to talk about these things, we get together to assist each other to *actualize* them, to live who we really are again. How many people want more of this quality in their lives?

Have you ever met an animal, plant, or person that was in a state of sovereignty? Have you ever been with a truly wild animal who is with you by choice? How does that feel? I found sovereignty a very powerful vibration to get reacquainted with, to reconnect with. It allows me to have the strength and clarity to follow my heart, especially when it might be telling me to do or be something a little different than what my friends or culture prescribe. We've found it really valuable to get reacquainted with and to move back into a strong sense of one's connected sovereignty.

SUZANNE - To me, it's inner trust, knowing.

LINDA - To me, it's something coming from the real me.

SUE - For me, it's inner-directed. I woke up at three a.m. and saw a vision of Keith in my room and was very aware the being in the vision was an aspect of myself. Up until that time I only felt safe in recognizing it as Keith. I am becoming sovereign enough to recognize my *own* wisdom.

JANET - When you asked that, I thought, "I have no clue." I don't know what "sovereignty" means. It was interesting because what I did was tuned in intuitively and asked, "What is it to me?" The answer I got was, "Freedom."

MICHAEL - To me, it's about being whole and complete, being firmly rooted, firmly planted. I keep seeing myself as the creator of my world. What I see in sovereignty is this thing that has been creeping into my life and I haven't been paying any attention to it. It doesn't seem too much of a surprise it would show up here.

ALLEN - My wife, Audrey, has been showing me sovereignty. What I love the most has been coming from the places she's coming from. I can get very centered and very quiet and feel this thing inside of me. I feel really big, and loving, and powerful. Sovereignty to me is setting myself free. And, for me, it's just... **(He runs around the room gesturing wildly and the group laughs.)** I don't allow myself that very much. Audrey said I may be one of the most intuitive people she knows. That was kind of a shock to me because I always feel so closed down. But something happened inside my heart; that acknowledgment went straight to my soul and kind of shocked me for a little bit, then I started giggling from my heart. I felt I have been keeping a secret from everyone, myself included. It was a mischievous part of me that came out and just started giggling. It's there and I recognized it. **(In a childish voice)** "I've got a secret." It's cool. This is freedom to me…not to be so friggin' serious all the time.

DAVID - I've got to tell you something. In fact, I've got to *do* it. I just had the image of running around like that about ten or fifteen minutes ago. I'm gonna do it! **(He's yelled and danced around the room.)** I wanted to do that. Thank you!

SUZANNE - I do too!

(The group laughed and clapped as Suzanne and David playfully ran around the room.)

DAVID - One of the things that I haven't allowed myself to express is joy. Because *I'm* so friggin serious…. **(To Allen)** we connect guy. Thank you.

KEITH - So there were three examples of people taking sovereignty over their domain, their universe. There's an approach to sovereignty in a book that has really helped me. Carlos Castaneda was being told by Don Juan that Carlos makes himself *too available*. He isn't consciously in charge of being available or not available, emotionally, physically, spiritually, or psychologically. Sovereignty is being in charge of when and how we're available to other people and the world. I strongly connected with the word "sovereignty." It felt good. It felt neutral and clean. It doesn't mean I'm withdrawing or I'm necessarily alone. I'm just intuitively being available or not available according to when it *feels right*. And that, I learned, is taking sovereignty over my universe, my energy. Shall we see what our knowingness, our heart has to tell us, personally, about sovereignty, in a *dream out*?

DREAM OUT: SOVEREIGNTY

If you would like, take a moment to gather your energy, your attention, your *self*. Allow yourself to be nurtured by the unique vibration that is you. Notice if there is some unauthorized energy out there that's stuck or fixed or tight somewhere, doing something on a forged hall pass. **(Chuckles from the group)** See if you have any energy or part of you that's in the past, in the future, somewhere you didn't know it was, and you don't want it to be. Just allow all of your energies to become present. For that part of your attention that's somewhere else, ask your intuition, your knowing for a suggestion. Intuitively, where else *could* my attention be right now? Where else could my energy be?

Allow a suggestion from spirit that's so attractive, so right and perfect, that your energy shifts in that direction. Allow such a suggestion to come. Allow your energy to flow toward your passion, your excitement, to where it wants to flow, to where your heart is calling. Sovereignty is being in charge of your attention, your energy, soul, spirit, life force. Allow your heart to guide you, your intuition to open you, to a time or place or directly to the vibration or energy that has to do with true sovereignty, connected independence, strength, taking charge of your life, your universe, your creation, your energies, to a time or place where you *knew* the nature of true sovereignty, spiritual sovereignty, divine sovereignty, when it was easy, fun, when you noticed it, when you felt it, saw it, experienced it in someone else or yourself. Go to a time when you just got a hit, an insight, a realization, a direct experience. "Ah, this is right. This is sovereignty. This is freedom, ownership, knowing." Allow your heart to open you to the perfect time, place, vibration or energy that will open a gateway to you, to what's right for you to know and experience right now, about sovereignty or about whatever's right for you to experience at this moment in your life. Allow it to unfold in its own time, in its own way.

Keith and the group took a break to assimilate their visions and stretch their bodies. This time, the group members reconvened but Keith was still out. They decided to start without him, a small exercise in sovereignty.

JILL - There are some of us who are repeat gatherers who this would have scared the shit out of a short time ago...to have started sharing without Keith in the room. Not that we're leaving Keith out. He will be joyous we could begin on our own. It's perfect for me. To some of you who are at your first *Gathering,* this might seem a bit odd that we would start without Keith. I could go into what my *dream out* was about.

Jill told a story about her past, a time when she was doing something considered socially inappropriate, but she recalled how present and happy she was at that time.

JILL - ...I was reminding myself I don't want to live my life that way any more, waste my time, with people who don't want to be *in the moment* with me, that want to tell me stories, that want to be in the past or the future. I want to be in *this moment* with whoever I'm with...I know what that feels like. I know the joy it brings for me.

DAVID - How do you feel now about having had the experience and telling it?

JILL - Wonderful. I never had shame and guilt, and I never understood why I did not. It didn't matter to me. I knew I felt good at that time. I didn't share it publicly for fear of judgment, but I personally never had any negative feelings of remorse about it. I felt good. I felt *alive.*

DEBRA - The present, for me, is changing. For a long time, being in the present for me was *this moment*, *this* experience, *this* day, *this* hour. This morning there's been much talk about the present. When it's the first of the month and, all of a sudden, I'm in the present but there's no rent money, what I realized this morning is that the present encompasses my past and my future. My present is being physically in my body and being able to look at my *whole life* the same as looking at this moment. And realizing the choices I'm making in this moment are part of all I am and all I want to experience.

My present includes looking forward to what my summer will be like. It's not that I'm rigidly attached to that summer plan, but for me I'm needing to broaden the perspective. It's just revealing itself moment by moment as I'm speaking, and it's still not crystal clear, but I'm getting more and more a sense of what I've been doing because I've felt, on my spiritual path, I've needed to stay *so* much right here that I didn't *dare* open to this part. Because of that, I've experienced some tremendous discomfort in my life. I'm ready to fully embrace the abundance available for me and to realize who should experience the abundance of the universe than those of us that who willingly seeking and *know* what's available and what's here.

For a long time, I was the perfect wife and the perfect mother. Something was always wrong, but I couldn't figure out what it was. It was necessary for *me* to destroy all that to find clarity. I would like to, from my knowing, encourage others to realize it's not necessary to leave your old life to experience the love and who you are. What I *know* is that I, in my life, thought I had to get *away from* everything I had created, so I could be me. What I *now know* is that being me, in that space, I had to deal with it *anyway. It doesn't matter what you choose outside.* To me, it didn't make any difference. I still had to go through that process. I look back now and know I could have gone through the process in my former environment. I could have remained in my old life and still come out of it with the same results.

PAT - I went on a *dream out* with most of you. I really had a *déjà vu dream out,* and we all went to another school; we were learning how to feel the environment. We all went to ancient Egypt, to the universal sandbox in the desert. I said, "But why are the faces the same?" And the answer was, "Because we've done it together *before.*" We were a *group* mind, or feeling, rather than only individuals. By coming together before, and then again now, means we are meeting to grow some more, to learn how to feel better.

JANET - I really felt the power of *sovereignty* when I was about seven. I did *whatever* I wanted to do. My mother was always on my back about being *so* independent. "You're *so* independent." What came up was, I was clapping erasers in parochial school and the nuns would say, "Whoever wants to stay after school to clap the erasers can stay and help us to clean the boards." I'd never experienced what it was like to take erasers and just clap the *shit* out of them so that all the dust flies all over. I thought, "I want to experience that." Well, I *knew* my mom wanted me home, but I didn't *care*. I thought, "I want to try this. I want to just *do* this. I want to *experience* this." And not only did I clap the erasers, but I did something you're not supposed to do according to the nuns. I took the erasers and threw them against the wall. So I got in trouble with the nuns, and I got in trouble with my mother. I told her, "I just wanted to clap the erasers." And she said, "You're always wanting to do something." I felt *so powerful* like, "I don't *care* what other people say. This is *so* much fun."

The second experience was, I had tried to convince one of my girlfriends whose father was the president of a dairy farm, to go see how they pasteurize milk. I *really* wanted to see how they pasteurize milk. I was about five years old. She said, "No, my father has warned me not to go in there." So, for *weeks* I worked on convincing her. Finally we went there. We entered a place where all of these people had masks on. I was fascinated. Wow, they're wearing masks. What was the reason? Then I went up the stairs and I looked right into a vat of milk. All of a sudden several of the workers noticed I was in there. They all started chasing me out of the place. I had ruined a *huge* vat of milk. The father called my mother, and I could never spend anymore time with this girl because I had brought her into the dairy farm with me. But it was *so* empowering. *Wow*, I just did *exactly* what I wanted to do. Since then I have shut down, but in those two instances, I didn't care about judgment; it didn't matter. I didn't care about the repercussions. I just wanted to *experience* it. And I did. That was exciting.

MICHAEL - In the *dream out,* I was looking at the first line of the Declaration of Independence, "When in the course of human events it becomes *necessary....*" It suddenly came to me, it's something I never realized before and that is that I, for a long time, have been in the process of declaring *my* independence from God which is pretty dangerous and pretty scary. It's so dangerous and scary I haven't allowed myself to stop and realize that was what I was doing. But I can see now, I had this feeling God controlled my life, God ruled my life. Not that *He* was controlling me but my *yearning* for God, my *desire* for God, for that connection, *ran* my life. Everything was about getting to the place where I could experience God *directly*.

The powerful message of the volcano also foretold the future of the *Gatherings* and how, by melting our hardened granite hearts, we can receive all of the gifts primal life force has to offer. Keith explained how to incorporate our re-discovered sovereignty into our present lives and carry it forward into the future:

THE FUTURE OF THE GATHERINGS

KEITH - Sovereignty is the new expression of the *Gatherings*. The *Gatherings*, as they were, died this last year. It was wonderful the way the old form died. The very aliveness of the energy that certain people brought to the *Gatherings*, the energy of pure, undiluted joy, aliveness, spontaneity, openness, playfulness, irreverence, love of life, *joie de vivre*—this pure, open, playful joy was too much for the old structure. The old *Gathering* had channels built for energy to flow through, but this new exuberant energy wouldn't and couldn't be contained. It flowed over the banks of the old channels of expressions we gave it in the *Gathering*. This energy of the volcano, that raw, primal force, fire, passion, literally disintegrated the channels we had built, the walls, paradigms, techniques, the ways of expression that had started to crystallize. These channels have been destroyed, and thus, the old form of the *Gathering* has been destroyed.

I held a funeral and a wake last year, and I now see the new essence, center, and heart of the *Gatherings* is sovereignty. If *The Dream - A Gathering of Equals* is to be fully realized on the planet earth, if that dream of people coming together to openly and fully express who they are, what they are, to each other, to themselves, and to the world is to happen, people have to first become sovereign over their own energy. If we aren't self-generating, we won't have the courage, power, or safety, to express who we are to ourselves, let alone to others in the *Gatherings* or in the world. Unless we have sovereignty over love, unless we have our connection with universal love, God, spirit, grace, fully open and flowing, we will feel alone, scared, separate, and shut down.

Sovereignty is realizing there's only one source, and that one source is yourself, your divine self, or God. Once you've opened to that one single divine source of all love, energy, power, safety, security, then none other is needed, and, therefore, outside sources can no longer have an effect on you. Your attention doesn't even go there. When you are fully living in the vibration of sovereignty, you have all your attention there. All your joy and awareness is immersed, nurtured, and fueled by this knowing, by this direct experience of being completely full, loved, supported.

There is no longer any attention available to look elsewhere. There is only attention engaged with living and expressing. There is no attention left to be conscious of or looking for love, attention, approval, or control of others. It's no longer necessary to control your environment, or others, to make sure you get energy or love. It's no longer necessary to resist, fear, or have attention on others, trying to control you or tapping your energy. You're living in an ocean of infinite love, infinite energy, infinite expression. If anyone else tries to control that or tap into it, it's of no interest or import to one who is sovereign. Others can do whatever they wish and reap whatever karma, results, consequences will come. It has no effect on a sovereign being. A sovereign being gives everybody else unconditional love, infinite space to be *just as they are*—even if they choose to be controlling, threatening, energy grabbers. It makes no difference to sovereign beings, because they're untouchable. They're connected fully to the fire within, to that essence that nurtures the fullness of one's being.

This is the next wave to surf in the *Gathering*. The surf's up and the big waves coming in are the waves of sovereignty. I'm seeing the dream I have is for a free expression of sovereign beings, sharing what they know. Up until now, what I have seen happening a lot in the *Gatherings* is that when the environment has been there to share, fear has prevented people from revealing who they are to themselves or to each other, and the veils win. The fear wins. It is necessary for people to tap more fully into the energy of the volcano, of the fire, the passion, the infinite security and power within so they have the courage, the heart, to *fully* express who they are.

A gathering of granite hearts cannot fulfill its dream. There is not enough connection, safety, flow, or love for a true expression of the heart. Beings with granite hearts don't even know what they're feeling anymore.

The next step in the *Gatherings* is to really assist people to more fully melt their own granite heart, to melt the armor, vault, and prison they've put their heart in, and to free their spirit. Only a freed spirit can freely share. Only a freed spirit can feel equal. Only a sovereign spirit can feel equal.

I've also seen very clearly, a person can only share with others what they've already shared with themselves. A *Gathering of Equals* cannot fully express itself as individuals sharing who they are with each other and with the world until they begin sharing with *themselves* who they are—until they begin sharing their own true energy with themselves.

The next step and focus for the *Gatherings* is naturally going to be on gathering oneself, gathering one's own energies, one's own power, one's own love, one's own fire—the message of the volcano—one's own sovereignty, one's own heart and courage. Only then, when we come together, will we be able to share who we are, what we are with each other and the outer world.

The *Gathering* is becoming a group of aware beings, coming together to share *with themselves first* who they are, what they are—fire, power, passion, primal force—and allowing these to ignite their true sense of loving, compassion, play, expression, creativity. Then we will have it available to share with others. We can't give to somebody else something we don't possess ourselves. If we don't have sovereignty, safety, security, universal love, universal supply within us, we can't share it.

The message of the volcano is to go to those places in our universe, in our experience, where we have tasted and touched primal life force. We can experience this force in nature by going to wild animals, forests, plants, rocks, and volcanoes. The true invitation of the volcano is for each of us to allow our spirit, our heart, our intuition, and knowing, to open us to a time, place, or vibration we have already experienced this lifetime when we have connected with primal life force.

Ask your soul to help you to re-experience those moments. They are the key to living your dream from this moment on. Allow your awareness to open to the moments when you knew the true nature of yourself, your power, your passion, and creativity, so your pilot light can be re-lit and your internal fire can burn more brightly. Let the heat of your truth warm your heart and satisfy your need for security, safety, and power. Opening to that power will enhance your dreams, your play, and your spontaneity. You will have universal supply and it will fuel your connection to love. It's time to begin living in the fire of your own love, security, knowing, and unlimited sovereign universal energy. As you access that primal life force, you can freely, spontaneously, and playfully share everything you are with yourself, others, and with all of life. This is the message of the volcano. It is now time to heed this message and begin living your dream.

THE WISDOM OF THE

Trees have played an important part in my life and in the writing of this book during the last year. Through them I have connected with nature and found a true and lasting bond with my own earth energy. In chronicling the *Gatherings*, I have been fortunate to experience the tropical Rain Forests of Costa Rica and the majestic oak tree canopy roads of Tallahassee. The sovereign giant sequoias near San Francisco taught me that all living beings have a personal, unique vibration. The cedars at Mayflower park in Austin reminded me about true serenity. An Aspen on a stream bank in the upper desert near Lake Tahoe inspired me to go to the East Coast. Then, at a *Gathering* in Philadelphia, I sat on a log under a tree and was inspired with the design of this book, including the layout and the tribute to the trees.

In Moraga, near San Francisco, a spirited eighty-something Gatherer walked through a grove when, much to her fascination, a tree actually spoke to her. It said, "I'm standing here being of service. What are *you* doing here?" While writing in my daily journal at the base of a huge maple in Discovery Park, I often felt the giant tree telling me, "Bring the spirit and the energy of the trees to the people." My message to you is to take the time to connect with the primal life force in nature. Trees have been a large part of that relationship for me. That is why we are returning some of the energy back by donating part of the proceeds from this book toward planting more trees.

Mark

A Note from Pura Vida Publishing Company

A portion from the sales of this book will be donated to *The National Arbor Day Foundation* which is dedicated to the advancement of tree planting and environmental stewardship for the benefit of this and future generations. We have combined our energies with the *National Arbor Day Foundation* in support of rain forest preservation and reforestation of our national forests.

The *Rain Forest Rescue Program* works to preserve one of the earth's most vitally important resources—some of its most beautiful and exotic regions. Over 96,000 acres of tropical rain forest are burned off every day. This is a frightening statistic because it means over 17,000 species of plants and animals will be wiped out each year, not to mention 70% of tomorrow's possible lifesaving natural drug sources. Each dollar donated, will preserve 250 square feet of dense rain forest in Central and South America. (The painting on the cover of this book is an artist's rendition of a rain forest jungle in Costa Rica.)

Through another effort called *Trees for America,* the National Arbor Day Foundation works closely with the U.S. Forest Service to replant areas of our national forests that have been destroyed. These trees provide habitat for a number of species of wildlife, including grizzly bear, moose, elk, and the mountain lion and restores beauty to these areas as well. For every dollar contributed, one tree will be planted.

To learn more about the National Arbor Day Foundation and how you can help, contact them at: The National Arbor Day Foundation, 100 Arbor Avenue, Nebraska City, NE 68410, (www.arborday.org).

INDEX

ORDER FORM

LIVING THE DREAM
IT'S TIME

A Chronicle of the Gathering of Equals

Name:____

Address:____

City/State/Zip:____

Telephone:____

Method of payment: _____CHECK

_____VISA _____MasterCard _____AMEX _____ Other_______________

Card number:______________________ Exp. Date:______________

Signature:_________________________ Date:_________________

______ copies of the book @ $22.95 $________
8.6% sales tax for books sent to Washington addresses $________
Shipping: $4.00 for the first book and $2.00 for each additional $________

(Check payable to: **Pura Vida Publishing Company**) **Total $**________

____Please add me to the Pura Vida Publishing Company mailing list.

TO ORDER:

Fax form to: (425) 744 - 0563

Email us at: PuraVidaPub@earthlink.net

Postal orders: Pura Vida Publishing Company,
P.O. Box 379
Mountlake Terrace, WA 98043-0379

Or simply call: (425) 670-1346 Order toll free @ (888) 670-1346